The Culture Wars

*How American and Japanese businesses have outperformed Europe's
and why the future will be different*

John Viney

Copyright © John Viney 1997

The right of John Viney to be identified as the author of this work has been asserted in accordance with the Copyright, Designs and Patents Act 1988

First Published 1997
Capstone Publishing Limited
Oxford Centre for Innovation
Mill Street
Oxford OX2 0JX
United Kingdom

All rights reserved. Except for the quotation of short passages for the purposes of criticism and review, no part of this publication may be reproduced, stored in a retrieval system, or transmitted, in any form or by any means, electronic, mechanical, photocopying, recording or otherwise, without the prior permission of the publisher.

British Library Cataloguing in Publication Data
A CIP catalogue record for this book is available from the British Library

ISBN 1-900961-253

Typeset in 10/14 New Baskerville by
Sparks Computer Solutions, Oxford
Printed and bound by
T.J. Press Ltd, Padstow, Cornwall

This book is printed on acid-free paper

Contents

Foreword by Karl Otto Pöhl — v
Acknowledgements — ix

1 Introduction: Towards the Twenty-First Century — 1
2 United by Difference: the Formation of a European Identity — 23
3 The Business of America is Business: a Consideration of How America Gained its Business Hegemony — 45
4 Miracle Workers: Development of the Japanese and German Economies — 71
5 Knowing the Field: the Asian Runners and Riders — 101
6 Towards a Definition of a European Company — 127
7 Confronting Culture — 153
8 The Cultural Iceberg: a Guide to Cultural Differences both Above and Below the Surface — 177
9 European Culture: Asset or Liability? — 207
10 Europe: the Practical Realities — 231
11 Conclusion — 259

Bibliography — 271
Index — 273

Foreword
by Karl Otto Pöhl

The single greatest political debate of our time in Europe is the question of the rate of integration and, from some quarters, the most highly charged aspect of the debate is the possibility of European Monetary Union (EMU). This has been a subject of heated political discussion across the continent, different postures have been taken on the pros and cons and few Europeans remain neutral on the issue. It has, after all, a significant impact on the status of the nation state and many citizens of those states, who cherish the symbols of nationhood of which currency is one of the more potent, have yet to be convinced of the benefits of union. For many ordinary Europeans further integration has few attractions; for Europe's businessmen, however, and particularly in large competitive enterprises, closer union promises quite dazzling opportunities.

The success of the business sector depends on the viability of corporations. Europe has an important number of flourishing, efficient, highly competitive corporations but is still does not rival the United States or Japan as enjoying similar world-wide acclaim for its best business enterprises, even when the separate European states are considered as one. It is not enough, furthermore, merely to support an array of superb world-beating larger corporations. To survive and flourish, an economy needs to encourage the development of new enterprises, to encourage entrepreneurialism and so secure the next generation of business and, of course, employment. Here Europe has been weak. Entrepreneurialism, if not in terminal decline, is certainly in suspension. It is clear that no one economy in Europe can outperform Japan or the US. However, if Europe as a whole can further integrate then it can become part of the triad of leading world economies alongside the US and Japan. From union at several levels could come a new momentum and a groundswell of entrepreneurial activity.

Business organizations today in Europe that are streamlined, professional and competitive, on a world-wide basis, with the best in their sector see rich pickings ahead. Monetary union will take financial decisions on interest rates away from the nation state and position them at the supranational level. New light will then more clearly fall upon European businesses in general, throwing into relief those that are increasingly uncompetitive. The opportunity to merge with others or take over these less robust businesses, and so achieve greater penetration and increased economies of scale and efficiency, is one that modernized European companies are anxious to exploit. Granted, non-Europeans stand to benefit too and the Americans, Japanese and Koreans are alert to the prizes of Europe; but still the biggest prize must be Europe's own. If Europe can achieve further integration it can confidently confront the possibility of its own economic renaissance.

Achieving monetary union, at the proper time and in the proper way, is but one step towards economic renaissance. Much more problematic, but less analysed and discussed, is the cultural imperative accompanying integration. Europe must develop the beginnings of a new and vibrant enterprise culture if European businesses are to take full advantage of the opportunities presented by integration. This culture must be truly European, not a pale imitation of the American business culture nor simply the strongest of the multitude of national cultures to prevail across the continent. It is, after all, a fear that national cultures will be subsumed within, for instance, a greater Germany or stronger Dutch, British or French enterprises, which, below the surface, gives rise to opposition to increased integration. Instead, this should be the clearer development of a pan-European business culture, a composite culture allowing for many differences, fusing the elements from the various cultures of which it is composed in spite of the very real differences Europeans see one to another. However, from the greater distances of, say, Japan or the US, Europeans do seem to be a more homogeneous group with a clear identity and one value system and culture.

If Europeans can succeed in forging a new business culture, one that sets value on diversity, then Europe will be extremely well placed to strengthen its economic position. The strong, uniform business cultures of the Americans and the Japanese that have served them so well in the twentieth century may lack the flexibility required by international, increasingly cross-border business activity in the twenty-first. *The Culture Wars* takes as its subject the role of culture – both national and company – as a primary differentiator in economic performance over the coming decades and considers Europe's economic chances set against those of the US, Japan and the economies of southeast Asia. It is predicated on the assumption that Europe cannot, indeed must not, resist integration and explores the precedents for culture co-operation that are the legacy of the long interrelation of Europe's nation states.

If the economic case is not properly made to the citizens of Europe and integration is achieved without a consensus in favour, then our politicians will have done us a disservice, for without that consensus the chances for building an appropriate, more integrated European business culture are negligible and the chances of Europe maintaining its economic strength infinitely weakened. *The Culture Wars* makes an important contribution to the debate.

Karl Otto Pöhl
President, Deutsche Bundesbank, 1980–91

Acknowledgements

Dedicated to my partners and colleagues at Heidrick & Struggles.

This book has been written over a period of six years and, compared with the changing world of international business, it seems like an eternity. The book has gone through a number of stages of development and draws heavily upon my experience as a business consultant and executive recruitment adviser to boards across the world. Anybody writing a book on the subject of culture is only too keenly aware that one's own position, upbringing and place in the world distorts one's views. I have no doubt that my prejudices and values give me a clear slant on the world but I am reassured that this would apply to anybody writing this kind of book! I am, to some extent, a recent convert to European philosophy and started out my business career with an attitude and outlook that focused me more on the business values of America. Although my experience is rooted in what I have observed, it has been of enormous benefit to me to have had the opportunity to work alongside some of the most talented business executives world-wide and to learn from them. I am keenly aware that this is a privilege and an opportunity that many have not enjoyed.

This book would not have been possible without a number of contributions and I want to ensure that generous praise and thanks are extended to them. The first is Heidrick & Struggles, for allowing me to spend the time and resources to ensure that this book has been written and published. I am most grateful to my partners and colleagues across the world who have allowed me this access and the opportunity to complete this book. Secondly, Judith Osborne has worked with me closely over a number of years, and the fact that this book reads as well as it does is to an important degree due to Judith. Writing and trying to edit a book with a punishing business schedule means that I have often not found myself at the same spot that I had left, and my various jottings and views have changed and developed significantly over the last few years. Judith has not only typed the manuscript, but played a huge part in making sure that it is consistent and well written. I owe an enormous debt of gratitude to her.

Thirdly, I would like to thank the business leaders and other contributors who took part in giving me their time to probe their thinking and to be able to test my ideas on them. Being able to do this with top business minds not only made my job easier and more enjoyable, but has also contributed in no small way to the strands and development of ideas in the book. Of course, any errors or inaccuracies in this book are mine and mine alone, and I must add that the views promoted in this book are my own and not necessarily those of Heidrick and Struggles.

John Viney

1

Introduction:
Towards the Twenty-First Century

'We may become the makers of our fate when we have ceased to pose as its prophets.'

Sir Karl Popper.

The final decade of the last century was dubbed, in Europe at any rate, the Naughty Nineties – it was a period of some moral laxity and bohemianism, the age of the salon and scandal, a final fling before the serious business of the twentieth century. And what a serious business it turned out to be: world warfare, totalitarian tyranny, pogroms, holocaust, nuclear detonation – a century of devastation and destruction. After such experience it is not surprising that the 1990s are not so much naughty as nervous. As we contemplate the past and try to project the future the mood is one of fearful prophecy. Thanks to our legacy of manufacturing and warfare, the planet faces the possibility of destruction from global warming, nuclear after-effects and pollution. The individual is atomized, split away from those forces which once anchored him or her. The family, the church, the nation state – all are in decline. The local, regional and national must give way to the global and in the seat of sovereign power, it would seem, is that absolute and terrifying monarch, the global corporation. The philosophers have run out of words to describe our predicament; we are post, post-modern and, so we are told, at the end of history ...

Is this stance mere scaremongering or justifiable jitters? Certainly, the environment in which we live is undergoing change and the institutions to which we have become accustomed are no longer as stable as they were. The impact of change is immediately felt and all the more shocking as the media brings information into our homes and offices on the instant. The age of global communications increases our anxiety by the simple activity of increasing our awareness. To what extent global communications accelerate the effect of change is incalculable, but change, by being communicated on the instant, takes immediate effect. This domino effect disallows delay or diversion of change. So, we are right to be unsettled and, after such a cataclysmic century as this has been, we are no less right to try and exert a degree of control over the next. Periods of taking stock, be they new years, new decades or new centuries, are important. Planning cycles offer a process by which contingency, if not circumvented, can be kept within containable limits. If the analysis underpinning plans is rigorous and comprehensive then the outputs should be sound, subject but not hostage to change.

The subject of this book is not so much prophesy as planning. What will the next century hold for business? Who will be in the ascendant in the coming decades? What form will business supremacy take? An artificial question, perhaps, but if the nineteenth century belonged to Europe and America laid claim to the twentieth, who will secure the prize of the twenty-first? For many it is a foregone conclusion that it won't be Europe. A few years ago most had written off America and were looking to Asia as the likely victor. Now, on the brink of the new millennium, declining growth rates even in the so-called tiger economies have called Asian might into question. It would seem there is all to play for and that Europe is most definitely in the running.

This book is written by a European from the intuitive position that Europe is very far from finished. In a period when much is written about the decline of the nation state only Europe offers an alternative paradigm for international government. When the call for international co-operation is heard on a daily basis, European states can be seen to be doing more than merely co-operating but considering extensive integration in the interests of securing the economic and political well-being of their citizens. Nowhere else in the world is there a similar model. As a huge literature accumulates on the subject of culture, it is Europe that can be seen to be a pioneer, considering the implications of integration upon identity. When the notion of the global corporation seems to be taking over from the mere multinational it is only the European business that appears to be grappling with the implications for governance. The signs are that Europe, having learned the lessons of the twentieth century, is taking the twenty-first seriously.

Such an optimistic, upbeat prognosis would not be shared by all observers. To some it would seem that Europe is united only by difference. The European Union with 15 members currently has 11 official languages; further enlargement could bring that number closer to 20. A third of the administrative costs of the Union are connected with translation services – even simple communication is fraught with difficulty. Historic enmities amongst the states are hard to erase and more modern ones (the ideological differences between the capitalist and former communist states) might prove every bit as indelible. Racial hatred, which we might have hoped had been expunged by the experience of the middle of the century, has resurfaced in the final years with the war and horrific campaign of 'ethnic cleansing' in former Yugoslavia. Concerns with sovereignty, fears of a Federal or United States of Europe, delusions of imperial grandeur grip the citizens of Europe and delay the process of integration. The tensions generated by the debate prove distracting and focus attention on single elements of a much larger process; hence European economies put themselves at some risk in their haste to achieve convergence criteria for monetary union. As our population's age and birth rates decline we nevertheless demand more and more welfare provision from fewer and fewer revenue providers. Far from revering those who generate new wealth we appear, through our veneration of heritage, to decry them. As John Maynard Keynes wrote: 'regarded as a means [the businessman] is tolerable; regarded as an end, he is not so satisfactory'. Written by a member of a cultural elite (the Bloomsbury group) this is not a bad summation of the European attitude to commerce – a necessary evil. What hope for Europe if this vision is the correct one?

What hope for Europe, furthermore, in the face of formidable competition? America and Japan have battled for business supremacy over recent decades and each has a cultural homogeneity which is the natural product of a single land mass with a consistent cultural tradition. Both have the certainty of substantial past successes, a stable polity and an array of world-beating companies. The fortunes of the two nations may rise or fall slightly but remain basically constant. The newly industrialized countries of Asia are no less formidable as competitors. Newcomers to the world business stage, they have the drive and cultural dynamism to supplant the more established, entrenched and so less flexible economies of their Pacific rim neighbours in Japan and the United States.

But all is not entirely well with these formidable competitors. Japan currently confronts economic and political crisis with confidence in its institutions at an all-time low. Innovation has evaporated and morality become lost in the morass of capitalist corruption. America on the other hand is in the grip of rampant individualism, with soaring crime and declining social stability. The collective will of the American people that made the nation the foremost business centre in the world has been dissipated and laid to waste. Even the newly industrializing nations of South East Asia are not immune from gloomy prophecy. Political instability is a reality – democracy far from consolidated, autocracy in some cases inevitable. A process of economic emulation has given rise to overproduction and an economic blood bath is possible at least in key industries like chemicals and automobiles. The skills and training of the work-force cannot keep pace with the demands of the economy and in a fickle global marketplace there are always new, cheaper labour markets to exploit. So, in the race for business supremacy in the next century there is, from the vantage point of the 1990s, no clear leader in the field. Indeed, we cannot even with complete confidence predict the major players. The accepted norm is that the triad of America, Japan and Europe are the real competitors, but to overlook the other nations of Asia beyond Japan would seem ill advised.

The aim of this book is to plot a course through this sometimes scarcely navigable territory. The fundamental questions it sets out to answer are:

- What is the place of European business in the global scheme of things? Does it have one or has it lost it irretrievably?
- What precedent does Europe have for forging a coherent culture?
- What chance does it have for evolving a new business culture – how, through whom and using which skills?

My starting point, that of a European more than a little reluctant to accept the inevitable eclipse of Europe, is perhaps partial but no more so than a member of a corporation who sets out to assess that corporation's likely path to success. I hope that, in the analysis that follows, the position taken will be impartial. The structure of the book is:

- A consideration of Europe's past: what has brought the continent to its current situation and what has united and divided her various states.
- A consideration of the legacy that Europe left with America and what America has made of that.
- How that legacy has been subsequently adapted by other economies, notably Japan and Germany; and, in a separate chapter, the other runners and

riders in the race for economic supremacy – the emerging South-East Asian economies.
- From a practical consideration of the key players we move to some cultural considerations and try to establish what is meant by a European company.
- Having arrived at a definition of what a European company might be we next consider what characteristics are required to lead that European company and so arrive at the definition of a European business leader.
- Since the principal challenge the European business leader will encounter is that of forging a new culture we devote a further chapter to the cultural characteristics the European leader will find above and – more threateningly – below the surface.
- The final portion of the book will return to the broad context in which European businesses and business leaders must operate. The focus, across two chapters, will be the big issues which impact on Europe – both cultural and practical, probing some of the assumptions that have bedevilled the continent and continue to excite debate and arouse concern.
- Throughout the text we will consider Europe's position relative to that of her primary competitors. The final chapter will present the synthesis of our findings and offer a blueprint, a strategic plan, for Europe's business well-being in the twenty-first century.

It is important to clarify the terms and assumptions against which this book is written and that will be the concern of the remainder of this chapter. In the opening paragraph I put forward some of the issues that concern commentators in the run-up to the next millennium. While such issues as pollution and global warming will have their role to play in the fortunes of Europe and we will need to find both political and commercial methods for eliminating (or at least stemming) the threat posed by each, these are considerations that fall outside the scope of this study. The supposed movement towards globalization, however, is the backdrop against which our drama is being played out and it is essential that we understand what is meant by the term and whether, in fact, we are going global. At the heart of this issue is the role of the nation state. Are we witnessing its demise? Should we be? Is there something in between – the trading bloc? What, in all this, is the role of the corporation? Has the multinational really given way to the global corporation and is the corporation the monster we are led to believe? One of this volume's presuppositions is that culture is an important, possibly the most important, element in the competition for business supremacy and we shall give some consideration to a work that considers culture from an economist's vantage point and gives some highly illuminating insights for the remainder of our text. Finally, where does all this leave Europe?

Going global

We are living in a global age. An age of global corporations, brands, communications. The word has become something of a universal, indeed a global, prefix. But what does globalization actually mean? Anthony Giddens offers a succinct definition:

> *'the intensification of worldwide relations which link distant localities in such a way that local happenings are shaped by events many miles away and vice versa.'*

In other words globalization is the intensification of internationalism, made possible by technology which allows the immediate transfer of information. Internationalism is nothing new – what are Christianity and Islam if not international movements that transcend local, regional and national barriers – the difference between globalization and internationalism would appear to be one of degree and extent.

The sphere in which globalization is most evident is the economic. Political scientist Jürgen Habermas writes:

> *'With the internationalization of financial, capital and labour markets, national governments are increasingly aware of the gap between their limited scope for action, on the one hand, and, on the other, the imperatives stemming, not primarily from world-wide trade relations, but from globally networked production relations.'*

Internationalization has been driven by the liberalization of exchange controls, leading to the freer movement of investment funds around the globe. Financial flows have become increasingly separated from the requirements of trade and manufacturing as speculation in international currencies via sophisticated financial instruments has become a more profitable activity. The deregulation of the money markets and the communications revolution allowing for 24-hour electronic trading, moving from financial market to financial market according to the time of day, have been additional factors enabling this process. For Habermas this has clearly been a process with far-reaching and sinister consequences.

The thesis is broadly the following. The architects and the beneficiaries of globalization are seen to be global corporations. These organizations, driven by the relentless logic of capitalism and without any national allegiance, compete in a global marketplace for market share and do so by the increasingly irresponsible direction of capital and production from one part of the globe to another, irrespective of social impact, driven only by the force of the market itself.

Given such a scenario, it is hardly surprising that the global corporation is taking on monstrous form in the public imagination. Science fiction, a medium that takes our fears of the future and turns them into present, if textual, realities, offers us an expression of our unease:

> *'That's all your standard big shits. Corporations. Very much a fixed landscape, you might say. Sometimes one of 'em'll grow an annex, or you'll see a takeover and two of them merge. But you aren't likely to see a new one, not on that scale. They start small and grow, merge with other small formations ... Bastard's bigger than anything ... and nobody knows what it is or who it belongs to.'*
>
> From *Mona Lisa Overdrive*, William Gibson.

There seems to be little doubt that the global corporation is a force to be reckoned with and can take a commanding position in world affairs. In relation to the financial markets the role of the corporation would seem greatly to exceed that of the government of a nation state, which may well be forced to resist certain fiscal measures it wishes to impose because of the potential effect upon the markets. This strikes at the heart of humane concern over the issue of globalization. Unable to raise revenues for fear of market consequences, governments cannot support defence or social welfare budgets. The individual is made vulnerable in a world economy that operates entirely uncoupled from the political and social arena. The nation state is being replaced, it would seem, by the global corporation.

Global corporations are sinister because, despite some disclosure of information and however public a public company may be, it remains, to most outside businesses and many within it, a closed world. A corporation is not a democratic institution; those in power are not democratically elected; those with voting rights of any description (shareholders) have those rights by dint of the money they have available to invest. The global corporation is therefore profoundly antidemocratic. The link between the corporation and the money markets again seems sinister. Few understand all aspects of the international money machine. The money markets exist in the realm of virtual reality – money moves invisibly, fluidly across international barriers, rarely taking tangible form, existing through esoteric instruments understood only by the statisticians and economists who invent them. In consumer societies where our status is defined and lifestyle determined by money, our innate lack of control of that money incites fear and that fear focuses on the global corporation. So the process of globalization is removing the individual from any sense of control over the personal or the public money supply. Further than this, globalization is seen to be reductive – bringing all peoples to a baseline of similarity. It is a levelling process, the icons of which are the MacDonald's hamburger and the can of coke.

There can be no denying that our society is undergoing something of the process of globalization as described by Anthony Giddens – the principal organ being the communications network which disseminates information. It is as possible that this form of globalization heightens as much as it levels difference, allowing access to information and making the variety that characterizes the planet more visible than before. Globalization might facilitate a decision or, equally, by giving access to too much choice, too many variables, may prevent action. In short, it is questionable whether globalization reduces or expands consciousness, enables or disables.

Much more importantly, it is also distinctly questionable whether the monstrous global corporation is real or a modern myth. We have noted, above, that internationalism is nothing new, nor is international trade. Indeed, substantial study has been made comparing the modern so-called global economy with the international economy prevailing in the late nineteenth century through to the First World War. Historian R. Zevin, surveying a wide range of the literature, concludes:

> '...every descriptor of financial markets in the late nineteenth and early twentieth centuries suggests that they were more fully integrated than they were before or have been since.'

Similarly, just as the economy is no more global than it has ever been, corporations are not the sinister rootless entities bent upon the destruction of human values that some would suggest. Indeed – as the extremely thorough analysis supplied by Paul Hirst and Grahame Thompson in *Globalization in Question* proves – corporations, irrespective of the number of markets in which they operate, have overwhelmingly national allegiances. Their evidence drawn from data on sales, assets, profits, subsidiaries and affiliates in some 5000 large scale multinational corporations in 5 countries for 1987 and 6 for 1992–3 suggests, overwhelmingly, that the multinational corporation is rooted in a single major national location. The global corporation is as mythical as the Minotaur.

Running directly counter to the global corporation myth is that of the demise of the multinational altogether – the small is beautiful, less is more, lobby. The assumption here is that small companies are the appropriate vehicle for innovation, that large companies bureaucratize and lack the flexibility to respond rapidly to changing market conditions. The model on which this hypothesis is based is that of the high-tech sector where small-scale operations have been able to undercut multinationals, as Steve Jobs and Steve Wozniak managed from their garage to take on the might of IBM. In recent years the trend has been towards downsizing on the part of large companies, to streamline decision making processes and free up intellectual capital to be creative and thus competitive. To extrapolate from these actions (which are, after all, direct responses to competitive threat) that the large corporation is in decline would appear absurd. Some sectors will ever benefit from economies of scale – hard to imagine a cottage industry for the development of aerospace engines. The design and apparel, *haute couture* businesses, on the other hand, would gain little and lose more by growing beyond a certain size. It seems unlikely that large companies will give way to small or vice versa. What is more probable, however, is that something in between will develop. The widespread practice of outsourcing and subcontracting is a clear precursor to a form of networked business where the needs of large companies can be met by smaller in close service-orientated relationships. Rather than global corporations we may come to see something closer to a global network.

While we can dismiss the notion that globalization is a wanton and destructive force bent on undermining the autonomy of the individual via the agency of a demonic corporation we should not be complacent about the extent to which the world is shrinking, making increased internationalism inevitable. The undeniable information revolution is creating an increasingly global market and the logic behind both producing and selling goods in a large number of markets around the world is compelling, offering economies of scale and protection from currency fluctuations. Parochialism has to be passé. The mind set of every manager must be multinational, sensitive to international difference, mindful of nuance – neither any more than this, nor any less.

The nation state – confronting its mortality, or merely metamorphosing?

And what of the nation state? If globalization is no more a reality than it was at the turn of this century, the supposed pinnacle of the nation state, can we really assume that it is in decline? The answer must be that the nation state emphatically is not in decline, merely in a state of evolution, as any organic entity inevitably must be. The nation state does not appear to have ever been a particularly stable entity. Opinions are divided as to its origin, its age, its extent and its purpose. There seems a consensus, however, that the nation-state emerged in early modern Europe, in the new monarchies of England, France and Spain in the sixteenth and seventeenth centuries. The extent to which these nation states engaged in the full panoply of state craft that has been seen in the twentieth century is open to question. Until the eighteenth century states were primarily concerned with diplomacy and warfare. The advent of industrial capitalism produced demand for a new range of state services: communication systems, infrastructural projects like transport systems, mass education systems. Then states became involved in health systems leading to the modern welfare systems. The five primary functions supplied by the nation state can be defined as:

- providing the capability to wage massive, organized war;
- providing the logistical capability to support both militarism and capitalism;
- providing the site for political democracy;
- providing protection for social citizenship rights;
- providing macroeconomic planning.

Not all of these functions are of equal importance and, while some have declined in the course of the twentieth century, others are growing in importance. There is considerable debate in Europe, with the development of the European Union (EU), about the need for individual nation states to maintain their sovereignty. By some observers the EU is said to undermine sovereignty. If we take sovereignty to mean the exclusive and comprehensive right of independent action maintained by a state, then it follows that every member of the EU has automatically relinquished the right to remain sovereign, retaining only the right to leave the Union. In any case, nation states in their dealings with other nation states, in their trans- or international dealings, routinely relinquish rights of sovereignty. Those Europeans who say that the most fundamental element of sovereignty is the ability of a state to defend or promote its own interests overlook the paradox that west European sovereignties in the area of defence were voluntarily given up to the United States in 1945. Since that date the defence of Europe has rested in the main, although not exclusively, with America. While nation states give up some of their sovereign rights, they take on others in their place. In particular, nation states are far more concerned with the regulation of the intimate private spheres of the life cycle and the family (regulations govern family violence, the care of the family, relations between men and women, even habits such as smoking are not immune from state intervention). Further, states are increasingly called upon by particular interest groups to play a role in environmental, gender or consumer issues. Central government, in general, has been increasing rather than diminishing in recent years. In some parts of the world, nation states are very much in their infancy, many having come into being only with the break-up of colonial empires in the post-war period – to talk of their decline, when some have been fought for so hard, seems absurd.

The balance of the national and the international

Nation states have never existed in isolation from transnational forces. Capitalism – which the nation state supported and made possible – has ever been transnational. In its earliest phase in particular there was virtually free mobility of capital and labour with most growth zones located in border or cross-border areas, such as the low countries or Bohemia and Catalonia. Finance capital has remained highly transnational. Cultural movements, the Romantic movement, the realist novel, modernism and postmodernism have all existed transnationally, alongside the nation state. There is no single reason why transnationalism should undercut nationalism – in its most positive sense. On the contrary, increasing transnationalism may give new force to nationalism (we shall consider this further in Chapter 7). Our sense of identity is bound up with the language we speak, the system of education we undergo, the geography in which we live – features of our national rather than our transnational life. The nation state provides an anchor and focus and so plays an important part in our emotional well-being. It also provides an important administrative vehicle for ensuring the protection of individuals in relation to civil and welfare rights. The challenge for citizens of the nation state is to balance the merits of transnationalism with the security to be derived from nationalism. Europe, which gave rise to the nation state, offers a strong example of the fluid relations between nationalism and internationalism. Town twinnings, student exchanges, professional and scientific conferences, tourism – all are routine elements of life which bring Europeans into easy relation with one another; and yet in no sense does this diminish our sense of being French, Swedish or Dutch.

We have seen from the above that while globalization is not the terrible force some fear, the various nations of the world are brought increasingly closer together and actions in one part can have considerable impact on the experience of another, potentially thousands of miles distant. This argues for some form of state or social apparatus which can help manage the numerous international issues that will arise, and which will increase the sense of responsibility in citizens that they are not just citizens of one nation state but of the wider world too. The EU is just such a vehicle. The citizens of each of the member states are also citizens of Europe, carriers of European passports who move freely across member states acquiring a sense of a more diffuse culture than the merely national. The Union has not eroded national identities (there is far greater concern about the impact of American popular culture); on the contrary, the only sense in which the Union seems to have eroded local cultures is in undermining xenophobia, national culture in its worst sense. The EU fosters a strong sense of internationalism, while also providing the economies of scale that enable its member states to compete effectively with the US and Japan (and, increasingly, the emerging Asian economies). This is not a point to pass over lightly. With the possible exception of Germany, no single European state has the muscle to compete on the world business stage against the United States and Japan. A cohesive, continent-wide economic unit is essential for the continued affluence of Europeans.

The influence of culture

Do Europeans, by dint of being members of Europe, gain anything over and above the experience of the Japanese and Americans who operate from the security and ease of large, homogeneous markets with a common language and generally common cultural traditions? It is the conviction of this author that assuredly they do. By dint of being European one learns the art of internationalism, developing the ability to be culturally dextrous, almost culturally neutral rather than culturally certain, in which certainty lies the way to cultural imperialism – the implicit danger of a strong and homogeneous culture. As international commerce penetrates more and more new markets, the more paramount becomes the ability to operate sensitively with people and practices that are foreign. The European saying, 'when in Rome do as the Romans do', reworked as the modern, 'think global, act local', resonates here. Both America and Japan have exported their cultures very effectively but both display elements of concern about the strength and different orientation of other cultures. The Japanese, famously, are slow to invest much faith in non-Japanese systems or workers, creating a situation where they rarely give top managerial positions to indigenous workers in their overseas operations. America finds problematic the Japanese practice of keeping business within Japanese networks even where the economic logic (an American economic logic) would appear to support that business being given to a non-Japanese (American) organization. This cultural pique has led to trade battles of a quite un-American kind. The American and Japanese experience shows that a strong culture can breed intolerance of other cultures which in an age of multiculturalism will be increasingly disabling.

As we have seen, the global corporation is something of a myth. However, of all the countries studied by Hirst and Thompson it was apparent that multinational companies with a European base have a wider regional focus than the multinationals in the homogeneous cultures of America and Japan. British and German companies are far more active in their regional market (taken to be Europe, the Middle East and Africa) than American companies are in either the Pacific Rim or the Americas outside North America and Canada, or than Japanese companies in Asia, beyond Japan. A manager now operating in a European company is likely, then, to have a broader international perspective than one in a North American or Japanese business, much less likely to fall prey to parochialism, much more likely to learn from the diversity of that experience.

Networking and trust

As we shall see in later chapters, a strong, unified sense of national culture has been a primary factor in the development of some of the strongest economies in the world. 'The business of America is business' – this comment from a President of the United States shows the extent to which there was a collective mission to make of America the consolidated business empire that it has been for the second half of the twentieth century. As we approach the twenty-first century, however, and in the context of heightened internationalism and the extension of worldwide networks, a culture that is more variegated might have something to offer those operating within it. Europe, by dint of being a collection of different cultures with areas of commonality as large as those of difference, may be peculiarly well suited to the conditions which will prevail in the increasingly global markets of the future.

Indeed, culture may come to be the key differentiator in business success. This is a large claim but in the many studies of economic prophecy and prediction that I have read in the course of writing this volume I have been struck by the extent to which the cultural, the human element is neglected. In the speculation about the horrors the global corporation will bring to bear on the societies which it is said so conspicuously to neglect, there seems to be little cognizance of the fact that a global corporation is the product of human endeavour and remains firmly within human control. Multinational corporations are seldom run by one individual and, while concern will be expressed about the degree of institutional control and the anonymity of those institutions, they are themselves scarcely run by robots. Increasing focus on governance and disclosure may demystify elements of corporate life and, while no corporation will ever be a fully democratic organism, the interests of shareholders and labour and, increasingly, the population at large will be better served in the future than they have been in the past. Witness the increasing incidence of committees to deal with the issues attendant upon the environment or the concern of the Maastricht treaty (the infamous social chapter) to harmonize labour practices. In short, corporations are ultimately run by and for people. To ignore the human element is extraordinarily myopic.

A number of modern economists do not so much ignore the human element as simplify human processes to a prevailing rationality. By this thinking individuals are actuated entirely by self-interest, by the narrow principle of utility and an unambiguous desire to maximize their material well-being. Any apparently irrational choice (so says rational choice theory) is the product of inadequate information. The argument continues that human association is also motivated entirely by self-interest – the recognition that a particular goal can be achieved better by harnessing others, even if the consequences of so doing are a necessary division of the spoils yielded by that joint endeavour.

While this neoclassical economic position may have a certain logic intuitively, emotionally it falters. Is it a rational choice to elect to have a child? Once, perhaps, the extension of family would secure one's well-being in old age. In modern society there is no guarantee that a child will provide that shelter but there is every certainty that that child will require substantial care, consuming large funds of both parental time and money, undoubtedly impinging to some extent on the material well-being of the parent. In the 1940s the psychologist Abraham Maslow identified a hierarchy of human needs. Principal amongst these was that of food and shelter, the fundamental requirements that allow life to continue. Once those needs have been satisfactorily met then the additional needs will surface – the need for safety, the need for intimacy and belonging, the need for self-esteem and respect and the need for self-actualization, the fulfilment of one's potential. Perhaps if we consider Maslow's hierarchy of needs against the act of having a child we will find that the extension of family is rational, assuming the parent has satisfied the basic fundamental need for food and shelter. Certainly, a child can satisfy the need for intimacy and belonging, by dint of being dependent. Childbirth can be said to satisfy biological potential and, by elevating the parents to a position of power, can generate self-esteem (if self-esteem is rooted in power relations), but are these the primary considerations that motivate parenthood? How would rational choice theorists deal with martyrdom, which may satisfy some need for self-esteem (to be able to believe one is doing something for a higher principle) but undercuts every other fundamental need? Human motivation is neither so clear cut nor so self-serving as a rational choice approach would have us believe, compelling though its logic may be in many instances. Nor is human behaviour. Human behaviour combines a rich network of inherited and observed habits and traditions, values, beliefs and abstract concepts. The human animal is a multifaceted, cultured being. Adam Smith, architect of political economy, was of the view that economic life could not be divorced from culture, a stance being increasingly taken up by modern economists, amongst them Francis Fukuyama whose recent publication entitled *Trust* has some useful insights for us.

Fukuyama's argument is that the ability of particular cultures to form associations based on trust has substantial implications for the type of economic environment that the particular culture will evolve. He divides cultures into low-trust and high-trust societies using several national economies as exemplars of type. In a well-argued, coherent and compelling thesis he demonstrates that there are three critical types of belonging: the family at the base, the state at the head and, in between, the associations which comprise civil society – church, social clubs, voluntary organizations, unions and businesses:

> *'There are three forms of economic organization corresponding to each path: the family business, the professionally managed corporation, and the state-owned or sponsored enterprise. The first and third paths, it turns out, are closely related to one another: cultures in which the primary avenue towards sociability is family and kinship have a great deal of trouble creating large, durable economic organizations and therefore look to the state to initiate and support them. Cultures inclined toward voluntary associations, on the other hand, can create large economic organizations spontaneously and do not need the state's support.'*

Of course, all companies generally start as small, entrepreneurial, frequently family-run businesses but the degree of sociability demonstrated by a given culture can have considerable impact on the ability of that culture to manage the transition from family to professionally managed businesses.

At the core of Fukuyama's argument is the notion of trust. To simplify, where family ties are particularly strong and loyalty focuses on close kin (or the extended family) there is little recourse outside the family for intimacy and a sense of belonging and hence little association with non-kin. The habit of trusting people with whom there is no blood tie does not develop – on the contrary, those with whom there is no blood tie represent competition and are unlikely to be trusted. Highly familistic cultures often coincide with those where there is a history of absolutism or where other strong state-like institutions predominate (such as the Catholic Church) either of which institutional type is intolerant of intermediary associations. It is ironic that family values should undermine the concept of trust. Amongst the low trust societies that Fukuyama identifies are China and cultures that have been heavily influenced by China (those of Taiwan, Hong Kong and Singapore) and in Europe, France and Italy. In Chinese communities the influence of the Confucian veneration of the family, coupled with the policy of equal inheritance amongst sons, led to the development of extended family units in which wealth was dissipated over a couple of generations. This gave rise to a community based on numerous competing families where family businesses, due to the pattern of inheritance, would decline within a couple of generations. While in Europe the policy of primogeniture ensured the development of noble families with huge stocks of capital, it also ensured that younger sons sought their fortune outside the family, forcing them to form associations beyond kin (the army, the church, the professions) leading, with the development of trade, to heightened entrepreneurialism. Fukuyama draws an interesting parallel between parts of Italy where familism has dominated and the Chinese pattern, describing a form of Italian Confucianism. The scenario in France, however, is rather different. France does not have a legacy of veneration of the family. Indeed, the prominence of the family as an institution has come about largely because of the absence of any other institutions to ensure social cohesion. Fukuyama traces this tendency back to the birth of a highly centralized French state as the French monarchy secured its absolute power in the sixteenth and seventeenth centuries. He cites Alexis de Tocqueville:

> 'there was in France no township, borough, village, or hamlet, however small, no hospital, factory, convent or college which had the right to manage its own affairs as it thought fit or to administer its possessions without interference'.

The habit of forming associations with equals or near equals was simply disallowed.

High trust societies, in contrast to low trust societies, are ones where there has been an enduring level of non-familial association that has operated below the level of the state. The German guild tradition which fed into the apprenticeship system and the different emphasis of Japanese Confucianism (venerating loyalty but not exclusively within the family) have both given rise to strong communitarian-based cultures where the wider community is stronger than the individual. Ironically, given its belief in itself as a culture of individuals the American nation has also been predominantly a high trust, communitarian culture where intermediate associations have been enormously influential – not least because they have been voluntary (America has no established church but has always had a high proportion of church-goers in its population).

As noted above the type of organization that emerges from a low trust or high trust culture is quite specific. Low trust cultures find it hard to develop professional management structures within the private sector where high levels of trust are required, where the notions of reciprocity and obligation are important. Large organizations in low trust cultures do exist, but they tend to be state enterprises (France is the obvious exemplar here). High trust cultures develop both large companies and complex sustaining networks around them (as we shall see in Chapter 4; these networks played an important role in the economic development of both Germany and Japan). Of course there are anomalies. Korea, which is a culture not unlike the Chinese model, nevertheless has an economy based on a few vast corporations – but these corporations have been developed via substantial state influence. This is not to say that the organizations that can develop in low-trust societies are intrinsically less economically viable than those in high trust cultures. China has experienced extraordinarily rapid growth on the basis of small businesses – but when the economy demands a transition to larger industry or existing small businesses outgrow themselves the absence of trust can become a barrier to success.

Although culture is something that matures over often huge periods of time, it is something that can be eroded and the American experience provides an interesting example. The pioneering individualism that unleashed such entrepreneurial zeal coupled with the communitarianism inevitable in a migrant-based population with a strong tradition of dissenting religions has given rise to the world's most impressive array of first class, world-beating organizations. However, American society has seen a dramatic breaking down of its intermediary associations in recent years and Fukuyama makes an interesting case that this is the consequence of the rights-based individualism that has always been a feature of American life, but which since the 1960s has come to dominate social interaction. Since any potential infringements of an individual's rights and liberties might result in litigation – and the probability is that the individual's rights will be upheld – the authority of a number of intermediary associations has been undermined:

> *'towns were less able to control the spread of pornography; public housing authorities were forbidden from denying housing to tenants with criminal or drug abuse records; police departments were enjoined from even such innocuous activities as setting up sobriety checkpoints ... the boy scouts ... has been sued by Jews for excluding non-Christians, by women for admitting only boys and by gay rights groups for excluding homosexual scout masters ... The organization ... has become fairer and less exclusive ... but has also lost those features which made it a strong moral community.'*

However well intentioned the American drive to protect the rights of the individual, a clear by-product is the loss of trust. Another by-product is a levelling effect. The virtuous American assumption of equality and the apparent eradication of moral, absolute or value judgments about individuals or groups of individuals blunts American sensitivity to other cultures. The erosion of trust, the levelling of all peoples to a baseline of uniformity have potentially far-reaching consequences for the American economy. It is trust and an imaginative understanding of difference which can enable diversification, innovation and flexibility. With the decline of American intermediary associations, where will future generations learn the art of association and so develop the skills to evolve new entities? Existing large American multinationals are increasingly slow to change themselves and the American management population is becoming decreasingly benevolent, paternalistic and nurturing. While the short-term consequences of this hard-nosed style may be beneficial rather than otherwise, the erosion of trust, reciprocity and obligation will lead, ultimately, to the monstrous inhuman corporation of modern myth. Such a corporation where mistrust is endemic runs the grave risk of becoming corrupt at the top and inefficient below.

The Fukuyama argument is interesting on a number of levels, for the focus it places on a positive virtue (trust) rather than a negative emotion (self interest), for the emphasis it gives to culture, and for the pattern it draws between cultures which appear utterly unlike (Italian Confucianism). Above all, perhaps, it is interesting for the emphasis it places upon association, on the coming together of unlike peoples for mutually beneficial purposes; and in the context of a European bid for economic supremacy this must be the most interesting application of Fukuyama's work. We have in these pages described a world which is shrinking, where peoples are coming closer together and on the one hand developing increasingly similar interests and tastes, while on the other becoming increasingly aware of areas of difference. The nature of communities is, inevitably, changing. There is no particular reason why the change should be seen to be negative, so long as a form of community continues to exist. The notion of an organic society, the golden agrarian age, has long since been ridiculed. Modern communities form themselves irrespective of geographies. Modern communication techniques give people the freedom to converse and correspond immediately. Familiarity and ease with these means of communication enable people to develop relationships that do not demand face-to-face contact. The popularity of citizens' band radio, the notion of pen pals, to take just two examples, testify that intimacy does not always demand either proximity or close personal knowledge. Far from disappearing in the modern age, community is being stretched over a wider area and is finding new forms of expression.

In an earlier epoch, the EU was called the European Economic *Community* and Europe, clearly, is a thriving community. The citizens of the various member states have formed a political association and, as we note above, numerous other voluntary associations (of which town twinning is one of the more extraordinary expressions). In the situations Fukuyama considers, the associational practices are confined within a national setting. In Europe we can see association operating on an international, indeed intercontinental level. High trust and low trust societies are increasingly coming together and the benefits of each, the paradigmatic business structures that evolve in the different cultures, will provide a pool of expertise to be shared. Above all, however, it is the act of international association which is remarkable. In a marketplace where the ability to form networks crossing international boundaries could prove a decisive factor in economic success or failure, Europe clearly has the edge on either Japan or America where strong homogeneous cultures preclude a certain degree of internationalism – only 9% of Americans hold passports, so inward-focused is the society. The coexistence of diversity and difference with tolerance and respect for that diversity and difference represents the primary advantage that Europe has in an age of increasing internationalism over her key competitors.

So what are the assumptions underpinning this book? The primary assumption is that culture will be, as it always has been, of critical importance in deciding the relative fortunes of the major world economies. Those institutions and organizations that recognize and articulate this fact will have the lead on those that neglect it. The intensification of worldwide networks is unlikely to be arrested, but equally this process will not undermine the strength of local and national units. On the contrary, in some ways increasing internationalism will reinforce nationalism, therefore necessitating a careful balance between the two potentially conflicting forces. The nation state will change as it has changed throughout its existence but it will continue to function, taking unto itself aspects that are currently not part of its remit. As a medium of government the nation state will probably also be supplemented by other transnational methods of government. Corporations, both of large and small scale, will continue to operate across a broad and widening market spectrum but not at the expense of local and national allegiance. As in the case of political systems of government, corporations may find innovative means of managing increasingly complex economic conditions, which may well include the development of international support and service networks. The economic unit that will make the most of such conditions will combine large- with small-scale corporations, and will lay claim to highly skilled, culturally tolerant and adaptable peoples who voluntarily enter into transnational relationships. The primary underlying assumption that this book will attempt to prove is that Europe, which meets each of these conditions, is better placed than either of her primary competitors Japan or the United States, or even the combined states of Asia, to be the pre-eminent power of the twenty-first century.

2

United by Difference: the Formation of a European Identity

'Whether the confrontation of cultures lead to conflict or adaptation and progress, it is now vitally important to develop a deeper understanding of what makes these cultures distinctive and functional, since the issues surrounding international competition, political and economic, increasingly will be cast in cultural terms'

Francis Fukuyama, *Trust*.

What is Europe?

Europe is an old continent. The etymology of the word Europe is a matter for debate, with some coming down on the side of Semitic origins, in which case the word would have associations with darkness and the direction in which the sun sets; others – more auspiciously – see its origins in the Greek language where it would mean broad-faced. Certainly, in the classical period Europa was both a person and a geographical region. The person was the daughter of the King of Tyre, who attracted the attentions of Zeus. In order to seduce her, Zeus turned himself into a bull and carried his prize away on his back to Crete. Eventually Europa married the King of Crete and bore several sons, one of whom was King Minos, the builder (appropriately enough for the son of Europe) of the labyrinth. The geographical region was originally merely the mainland of Greece as distinct from the islands, but with the spread of Greek civilization north and west so the boundaries of Europa extended in contradistinction to Asia and Libya. Jacques Derrida, one of

Europe's greatest living philosophers, has found a metaphor which embraces some of the complexity within one idea:

> *'In its physical geography, and in what has often been called ... its spiritual geography, Europe has always recognized itself as a cape or headland, either as the advanced extreme of a continent, to the west and south (the land's end ... Europe of the Atlantic or of the Greco-Latino-Iberian shores of the Mediterranean), the point of departure for discovery, invention, and colonization, or as the very centre ... the Europe of the middle, coiled up, indeed compressed along a Greco-Germanic axis ...'*

This gives some sense of the range of peoples and influences that have come together in this arbitrary alliance called Europe. He attributes his use of the term cape to another French thinker and poet, Paul Valery who wrote:

> *'What then is Europe? It is a kind of cape of the old continent, a western appendix to Asia?'*

and, for all we talk about Europe as an old continent, it is young when contrasted with the ancient Asian civilizations that once enjoyed hegemony. Indeed, while Europa may be a classical concept, the term European does not find expression until the Renaissance when it was coined by Pope Pius II.

From the Renaissance (or more particularly from 1492 until, perhaps, 1992) some would say that Europe has looked outwards to other shores and that Europe's culture derives from being no more than the happy confluence of fertile lands and navigable seas, from which sprang pioneers who set sail to colonize and stamp their culture on distant lands (and, as Derrida again points out, the Latin-derived words culture and colonization have a common root) only, in the twentieth century to find themselves being colonized in turn by the Americans and Japanese. In reality, there has been a continuum of distinctly European experience from classical to modern times, a merging and co-mingling of histories, trends, ethics to create an identity that is distinctive, functional and the clear product of adaptation and progress. Given the inevitable role that culture will play in any political or economic competition in the twenty-first century it is essential to understand something of the labyrinthine process by which Europe has become the entity we understand her to be today. What emerges and is of relevance to Europe's businessmen is a tradition of unity both of thought and action, coexisting with local difference and distinction. As François Mitterand once noted: '[Europe] is returning in its history and its geography like one who is returning home', after long years of looking outwards, we are looking inwards at one another. However, even at its most splintered Europeans have been held together by factors other than geography, factors that this chapter will trace. What this chapter will conclude is that our dilemma now is no different than it has ever been – the requirement to maximize difference within loose union.

European Union – Roman style

Despite the affirmation by Derrida that Europe is, traditionally, innovative, it is not fashionable to see Europe as in any sense pioneering. Can we deduce from this, then, some lost European homogeneity of culture and purpose? Certainly, Europeans have been united before but the most enduring, longest-lasting period of union was the first. Interestingly in the light of the metaphors we have seen in the context of a European character, the first exemplar of a homogeneous (broadly) European empire comes not from a sea power at all, but from those great mobilizers of land power – the Romans. The first European civilizations were founded in Western Asia and the Nile valley and then around the shores of the Aegean in Crete, Greece and Western Asia Minor. To these cultures modern Europe can trace many of its myths and values but it is the Roman Empire which brought together a diversity of peoples and, remarkably, held them together over a process of acquisition spanning seven centuries. No other empire has yet to emulate the Roman achievement of retaining conquests. The minutiae of Roman imperial expansion and ultimate dissolution is not the concern of this chapter, nor shall we dwell on the dependence on a slave economy (characteristic of so many imperial endeavours) and the bloodbaths that marked the hand-over of power from leader to leader. Instead, we shall concern ourselves with the key elements in the maintenance of empire.

Decentralization and empowerment in the Roman Empire

In the first place Rome had to acquire the territories that were to form its empire. This it did by means of its army and the army came to dominate the economy and infrastructure of the Roman Empire. The Roman Head Office – as it were – was a lean machine; from about 100 BC to AD 200, Rome supported only around 150 civil servants, another 150 senatorial and equestrian administrators and the small staffs of these. For an empire that stretched some 3 million square kilometres and embraced, perhaps, 70 million people this low bureaucratic level is extraordinary. The Roman army – the legions – was the primary source of power, although over the centuries of the Empire's existence the army went through modifications and to impose one unified identity upon it is to distort the truth. There was nothing novel in an empire that ruled through native elites backed by imperial governors, garrisons and legionary camps – the Romans merely followed the established model in their government of acquired territories. What is novel about the Roman approach, however, is the policy of allowing local rulers to stay in place – harnessing the defeated seat of power to assist in pacification. The Romans, then, are the first exponents of the 'think global, act local' philosophy. This process of pacification brought with it several benefits. In the first place Roman culture took hold of conquered peoples (or the ruling classes of those conquered peoples) with a conscious policy to teach language and literacy, build theatres and amphitheatres and integrate local cults into Roman ones. Indeed, the process of Romanization was so thorough that, after about a century of Roman dominance local cultural distinctions disappeared from view. Further, membership of the senate and even imperial succession was diffused across the empire, passing through Roman aristocrats to Italian bourgeois, thence to Italian settlers in Spain and southern Gaul, onwards to Africans and Syrians and ultimately to men from the Danubian and Balkan areas. This subtle integration of diverse cultures into one homogenous unit, coupled with a recognition of Rome as the centre of the Empire, brought both peace and power. The army, with the completion of conquest and pacification in one area could then extend itself to more outlying areas, drawing upon the manpower and the trading wealth of the newly subdued states. We risk distortion again by using too liberally the term 'peace' – one feature of the Roman Empire was that it was always at war.

European Monetary Union and standardization

A warring economy can be a stable one. The provision, by war, of a communications and trade infrastructure and a consumption market in the legions (and of course in Rome itself) served to boost coinage, trade and economic development. The Romanization of culture is no less striking than the Romanization of coinage and from AD 40–260 the empire was a single monetary unit. The legions accounted for some 60% of all Roman expenditure but the conquest culture, while it drew from Roman coffers, substantially added to them too. Roman conquests dispensed with political boundaries and gave access via the opening up of the north-west to highly lucrative trading networks to the south and east. While trading riches formed one prong of the economy, taxation was another (and monetary taxes were exhorted from the richest provinces – Spain, north Africa, southern Gaul and Asia Minor) and rent still another, with the use of slaves, serfs and free labour by landlords increasing the surplus, cash flow and, of course, trade.

This foray into Roman history affords us a glimpse of a united Europe, although by no means a united Europe that embraces all the territories that now come within the European frontiers. Nor was the Empire exclusively European. Qualifications aside, the Roman empire brought a degree of standardization (rather than homogeneity) of government, of coinage, of trade, of language, of law and, eventually, of religion too. That these standards, with the exception of the religious one, were coerced – set in place through conquest and held in place by a form of tolerant coercion – it is perhaps only fair to state. The Roman Empire, like any extensive and aggressive one, was not benevolent, or was only benevolent in so far as benevolence served the ends of the city state and thence the empire itself.

Christendom and the need for a coherent European identity

The rise of Christianity – and the development of a spiritual empire – did not depend on coercion. The movement was a popular one, in the sense that its ideology was for and of the people (the term 'people' is used here to denote those not of the ruling classes rather than the masses, but broadens in time to include both ruling classes and masses alike). There are a range of explanations for the rise of Christianity but that which to me and to the thesis of this book is most striking is the need amongst conquered peoples in an extensive empire for a coherent identity. Michael Mann, eminent sociologist and author of *The Sources of Social Power* (to which this chapter owes a significant debt) makes the point with precision:

> *'Christianity was not a response to a material crisis, nor was it a spiritual alternative to the material world. The crisis was one of social identity: what society do I belong to? This was generated by the very successes of the Roman Empire and of Hellenistic civilisation, which produced transcendent principles of social organisation interstitially from within their own social structures'.*

The message of Christianity in its simplest form – that the kingdom of God is open to all and requires no qualification for entry beyond faith – has an innate universalizing tendency that sweeps away the secular hierarchy within which few had either power or authority. The Roman Empire had extremely efficient (which is not to say official) communications networks which were swiftly mobilized to spread the Christian Gospels. Of these the most important was the mercantile and artisan axis. This class drew on rural agricultural production and so had access to the portion of the population under the rule of large landowners, but were organized within towns that were also governed by large landowners. Merchants and artisans had their own organizational structures that were independent of those set in place by the Empire – the guilds – and so, with a foothold in both urban and rural communities, access to extensive trade routes and high levels of literacy (and Christianity is a religion of the book) formed an effective fifth column. The spread of Christianity, being outside (or underneath) the official administrative channels of the Empire, was largely invisible to the state and this explains the speed of communication and the concomitant harshness of Roman efforts to suppress 'secret societies'. A crucial tenet of the Christian gospel is that man must help his fellow man; hence class barriers were no inhibitor to the rise of Christianity and the notion of 'fellowship' and 'brotherhood' rapidly took hold across the empire. The Emperor Constantine was the first to convert to Christianity (AD 312) but while his personal motives may have been confused there is little doubt that the ethic of Christianity was one that the Roman elite saw in action as a profoundly efficient model for social organization.

The marriage of two empires

The marriage of the Christian Church and the Roman Empire has a compelling logic. The Roman State lacked the apparatus to penetrate the everyday lives of those it governed while Christian communities lacked the organizational apparatus to provide the necessary level of infrastructural and social support. The church borrowed organizational forms from the Empire – developing a municipal structure with bishops in place of governors and tithes as taxes by another name. In turn, the Empire carried Christianity to the limits of its territory – although the marcher lords, the German barbarians, were not exposed to this missionary zeal. Although tied to the Empire in significant, largely organizational ways, the orthodox Catholic Church (which dates from around AD 250) remained a distinct entity and was able to survive the collapse of empire. The birth of Christendom marks a second (and despite later schisms) much more enduring unification of Europe. Without reference to its spiritual significance (this is, after all, a secular study) the central creed of Christianity was a universalizing one. It was an ideology that could unite the unlike and transcend the traditional barriers of allegiance, tribal origin and language. The other great legacy of the Roman Empire to the Christian one was the Latin language that gave, to the literate and educated sector of the population, a common standard until the reformation and the celebration of the vernacular. The marriage of the two empires is interesting within the context of the Fukuyama thesis on trust and the need for civil association – here we see a precedent for Europeans to mix on the basis of shared faith rather than shared kinship patterns and to communicate by dint of the apparatus of trade and government held in common through an efficient bureaucracy. In the marriage of these two empires it is possible to see the birth of European commercial greatness with a culture of trust and association clearly being developed.

The fragmentation of the secular empire

Our use of the term Europe above in the context of the Roman Empire is misguided. It was not until the ninth century that a recognizable European map comes into being. Thus far in our discussion we have not yet mentioned the Germanic tribes who, responding to the aggressive influx of nomadic peoples from Central Asia (who penetrated the Chinese, Indian and Persian civilizations at the same time as they mounted an assault on the Romans), moved from their settled positions in north and central Europe beyond the reach of the Empire. There followed a sequence of Germanic invasions. The Visigoths defeated the Roman emperor at Adrianapole in 378, sacked Rome in 410 and were settled in Aquitaine by 418. Following in the wake of the Visigoths came the Alans, Vandals, Sueves, Alemans, Franks and in the rear, the Ostrogoths who gained control of Italy by 493. It was to take nearly another two centuries before the Germanic tribes could finally gain control of Britain although the Anglo-Saxon invasion began around 440.

Roman rule in the heartland of the Empire withstood the invasions by less well-organized tribes and a major counter-offensive was launched and won by the Emperor Justinian in 533. However, the victory was short lived, for the resulting chaos of war made the Empire vulnerable to attack from the Asian Avars who drove the Lombards into Italy. For a period Italy was divided between the Lombards, the Byzantine Emperor and the Papacy but fearing the rise of the Lombards the Pope sought assistance from the Franks. Ultimately this was to lead to the invasion by Charlemagne (Charles the Great) and subsequent conquest and annexation by the Carolingian rulers of the Lombard kingdom in 774 – here lie the origins of the Holy Roman Empire. Charles' greatest victories were against the Bavarians, the Avars, and the Saxons – which last were finally subdued in 804. This last victory postdated by four years Charles' coronation as Emperor by Pope Leo 111 – the very apogee of Frankish success. The Carolingian Empire was a short-lived one – it had collapsed by 888 but it left behind a legacy of land unions which comprise much of Europe as we now know it.

Still there is the Scandinavian legacy to consider and for the northern peoples of Europe the latter two centuries of the first millennium mark the invasion and subsequent settlement by Norwegians and Danes in the north and west. Meanwhile, to the south the Saracens led attacks while the Magyars moved into northern Italy and Germany before colonizing the Hungarian plain. Invasion led to political disruption and the decay of royal authority, leading in turn to the rise of local magnates, from which sprung the upsurge in feudalism and the polarization of society into nobles and serfs. The English kingdom of Wessex seemed a lone example of a European kingdom that withstood outside invasion whilst sustaining Danish attacks which destroyed its fragile unity. England would have become a Scandinavian stronghold but for the Norman conquest whereby William was able to subdue southern Britain and align it with the Christian and feudal civilization of mainland Europe.

Fragmentation as a source of power

This canter through several centuries of early European history shows the endurance of the Christian religion – missionaries were active amongst the Germanic tribes and the Germanic peoples acquired Christianity as part of the route to power – but also what, in the wake of the Roman Empire, might seem a disturbing fragmentation of a settled group of lands. Paradoxically perhaps, this fragmentation might be the very source of the power that developed in Europe and dominated the world until the twentieth century. Paul Kennedy points out in *The Rise and Fall of the Great Powers* that European geography, with is mountain ranges, large forests and therefore necessarily scattered centres of population, did much to ensure that no one centralized power was able to gain absolute control. Extensive development of power across a vast land mass, mobilizing, through coercion, seemingly endless resources of human power, can be seen to preclude intensive development. Much is made in commentaries on the decline of the Roman Empire (although all such ideas are subject to considerable debate), of the failure by the Empire to innovate. Critics of the Empire note that such technological innovations as the water mill (known in Palestine in the first century AD) and the reaping machine (known in Gaul at the same time) were not carried around the Empire. With no shortage of human labour there was no need to invest in labour-saving technology and indeed, given the requirement to subdue conquered populations through labour, there might have been every need to resist such technological advances. With the fragmentation of the Roman Empire comes the concentration on intensive development – such inventions as the heavy plough and the three-field system, which were revolutionary to agricultural development – and extensive development during the period remained the province of other groups, notably the Mongol Empire (1206–1696). So from the experience of the Roman Empire and its annexation of Christendom several features of relevance to a new European Union emerge:

- that decentralization, local decision making and tolerance towards indigenous peoples by colonizers within one unifying system of loose bureaucracy can lead to long-standing hegemony;
- that a need for a common identity over and above the identities wrought by class, region and family is a common historical trend;
- that a large, geographically diverse region can be susceptible to rapid networks and the growth of interest groups between people apparently very unlike one another;
- the preservation of areas of significant difference and the legitimization of intensive development is the primary means of ensuring sustained innovation.

The free movement of persons – the historical precedents for a single market

It is perhaps just a happy accident that no one state developed firearms which could give them the potential to overrun neighbouring states so that this fragmented Europe was able to develop at its own pace without the imposition of rule from outside. Communities were able to develop to some degree in isolation, intensively, on a broadly feudal model but were linked by the enduring trading networks. It is stating the obvious to say that trade is as old as civilization itself but in the context of a book about business, which is the scion of trade, it is perhaps pertinent to identify the role of a mercantile, artisan and trading class in the growth of European power far in advance of the agricultural and industrial revolutions that solidified that power. Geography again played a part in the development of a trading culture. The range of climatic difference led to a range of differentiated products across Europe that were suitable for exchange and barter. Where the oriental caravans carried luxury items, fine silks and spices, European trading routes were reserved for more prosaic, bulk items of which the staples were timber, grain, wine, wool and fish. Trading via navigable rivers gave way to trading by sea which, in turn, necessitated the development of ever more sophisticated seafaring vessels. As new centres of wealth grew (like the Hansa towns and the Italian cities) so too did the financial structures to support growing international trade. Bills of exchange, banking and a credit system have their foundations in this period. Merchants carried goods, but also spread news, demonstrated new advances in technology and, with catastrophic effect, also took disease (notably plague) from one part of the continent to another. The mercantile class was a necessary one, but to the ruling classes something of a necessary evil. Large landowners feared the insurrection of the towns where the merchants clustered and the papacy made pronouncements against usury and the generation of wealth as alien to the word of the gospels. It was, however, convenient for many to connive at the continuance of trade and to take a share in its spoils. Thus, despite systematic attempts at the oppression of visible mercantile groups, such communities were able to uproot themselves and take their expertise to more welcoming lands – hence the migrations of oppressed Jewish traders, ruined Flemish textile workers and persecuted Huguenots.

The movement of merchants across the continent is matched only by the movement of religious communities. This involved not just the monastic communities but clerics and of course the laity who undertook pilgrimages over great distances, through diverse lands in pursuit of expiation of sins. Differences were leavened by the solidarity of shared belief systems. These shared belief systems were reinforced by the edicts of the Church, which governed man's very soul and in so doing could assign or withhold social status. The act of excommunication, of setting an individual outside the boundaries of acceptable social organization, was one of the manifestations of the cohesion of Christendom. Differences, nonetheless, existed. The Middle Ages were as much a time of warfare as any other – and, throughout the period, there was an arms race of a primitive kind but not one that resulted in supremacy by any one of the emerging states. Schism in the church divided the orthodox Eastern regions from those with their head in the Roman Papacy, mirroring the old east/west divide of the Roman Emperor, but the period was one of a continent gaining momentum in readiness for the expansionism of the sixteenth century. It was a period of agricultural revolution and a movement from hill top farming to the valley floor, of improved diet and flourishing trade interrupted by a devastating climatic change (the mini ice age) and the Black Death, which decimated a population already suffering from the harsh weather that had diminished yields. Historians of comparative civilizations point out that Europe was not recognisably poised for its great leap forward. In the absence of one unifying structure of rule, however, Europe was able, through a process of contest, discovery and established patterns of diffusion of knowledge coupled with the new invention of the printing press, to develop some of the systems that would ultimately lead to world power.

Expansionism, reformation and the origins of the market economy

At this point we might recall Derrida's allusion to Europe as a cape or headland – a point of departure. His philosophical concerns have often focused on language and so in his treatise on *Europe Today (The Other Heading)* he uses play upon language to illuminate a cultural tendency:

> *'The word cap* (caput, capitis) *refers ... to the head or the extremity of the extreme, the aim and the end, the ultimate ...'*

and while such playfulness may seem fanciful to a more pragmatic reader the exercise has a curious appropriateness in the context of the next phases of European development. The sixteenth century is marked across Europe by two parallel, distinct but interlinked movements. One was a physical movement, a heading off from home shores, the expansionism across the seas and development of arm's-length empires which were to fuel further discoveries (geographical and scientific) and the other was a more cerebral movement away from the orthodoxy of Catholic religion and its all too corporeal manifestations (a hatred of abuse by clerics being a primary motive behind reform). Expansionism and reformation were the twin movements which, on the one hand, highlighted division and difference while, on the other, threw into relief new similarities between peoples and places essentially unlike. In their separate ways both were to contribute to the rise of the market economy and the subsequent industrial revolutions.

Protestantism, the hard work ethic and the rise of capitalism

While Europe's seafarers were looking to other worlds, so too were the critics of Catholicism, but the end to which first Luther and then, much more incisively, Calvin looked was profoundly other-worldly. The principal tenets of Protestantism were a belief that salvation was dependent wholly and utterly on the will of God, refined by Calvinism to a belief in predestination, whereby the status of the elect (those who would find salvation) was predetermined by God. Protestantism in its strongest form rejected absolutely the notion of any intervention by human means in the preset outcome of individual salvation. This, naturally, took from the Church and all its officials the hitherto God-given right to mediate between the sinner and his/her God and threw that sinner entirely upon his/her own devices, the imperative to follow his/her *calling*. Max Weber in his publication *The Protestant Ethic and the Spirit of Capitalism* (1930) identifies a link between this focus on the individual and the eventual rise of capitalism (although his concerns are more with tracing the development of religions than with unearthing the catalyst to capitalism). He writes that one aspect of this new creed with its belief in one inscrutable, transcendent God is:

> *'the entirely negative attitude of Puritanism to all the sensuous and emotional elements in culture and in religion, because they are of no use toward salvation and promote sentimental illusion and idolatrous superstition.'*

Combined with the rejection of salvation through single acts, this denunciation of the sensuous gave to the individual a requirement to subject the personality as a whole to interrogation and so steered the individual in the direction of a methodical lifestyle, one which favoured asceticism over hedonism. Value came to be set upon hard work. Traditional power relations were undermined by a recognition that change could only be exercised from within and, it may not be far-fetched to claim, a disinclination to accrue personal and ostentatious wealth led to a predisposition to reinvest. Protestantism, which undercut the noble classes by a thoroughgoing denunciation of conspicuous consumption, resonated most with an emerging middle class in Europe although even kings could turn the new faith to their advantage (witness Henry

VIII in England). Weber wrote: 'rational conduct on the basis of the idea of the calling was born ... from the spirit of Christian asceticism', meaning that while there cannot be traced a direct causal link between Protestantism and Capitalism, the spirit of Protestantism was to inform that of Capitalism. An interesting aside to the classical Weberian thesis is that put forward by Colin Campbell in *The Romantic Ethic and the Spirit of Modern Consumerism*. He charts a link between the suppression of hedonism, and the pursuit of pleasure and the development of internalized forms of pleasure. Socially constrained from conspicuous forms of pleasure, Puritanism – Protestantism in its most severe form – led to the divorce of inner feelings from outward actions. Pleasure started to come from inner contemplation rather than external stimuli and so fantasy and imagination come to be important to modern man. From fantasy and imagination it is a short step to the notion of aspiration, a dreaming of being better circumstanced. Over time, paradoxically, the aspirational element of Protestantism feeds into the development of a consumer society, ever aspiring for better and better. Interestingly then, Protestantism might be said to inform not just the ethic that allowed for the development of capitalism, but also the imaginative stimuli that sustained it in the form of innovation and, crucially, demand.

Protestantism and the delineation of difference

Before this contribution to the rise of capitalism became evident it could be seen that Protestantism had contributed to the destruction of Christendom, by which name during the Middle Ages, Europe had more commonly been called. Christendom gave an ideological unity to the land mass but the Catholic/Protestant divide continued to bring together peoples from different localities – and it is worth remembering that the European map was still far from a consolidated collection of nation states. The doctrinal differences that emerged during the fifteenth and sixteenth centuries gave additional impetus to border, territorial and interdynastic wars, as the leaders of the key families across Europe took on the banner of either Catholicism or Protestantism. The populace proved more tolerant of war fought under a religious battle cry and to this manifestation of piety – or perhaps mere expression of identity – can be accorded the length of wars such as the 30 years war and the 80 years war.

Whereas an earlier schism in the Church had brought about a west/east distinction across the continent, the reformation gave rise to a sharper distinction between the north and south, with the English, Dutch and Swiss firmly Protestant, Spain and the Habsburgs Catholic and the French royalty also Catholic despite considerable regional Protestant dissent.

If Protestantism in part gave an emotional and behavioural impetus to the still distant industrialization then expansionism and subsequent exploitation of new worlds gave some of the wealth that was to lead to enhanced living standards and thence to increasing population, which in time, coupled with agricultural advances, free labour from the necessity of working the land and thus the increased urbanization and industrialization. Expansionism also brought into being a greater consciousness of belonging to a particular colonising nation or state as European countries vied for the spoils of empire – hence the rise of state-approved pirates like Sir Francis Drake. The post-reformation period continues the trend of aspirants to empire fighting both for the acquisition of far-off lands but also to bring under dominion the greater part of the European continent itself. The sequence of alliances by the Habsburg family, which reached its zenith under Charles V, Holy Roman Emperor, gave rise to the possibility of an Empire of the proportions not seen since the fall of Rome. However, a series of counter-alliances on the part of those threatened by the advance of the Habsburgs, coupled with the geography of the continent which rendered impossible centralised control, ensured that no one power would rise above another over the following two centuries. A policy of containment was exercised through judicious and relentlessly changing treaties and alliances.

The nation states and systems of commerce

The late fifteenth through to the late seventeenth century saw the emergence of nation states. In particular the so-called flank powers, those on the outer edges of the continent, rose in prominence as much through the activities of entrepreneurs who generated wealth as through systematic state-craft – as in Holland, Sweden and Britain. By the mid-seventeenth century the nation state system was polarizing into the Great Power system, focusing on France, the Habsburg Empire, Prussia, Britain and Russia. The emergence of these great powers owed much to the development of the apparatus of state by an absolutist monarch – led by such great state builders as Louis XIV in France and Peter the Great in Russia. Standing armies and navies were trained and maintained, and military power was subsumed within state and civil power, so freeing states from the expense of mercenary armies. The development of nation states, however, owed less to the development of great armies than to the development of the financial systems which would support an army in time of war. We have seen, already, the development of bills of exchange and a system of credit to support trade, but by the seventeenth century there had grown a cluster of financial centres, principally Amsterdam, but also in London, Lyons and Frankfurt, where grouped money-lenders, commodity dealers, goldsmiths (dealers in loans), bill merchants and jobbers in shares of the growing number of joint-stock companies, which latter had arisen as a requirement of expansionism and exploitation of new wealth. It was the United Provinces (Holland) which led the way as a financial centre, issuing loans on the basis of strength and means to pay rather than assessing governments on the basis of religious or righteous justification. This polarization towards a financial state was not, ultimately, to the advantage of the provinces which failed to develop a manufacturing base at the appropriate time, but the availability of credit and the method by which it was granted did much to define the final alignment of Great Powers.

The eighteenth century saw the development of sophisticated financial services. The Bank of England was founded in 1694, initially as a war-time expedient, and following from this Britain undertook the regularization of national debt and encouraged the growth of the stock exchange and the development of country banks which boosted the money supply available to governments and, critically, businessmen. Such financial institutions were of course supported by centralized tax collecting regimes and it was the legacy of organized fiscal apparatus that enabled Britain to raise funds that were significantly in excess of those raised by the much greater and enemy state, France. The bureaucratization of states and their manipulation of the money supply could not alone account for the Great Power system. Geography again played a significant part. Power depended as much upon one's neighbours as anything innate to a given state – Britain with its island status is a clear example of a state that could develop without the inhibition of aggressive neighbours on the other side of a relatively arbitrary land border.

Revolution – democratic and industrial

From the two great powers Britain and France come the two great revolutions which were to define the nature of the modern world. The first of these was the Industrial Revolution by which scientific and technical innovation led to the exploitation of rich natural resources in Britain, the birth of towns and the permanent change in the constitution of society away from peasants towards workers. While, from a variety of factors, not least the absence of war on home territory, Britain became the architect of the modern industrial world, it was France that fathered the democratic revolution. The French Revolution of 1799 brought to the powers of Europe the novel concepts of egalité, liberté and fraternité. The power of the people was recognized and mobilized and the entire foundation of human organization was upturned. Without dwelling on the details of either of these revolutions it is important to state that, taken together, they represent the final break with an old world order as the shock waves from both were felt across the continent and states rushed to acquire and customize elements of each.

The French Revolution also brought to the fore one of the great figures of modern history: Napoleon Bonaparte. Not since Charlemagne had there been so systematic a bid to build a European empire as that launched by Napoleon. To characterize his ambitions and achievements in such a way, however, is to deny the very kernel of his achievement which was to construct the apparatus of a modern state in his reconstruction of revolution-tattered France. As early as 1800 the 83 *departements* which had been divided the year before were reorganized under prefects, reporting in to the First Consul. The Napoleonic Code of 1804 confirmed the property rights that had been conferred by revolution, which won the enduring support of the peasant proprietors who were a vocal force across the country; and through a system of state schools and universities put in place in 1802 Napoleon also instituted the first elements of a meritocracy. Napoleon gave to the *people* of France (in itself a novel appellation) a sense of security and the focus for that security was the nation; and so we glimpse the emergence of a trend which was, ultimately, to lead to two world wars in the twentieth century – nationalism. Napoleon's own credentials were military ones and his career was permanently embattled. His enormous administrative successes might have given him the banner of national unity under which to march, but the obligation to march would have existed whether or not there was for him the opportunity of imperial control.

Nationalism – source of unity, force of destruction

The thrust of this chapter has been to understand key movements in European history which have united its peoples divided by geography. It is perhaps ironic that a unifying creed such as nationalism was to lead to intense emotional and intellectual division, that a common cause, differently expressed, should have ignited hostilities of the scale seen in the twentieth century. Throughout this cursory look at a score of centuries we have seen that running alongside any new developments has been the common urge for containment, the sequence of alliances that have held in check any one superior power, the singular *geopolitical* advantage which maintained a balance of power allowing for the subtle exploitation of difference, which was then communicated and shared. As British industrial innovations were spread, refined and extended across the continent, so too were notions of nationalism. The nineteenth century can be characterized as an age of revolution, an age of empire – as the superior European powers raced to subdue and subsume the farthest reaches of the world – and of nationalism.

As in any effort to muster a range of different events and motivations under a single umbrella it is misleading to talk of an age of nationalism. A nationalist spirit was no more pervasive among the bulk of the population – the labouring poor – than was the Protestant spirit or the capitalist spirit. Nationalism was the brainchild and creed of a startlingly small number of individuals in reaction to outmoded forms of government but these people are united by a singular gift, for propaganda. The rise of the press and the effective use of the media machine by Italian and German nationalists (principally Bismarck) has tremendous influence on the outcome of both campaigns. It is without question the rise of a unified German nation state that has done so much to decide the future of the continent. At the hub of this German state, from which sprang that arch-administrator Bismarck himself, was Prussia which, at the conclusion of the Napoleonic wars gained much of the Rhineland, a territory that was to be a primary feature in the consolidation of German unity as it supplied so much of Germany's wealth. The success of German unification in particular was that it brought together peoples of shared language and cultural/religious experience. Once brought together these people were then harnessed to produce a second industrial revolution as the German/American phase of industrialization is often dubbed. (We will consider this in closer detail in Chapters 3 and 4.)

There is neither time nor space to chart the origins of the First World War, save to refer briefly to the spread of nationalism to the Balkan states, the system of allegiances entered into in the age-old spirit of containment that came to have a stranglehold on the various participants, the jealous protection of empire by established imperial powers against the ambitious Germany, and the financial and engineering wealth that led to the stockpiling of weapons on an unprecedented scale. The eruption of war and the eventual institution of conscription brought into the homes of the entire European populace the notion of a recognizable enemy in a particular nationalist guise. For the sake of victory certain age old hostilities were overturned (at last the English and the French were allies) while others took their place. The growth of mass communication systems like the radio led to the reinforcement of national propaganda which was to become a feature of the second great conflict of the century. The Second World War – however much in retrospect we can see it as a just war – was fought initially against imperial ambitions on the part of Hitler who, like the Roman Emperors whom he revered, Charlemagne, Charles V and Napoleon, fell as a result of fighting on too many fronts.

The twentieth century has seen more savage and widespread enmities across Europe than any other century before it and it is easy to infer from these a cultural unease, simply because human memory is a conservative thing. Human endeavour, fortunately, is not and despite wholesale catastrophe the twentieth century has also seen the greatest historical efforts at peaceful integration, with substantial American support. Between the wars the ill-fated League of Nations was a fledgling effort at unity, greatly superseded by the United Nations on an international level and, on a more local one, the emergence of the European Community. I save a detailed analysis of the achievements of the Union until Chapter 10 but what is remarkable about Europe at the close of the twentieth century is that history, in its inevitable way, is repeating itself and a set of states are combining in such a way as to ape, although without the coercion and, it is to be hoped, with more innovation, the Empire of Rome. Perhaps this was the homecoming to which Mitterand referred?

This chapter has trod steadily within the tracks of historical events and movements to show the similarities and emphasize how dissimilarity has been harnessed to the defence of these similarities. Empire, Christendom, Protestantism, capitalism, nationalism and empire again have been recurrent trends that have held together the peoples of Europe as often as they have thrust them apart. There has been no mention here of the intellectual movements that have operated alongside the political ones to cement together those born in widely disparate geographies. Rationalism, the Enlightenment, Romanticism and Modernism have each in their turn brought together the minds of peoples who, physically, occupy very different spaces and we shall give closer consideration to some of the common systems of thought that have dominated in Europe in Chapter 9. Great figures such as Copernicus, Darwin, Marx and Freud have each contributed to the cultural currency that we hold in common and French, German and British traditions of thought have extended well beyond the lands that gave them birth. The influence of patterns of thought and intellectual systems should not be underplayed. While we have considered some of the trends that contributed to several centuries of European economic (and political) hegemony it is worth noting that, while it is remarkable that Europe attained its particular point of development, it is equally remarkable that other cultures did not. China, for instance, was far more technologically innovative in the fifteenth century than any European nation. What Europe developed was a scientific method that allowed for progress through empirical observation. That method was based on a belief in transcendent causality (on there being a higher truth governing reality), which was directly fed by the monotheistic, Christian ethic that has dominated in Europe and contrasts sharply with the Asian polytheistic or Confucian cultures.

A modern European identity

Much is written about the death of national identities. The French obsession with the preservation of its language is one striking manifestation of this concern and certainly in an age of mass communication there must be some fear of lost distinction. Every city in Europe has MacDonald's burger bars lining its routes and from every bar will come the music of other nations (predominantly British and American), while the designer labels in the clothes of European youth betray a common street culture. Europeans move around the continent freely – witness the number of non-nationals playing in the different football leagues – and the sense of national stereotypes is waning. Certainly opinion polls show that national rivalries between Europeans have substantially declined, remaining in healthy competitive outlets such as soccer or the much-lampooned Eurovision Song Contest. Indeed, extremity does seem to have declined with the absence of far right and far left groups and the predominance of a benevolent middle. Michael Mann, in a consideration of the fate of the European nation state, writes:

'The new Europe is harmless. It is also unthreatened. Europe has the geopolitical security it has always wanted, as well as client states and even supplicant states, between itself and any threat coming out of the East. And the Americans remain to defend it ... If this is postmodernity, it is closer to being a utopia than a crisis.'

European identity would seem to consist of prosperity and security and perhaps the greatest risk the continent faces is that of complacency. Harry Lime's parting speech in *The Third Man* puts the point nicely:

'In Italy for thirty years under the Borgias they had warfare, terror, murder, bloodshed – they produced Michelangelo, Leonardo da Vinci and the Renaissance. In Switzerland they had brotherly love, five hundered years of democracy and peace, and what did they produce ...? The cuckoo clock.'

So Europe, in its modern incarnation must learn to innovate from a position of peace and prosperity.

The initial purport of this chapter was to gain some understanding of what it is that we mean when we use the term 'Europe' and what emerges from it is a multifarious entity to which union of thought and action is by no means alien. The weight of tradition can be a heavy one but to see tradition in purely local terms, as can be the tendency of those of us who base an understanding of tradition on the perimeters of human memory, is misleading; the very traditions that seem to have become enshrined in national identities, like the very languages that express those identities, come from common roots. Tradition, however, is not immutable and new traditions, as we have seen, can emerge in the space of a lifetime. Paul Valery, celebrating the traditions of thought that built Europe and decrying the traditions of policy that undermined that same Europe, wrote: 'Europe will prove not to have had the politics worthy of her thought'. The challenge for modern Europe is to refute that charge and to ensure that in its institutions of government and commerce the traditions of thought, old and new, will find their best expression. More than this, Europe must maintain the peace and prosperity that have been achieved at such cost but resist the comforts of complacency and *laissez faire*.

3

The Business of America is Business: a Consideration of How America Gained its Business Hegemony

'A salesman is got to dream, boy. It comes with the territory.'

Arthur Miller, American playwright, put these words into the mouth of Willy Loman, the eponymous hero of *Death of a Salesman*, and these sentiments from small-town America encapsulate a national cast of mind, a predilection to look forward in hope, to start from small and make it big, and to make it big through business. Miller depicts the underside of the fabled American dream, and in Willy Loman we see, perhaps, the detritus of such a vision, one whose dreams are washed up on the shores of disillusionment. But, for all we are reminded of the failure of the fanciful American dream that never was, the notion of the little man making it big through hard work and endeavour and realising dreams of wealth and status is one that lies at the heart of American society. That society is itself, unlike any other before or since, underpinned by business, its outputs and values. There has long been an explicit understanding that this is the case; we have already noted President Coolidge's remarks on business that gives this chapter its title but, still earlier, President Woodrow Wilson indicated the profoundly commercial foundations of the nation: 'Business underlies everything in our national life'. Enterprise and self-improvement, the exercise of an individualistic (even at times self-serving) spirit of endeavour can be seen as an expression of the American spirit, of American culture.

The concern of the preceding chapter was to look at Europe in isolation without pausing to consider the legacy that Europe left with its former colonies (and in particular the legacy of the English to the North American colony) or the efficient use to which that legacy was put. Nor did the chapter refer to the manner in which European peace and reconstruction owed a huge debt to American intervention. There is, however, a symbiotic link between those peoples on either side of the Atlantic divide which can be conceived in familial terms. Europe gave birth to the United States, which in youth reacted against the standards of the parent and fought for freedom. This adolescent state came to maturity through the rigorous application of the skills learned from the parent but refined and enhanced with the vigour and vision of youth. Eventually the time comes when the child is stronger than the parent and in middle age the child must come to the aid of the parent and show how life is lived in the modern world. But what of the child when it reaches old age? This is the very juncture at which we began this book, a new generation of Europe rebelling against the standards of the now parental United States. This chapter will seek to look more closely at how the United States achieved its business supremacy and how Europe has been able to make use of what it has learned from the American model.

A mongrel society but a pedigree culture

Although it is clear that modern Europeans have tangled tribal routes few of which are any longer discernible, the same must be even more true of the United States, which is a society whose members are drawn principally from Europe, Africa, the Caribbean and Latin America. Within the sector of the population who can trace their origins back to Europe there is as much diversity as exists in the old continent itself, with huge numbers originally emigrating from Britain, Ireland, Italy, the east European states, Holland, France – from any corner of the continent where there was oppression, poverty and a paucity of opportunity. Indeed, in the 50 years prior to 1914 some 50 million Europeans made the journey across the Atlantic. In 1907 two-thirds of the 23,000-strong work force in the Carnegie steel works in Pittsburgh were immigrants. In 1915 a survey of the work force at Ford's Highland Park revealed no fewer than 50 different spoken languages. America is typically – and with some logic – depicted as a melting pot of race, religion and national identity and this being so it is all the more extraordinary that we can speak in terms of a homogeneous culture. On the face of it America would appear to be the very paradigm of heterogeneity and yet there is a very clear international sense of an identity which is profoundly American and which appears to be thoroughbred. Much of that identity has to do with the two greatest exports of American life – the Hollywood dream factory and the mass brands of high-quality consumer products that have been developed by her corporations. Indeed, the American corporation is paradigmatic of American national culture – strong, unified, enduring, flexible. It is telling that the phrase by which Hollywood is referred to includes the term 'factory', with its implications of manufacture. My semantic interest here lies less in the possible artificiality of the dream than in the fact that industry and business underpin that most American of inventions. For when Coolidge made his comment in 1925 about the business of America being business, he was right. Europe gave the world industrial capitalism and liberal democracy. America's gift to the world has been the harnessing of the latter and the organization of the former via the corporation to create a business environment that has been, quite simply, world beating. That this has been the achievement of such a heterogeneous group of peoples is hardly surprising. The difference and diversity of a migrant population has been of infinite importance in the development of a thriving business culture, as has the existence of a common sense of motivation, a common goal – the desire to prosper. It is ultimately no surprise that a migrant community, both freed and constrained by the immensity of a continent with no immediate enemies and few natural barriers, should forge a homogeneous culture from initial extraordinary diversity. The task of this chapter is to plot some of this terrain.

The early migrants

Initially the lure of prosperity was the primary reason for migration. Religious intolerance around the world was never so great a spur to migration as was simple money motivation. The new émigrés were not the lean, underfed Europeans we now associate with arrival at Ellis Island, but corporate entrepreneurs, members of chartered stock companies who were allowed by the crown (of England) to take on the business of colony building. Shareholders were to be disappointed when vast and quick profits failed to accrue but this entrepreneurial colonizing spirit is an important one in the origins of a state. The internal market proved too small and the external market too distant for the vast riches to come from commodity production and, in any case, it was the land that was a lure for early settlers. That it was soon found not to be the case that the promised land would deliver up quick fortunes may, in part, explain the subsequent rise to independence and greatness. Few colonizing empires wished to sink the huge start-up costs into a venture that might yield less than invested. Instead, America was left largely to the individual efforts of settlers. In other words, rather than being fully colonized and having a culture imposed upon it from without, the New World was enabled to develop its own culture from within.

The constitution of those settlers themselves is a factor in America's rapid rise to greatness. It is seldom the sick, the infirm and the failing who strike out on new ventures and this truism is illustrated by the migrants to the new world. Opportunity appealed more to young able men, unfettered by family ties, who came from the strongest (in physical terms) sector of the population. This enterprising migrant also tended to be intellectually stronger than his social peers who remained at home – to have greater vision and superior confidence in his personal ability to realise that vision. It was perhaps less courage than personal conviction that spurred the migrants to William Penn's colony, which began as a refuge for persecuted Quakers but, whatever the initial motivation, it was a desire to prosper that led the community to extend itself through advertisement – a feature that is of huge importance to the American miracle – via the assistance of German and Scottish migrants.

The European legacy

Those who made the arduous journey across the Atlantic brought with them the legacy of European economic lessons – a belief in private property rights, an understanding of an economic principle whereby potential profits could accrue from shrewd investment and a knowledge of accounting procedures. Significantly, another lesson learned from Europe was that political stability is a factor in individual enterprise and during the early decades of America's colonization there was an absence of political factions and instead a common concern for individual enterprise. Strangely, the status of a satellite nation, a colony of the English crown (the Dutch and the Swedish efforts at colonization were put down by a British military expedition by 1664), was a factor that encouraged rather than diminished American enterprise; there was no need to invent or establish from existing models the institutions of government – these existed at a remove.

The new colonists could concentrate, instead, on overcoming the natural factors – the labour shortage, the inadequate monetary situation and poor internal transport, which were the primary obstacles to economic expansion.

Another element of the legacy from Europe was the notion of religious dissent. It would be wrong to underplay the importance of religious dissent in the building of America. The first settlers on the Mayflower were a religious community seeking a new start away from religious intolerance and there has been a strong Puritan element to American history as two major works of American literature testify. Nathaniel Hawthorne's *The Scarlet Letter* and Arthur Miller's *The Crucible* both chronicle the sinister effects of Puritanism (the latter being, of course, an allegory about McCarthyism). The effects of Puritanism have not all been sinister. As we saw in the preceding chapter, the spirit of Protestantism was important in the development of a hard work ethic; the fission between the inner and the outer life wrought by Puritanism was important in the development of an innovative, dreaming, ultimately consuming society. More than this, those who engage in religious dissent are by their very nature questioning of the status quo. The individualism of the religious dissenter combines with the strong evangelizing tendency, the desire to share an alternative vision with others, and so builds a strong new community; and that coupling of individualism with a strong associational ethic, in line with Fukuyama's thesis, is a powerful one in the building of any new enterprise.

Independence and a constitution for business

Initially the staples of the American economy were fur and fish, but during the eighteenth century there emerged a divide between the mercantile north, exploiting the British colonial markets in the Caribbean as well as the European markets from a New England base, and the plantation culture of the southern states where the major export crop was tobacco. It was to be the British government's attempts to inhibit trade via monopolistic measures and its efforts to extract higher taxes from American subjects to pay for costly wars fought by the British against the French on American soil which led to the revolution. After the revolution there followed a period of confederation which bound the various states together in an extremely loose union and then in 1789 the American Constitution was drafted to create a centrally managed federation of states.

Modern commentators on the Constitution would quarrel with the statement that its motivation was mainly economic, but there can be no doubt that economic factors were important. The loose confederation that existed after the 1776 revolution led to a range of anomalies. Conflicting state monetary policies were disruptive of trade while interstate rivalries led to discriminatory taxes with New Jersey, Connecticut and Delaware levying no duties on foreign goods, while New York and Pennsylvania depended upon such levies for finance. By the late 1780s a group of federalists had come to see the sense of greater centralized control both to resolve some of the financial problems, to take control over the wilderness regions to the west and to regulate trading tariffs and so eliminate interstate trading rivalries. The resulting constitution gave the state the exclusive power to set taxes, to arbitrate between rival states, and ordered the government to establish a postal system and so enhance interstate communication and to encourage innovation through patent and copyright protection. Critically, of course, the constitution gave to the federal government the exclusive right to coin money and to set its value. It should be noted, however, that the state the constitution created was not a highly centralized machine like, for example, the French government. The model was a federal one and America did not truly become a strong nation state in the European understanding of the phrase until the twentieth century, when some state level responsibilities were brought to the centre and military power began to be consolidated. Nevertheless, the outcome of the commercial elements of the constitution was the creation of a large, unified national marketplace. It is hard not to see a parallel between this attempt to create a consolidated trading nation and the attempts by the European commission to do the same – the Europeans belatedly putting into practice lessons learnt from the Americans. This, however, plays to the fears of some Eurosceptics that Winston Churchill's vision of a United States of Europe is, indeed, at the heart of the endeavour towards European Union. Such considerations aside, we can see how, in the American constitution, business concerns were enshrined in one of the nation's greatest political and cultural edifices. Business values and national values were broadly synonymous.

Innovation

Innovation was a key to American development as, of course, it has been critical in the development and indeed, by its absence, the decline of any major state.

In America the difference was that innovation was not confined to a small group of inventors or designers. The colonial lifestyle which necessarily became the American lifestyle was one of dependence on home-grown skills. Settlers built and furnished their own homes, clothed their own bodies and fed their own stomachs, and skills were pooled in order to arrive at a decent level of community life. The ethic of sharing expertise was to be influential in the spread of new ideas and the community spirit was also to inform the manner in which, once industrialized, the American nation organized itself – into corporations of shared skills. The American population was, however, a flexible one of people who were prepared to learn new skills and apply new technologies in a concerted effort at self-improvement. In this climate new innovations spread rapidly and the invention of the cotton gin to separate cotton fibres from seeds, and the subsequent development of milling techniques along British lines, led to the growth of the cotton crop, which replaced tobacco as king during the nineteenth century. There were to be numerous innovations during the course of the nineteenth century – the Singer sewing machine, the various processes for canning and preserving foods – but almost more important were the innovative methods of organizing business.

The growth of the corporation

In the early years of American enterprise business was conducted individually or in partnership. Either route was risky and the businessman could stand to lose his entire investment or his family be rendered destitute by his untimely death. The corporation was a vehicle that grew up rapidly after the ratification of the constitution and soon came to incorporate a limited liability clause that minimized all risk. The granting of corporate charters was in the gift of the individual states. Whereas monarchical European governments were at best reluctant to grant corporate charters, the American states saw such activity as a move to encourage business as they felt responsible and mandated to do. Although early corporations did not include limited liability protection, this was shortly to become an integral feature so that investors were liable only up to the value of stock purchases. The huge benefit of corporations was that they were enabled to conduct business far beyond the wealth of one individual. Corporate shares could be sold on the open market and were available in sufficiently small denominations to encourage the small investor; thus the scale of the enterprise was not such as to exclude the little man. Further, many charters allowed corporations to borrow money by selling bonds and hence financial communities developed specializing in the exchange of bonds. The management of a corporation could differ substantially. Stock could be held solely by a group of active managers, shareholders could seek representation in management or, as became the norm, shareholders would involve themselves on an investing basis only and leave the management of the corporation to a few professionals. The fortunes of a large number of people, thus, could depend on the skill deployed by managers and the need to manage effectively became in America far more pressing, far more socially desirable, than in European companies, which tended to be family owned and managed.

The corporation became the vehicle by which the railways were developed across the United States and to the railways much of America's future prosperity was owed. Equally, the railways became the vehicle by which the corporation was developed. Unlike any other advanced economy the provision of a railway infrastructure was undertaken by the private rather than the public sector. The sheer scale of the enterprise and the land mass to be covered called for the development of corporate structures and the widespread trust in those 'managers' empowered to enforce company policy at often vast distances from corporate headquarters. In more general business terms, the network linked together far-flung territories, and so brought closer a growing home market and also allowed for the passage of goods and people across vast tracts of land. The railway boom also led to the increased development of the iron and steel industries. All the same, for the first half of the nineteenth century America was held to be an agrarian rather than an industrialized nation, drawing wealth from the cotton plantations to the south which depended for their vast incomes on the labour of black slaves. However, industrialization was rapid in the north and integrated manufacturing processes that took place under one factory roof led to the spread of towns that could easily absorb the fast growing number of European immigrants. During the civil war (1862–5) over 800,000 immigrants arrived on northern shores.

The impact of war on industrial development

The American civil war, which was to lead to the prohibition of slavery, was won by the North precisely because the North had become industrialized. Industrialization is fuelled by and in turn fuels urban growth. The Northern states could call upon a population of some 20 million against a white population in the South of just six million (and it was only in the final two months of the war that the Southerners enlisted its black population). Around two million men served in the union army against less than half that number (900,000) in the confederate army. To build an army to this size necessitated the removal of labour from the land, from mines and foundries, which undermined Southern efforts still more. The North's great advantage, however, was that its industries produced the goods that were essential to a war that was to be won ultimately on the basis of endurance and longevity. The North numbered some 110,000 manufacturing establishments against the South's meagre 18,000 and many of these 18,000 depended upon Northern labour and technological expertise. The North was able to manufacture weaponry and to maintain its railroad so that the all-important shipment of goods and men to far distant battle grounds could be achieved with efficiency. The North was able to build ships, which were to break down the efficiency of the Southern blockade breakers who were bringing in goods from Europe; and from maritime power came inland water power, giving the North control of the Mississippi–Tennessee region. Most crippling for the South was its dependence on just one crop – cotton – which was the main source of income. When this dried up the Northern victory was secure. The North had a spread of income sources and was able to maintain outputs throughout the war. Importantly, too, the North was able to feed its troops both by making use of such innovations as food canning and by the huge output of western wheat crops and the rapid mechanization of agriculture, which was to be a lasting achievement of the war. The civil war was won, ultimately, by dint of the industrial and technological advantage of the North over the South. By the close of the decade in which this war was fought (with greater loss of American life than the first, second and Korean wars combined) America was to emerge, with Germany, as one of the world leaders in industrialization.

The importance of peace to industrial development

In the previous chapter we made much of the geopolitical advantage of Europe and the same is true of America. The absence of significant hostile enemies on the other side of land borders left America fairly free from the need to support a standing army with the necessary dilution of state funds. During the nineteenth century the apparently parallel growth of Russia and America was much remarked upon; comparators, however, show how rapidly the United States had developed. By 1860 America had just 40% of Russia's population, but an urban population that was twice as large and energy consumption levels (from modern fuel sources) 15 times greater and railway mileage 30 times greater. Whereas Russia in 1860 was obliged to keep an army of some 862,000, the American regular army numbered a mere 26,000. The necessity for defence was not a variable to which the Americans needed to give serious consideration; instead they could deploy their peoples in economic enterprise and, when the need to mobilize came, then that economic enterprise could support victory and war itself could sustain the economy. The industrial heritage of the northern states is still visible today in the high incidence of CEOs who come from northern towns.

A nation of shopkeepers?

Industrialization brought with it an increasing number of industrial giants, entrepreneurs who made vast profits from burgeoning business enterprises, who came to be as much vilified by some as they were vaunted by others. America, however, was still the land of opportunity for the lone operator and in 1850 it was the small town storekeepers who constituted the central plank from which American conurbations developed. Indeed, during the first half of the nineteenth century it was common practice for land operators to offer inducements to would-be store managers to set up shop in remote areas and so lead to the development of small towns. The management of a store gave for some the opportunity for direct management of an investment and the flexibility to operate other trades outside commercial trading hours. We began this chapter with the image of Willy Loman the salesman and it was tradesmen and salesmen who were at the base of the economic pyramid that developed during the nineteenth century, carrying goods and news across miles of the developing countryside. At the tip of the pyramid were figures such as John D. Rockefeller, the creator of the first trust in the United States whereby a separate Standard Oil company was incorporated in each state (so getting round the laws preventing a corporation from owning property outside its home state) which multiplicity of companies were then overseen by a board of trustees from a New York City base. Shareholders in the various companies received trust certificates for the shares that the trustees technically held 'in trust'. In reality, Standard Oil was run from New York with the founder John D. Rockefeller personally owning four-ninths of all the stock transferred to the trust. His personal wealth in 1890 stood at $37 million – a mere fraction of what the Rockefeller fortune was subsequently to become. Even the retail sector, traditional home of the small trader, was to breed its own superheroes. As towns developed so did shopping areas and diversified merchandising was pioneered shortly before the civil war in A.T. Stewart's dry goods emporium – the first department store. The founder of the modern department store, John Wanamaker, introduced the money-back guarantee and the financial arrangements of department (and later chain) stores set them apart from the small general store trader. Fixed prices were set for all goods instead of the bargaining common in smaller stores. Volume of trade allowed for negotiation with wholesalers and these price reductions could be passed on to the customer or put to such use as reinvestment or advertising.

Technology and the shrinking nation

This consolidation of business was evident throughout the closing decades of the nineteenth century as the country seemed to contract with the development of first the telegraph and then the telephone (AT&T was founded in 1885) and the widespread use of electric power which improved transport (the trolley car, the electrified underground railway) within large and still growing cities. The telescoping of the country in this way brought a mass market within reach and that market seemed a prime target for exploitation by large, co-ordinated corporate machines. The Standard Oil Trust had illustrated the vast profits to be made by near monopoly and manufacturers were beginning to strafe under the destructive and inefficient competitive practices that were the product of a free enterprise system. Manufacturers were aware of the cost reductions to come from consolidating enterprises into one unit and pools developed not unlike the German cartels (see Chapter 4), but these were a brief experiment that went out of fashion very rapidly. The Sherman Act of 1890 made trusts subject to litigation and so this method of consolidation also enjoyed only very short-lived popularity. It was the relaxation of incorporation laws by individual states (the first of which was New Jersey) that allowed for a business incorporated in one state to have stock in out-of-state companies, which was to give rise to the interstate holding company and thus to the modern business organization we know today.

The automobile industry – Fordism and Taylorism

It was the emerging automobile industry that was to crystallize American business in the form in which we would now recognise it and Henry Ford who was to tap the potential of the mass market for the first time and to revolutionize manufacturing, so that the demands of that mass market could be fulfilled constantly and immediately. Ironically, Ford, who was to become another in America's pantheon of business giants, started his career with a major court battle against the then automobile establishment. When that was won he was able to launch in 1908 his Model T – the most efficient car yet developed, with a price tag of $825 which was later to fall to below $300. He offered pricing incentives to keep interest in his product alive, offering rebates if sales went beyond the 300,000 mark in 1914. Although Henry Ford knew how to manipulate the market it was his understanding of production efficiencies which was to revolutionize the manufacturing industry. Working with a consultant (surely one of the earliest examples of the breed), Frederick W. Taylor, Ford built a process of scientific management based around the principle that all unnecessary and awkward worker movements should be eliminated to maximize production output and efficiency. In his autobiography Ford wrote:

> 'The first step forward in assembly came when we began taking the work to the men instead of the men to the work. We have now two general principles in operation – that a man shall never have to take more than one step, if possibly it can be avoided, and that no man need ever stoop over.'

Such were the origins of the modern assembly line product – a far cry from the first produced automobiles where artisans and craftsmen built by hand. In just one year the time to assemble a Model T dropped from 12 hours to 1½, with a concomitant drop in labour costs that allowed for pricing cuts and made Ford the undisputed leader of the automobile sector.

If Ford was the practitioner of mass production, then Taylor was the theoretician. His book *The Principles of Scientific Management* codified the 'laws' of mass production and contributed to a considerable dehumanization of the industrial process. Where Ford recognized the merits of incentivizing staff (giving them a $5 day in 1914, thereby doubling the rates of pay) and operated a paternalistic although intrusive surveillance system ensuring that his workers lived in acceptable conditions and behaved to an acceptable social standard, Taylor's creed denied the worker the right to any individuality. Strict lines of demarcation were drawn between the levels of worker and maintenance of machinery given to a separate department, so that the individual assembly line worker need worry about no more than the narrow task assigned to him. It was precisely this inhuman, mechanistic treatment of the worker that inspired such grim allegories of factory and industrial life as Fritz Lang's *Metropolis*. The so-called scientific management philosophy led to a similarly scientific response from the unions who called for equally legalistic and formulaic agreements and in the exchange between management and unions came the 'them and us', combative culture, which was later to bedevil the American car industry and give a loophole to the Japanese with their 'holistic' approach to manufacturing. Nevertheless, the principle of organized, Fordist style production represented a tremendous innovation and one which remains the common model in newly industrializing economies.

Sloan, General Motors and the development of brands

During the 1920s Ford's ascendancy was to come under threat from General Motors and the unlikely figure of Alfred P. Sloan. General Motors was the brainchild of William C. Durant, who pieced together the future automobile giant. He was not, however, a manager and in 1920 he lost control of the combine to Pierre du Pont, the founder of the Du Pont empire who was in fact retiring from that business when he poured his money into General Motors. Du Pont put Alfred Sloan, the thinking man rather than the entrepreneurial man of action, in control of the business and so gave rise to a system of business organization that has been emulated across sectors and markets. The basic tenet of Sloan's plan was that the management of manufacturing operations should reside with divisional executives able to exercise considerable autonomy. To assist these operators an elaborate centre was devised which took charge of capitalization, marketing, planning and procurement. Legal and financial experts also had their pivotal place at the centre from which they monitored operating performance and made suggestions that were then taken up and discussed by the executive committee, which met frequently to devise policy and authorize proposals from the operating companies. The plan was geared around profit and was designed to ensure that supply would keep pace with demand. Sloan also had a scheme to ensure that demand would keep pace with the rate of supply he favoured and here his genius is made manifest. Whereas the Ford Motor Company traded on the basis of perpetually reducing costs Sloan recognized that there was only a finite market for a standard new car – particularly since the used car market had already opened up by the 1920s. He also recognized that a car had far more than mere functional value, but was a statement about the owner's status. He set about rationalizing the company's portfolio so that he constructed a range of models to suit a range of pockets and then set about a policy of undermining the old model in the light of the new, so that with each year he could market a new, superior product. Every three years the General Motors products were completely redesigned and in the intervening years given a face-lift. The strategy proved well founded. Before Henry Ford came back with a new product in 1932 General Motors very nearly put him out of business. In devising a marketing strategy for GM, Sloan was also devising one that was to be the starting point for an entire sector of manufacturers catering for the mass consumer market.

Latter day innovators

The lessons of the early automobile business heads have been well learned by future generations of businessmen. The Apple phenomenon is a well-known tale, but for its parallels to the Ford story is worth repetition. The alliance between marketing wizard (unschooled, but instinctive) Steven Jobs and technical expert Stephen Wozniak who met during Jobs' summer job at Hewlett-Packard (then still a pioneering electronics company) is the stuff of legend. As Henry Ford made his first models in his spare time so the Jobs–Wozniak team worked on the prototype of the first marketable computer in the Jobs family garage.

Jobs managed to sell the model to an electronics firm who ordered 25 machines and the pair sold everything they owned in order to fund the production of the Apple I, a ROM computer that retailed for $666. The profits from this venture financed the development of their Model-T equivalent, the Apple II, a RAM computer that could be hooked into a television set and which sold for the extremely modest $1350. Wozniak's technical brilliance was matched by Jobs' marketing flair and his decision to invite independent programmers to design software for the Apple II was one of several critical decisions that were to lead to the Ford-style rapid growth of Apple. Just six years after the launch of the Apple II some 16,000 software programs were on the market, the majority of which were compatible with subsequent Apple machines.

If the Apple phenomenon shows some parallels with the Ford experience then the MacDonald's retailing miracle has some similar parallels with the General Motors experience. The founder of the fast food chain Roy Kroc took his inspiration from a one-off burger bar in San Bernadino, California, run by the MacDonald brothers. The mini-miracle he saw performed was a production line assembly of products that differed in minor ways and gave a broad offering on price. Streamlined production à la Henry Ford was harnessed to an understanding of market needs à la Alfred Sloan. Kroc studied the urban market and sited his restaurants in downtown districts where low-paid clerks and office workers needed a fast and cheap midday meal and gradually came to cater for the major child market with its playgrounds and parties. The consistency of the product, the consolidated brand name and the power of advertising led to the outstanding growth of the business.

The automotive industry was not the sole source of innovation by any means, nor was innovation confined to the early years of the century. The post-war electronics boom which spawned Apple also gave rise to the rapid development of such companies as IBM, which were to provide innovative techniques in terms of sales, service and the perception of company identity, company culture. Again, we see the influence of one charismatic leader in the shaping of a solidified company image. In the case of IBM that leader was Thomas J. Watson. Watson began his career as a travelling organ and piano salesman before he was recruited by the National Cash Register Company. It was there that he learned many of the techniques that he was to use to energize IBM. The National Cash Register Company was run by a charismatic leader, John Henry Patterson, who set rewards as incentives for earnest young salesmen and held sales rallies that had an evangelical atmosphere with a constant emphasis on the team. Salesmanship and team building were not the only elements that made NCR a successful company – research kept the organization permanently one step ahead of its competitors. Unfortunately, NCR began a systematic attempt at sabotage of competitor reputations and equipment, which led to a court appearance and the breakdown of relations between Watson and Patterson. Watson escaped a jail sentence but found himself out of a job, although he maintained his innocence of personal misdemeanour.

Watson moved on to the Control-Tabulating-Recording Company as General Manager, later to become President. Here he implemented many of the initiatives he had participated in at NCR. Having first streamlined the business (which dealt in manufactured scales, calculators, business machines and technical instruments) he established a centralized research department and personally directed training and motivational programmes for his sales force. Within half a decade the company had so prospered in the home market that it was able to expand overseas and in 1924 Watson changed the company name to the International Business Machines Corporation. The success of the organization derived from several factors, not least of which was the charisma and drive of Watson Sr and his son who took over from him in the early 1950s. The research department ensured that IBM was there in the vanguard of electric typewriter and then computer development, with the strong and committed sales force guaranteeing huge sales. A further pioneering step was to concentrate on service – distribution of equipment under leasing contracts enabled IBM to corner the market in fast and efficient maintenance. Watson's motto, an early buzz-word, was 'think' and he wrote of the underlying purpose of IBM:

> *'The real contribution of improved machines and methods is to relieve thinkers from routine operations, giving them more time to think.'*

The cult of culture

While this may well have been the guiding spirit that spoke to Watson and hence infused IBM, there is some sense in which the company he created was in the image of its products. Corporate culture was so homogeneous that the

IBM worker came to typify the breed of big company man, a work automaton. Such numbing corporate cultures had their critics and William H. Whyte, writing *The Organization Man* in 1956, decried the mediocre manager spawned by the charismatic leader:

> 'The premise is, simply, that the goals of the individual and the goals of the organization will work out to be one and the same. The young men have no cynicism about the system and very little skepticism – they don't see it as something to be bucked but something to be conformed to.'

From this viewpoint we can see that the businessman or the man of business, the executive, had come to be integral to the system to be, in fact, a veritable pillar of the establishment, an expression of the aims and objectives that America held dear.

This image of a highly conformist American Manager seems to run against the prevailing modern view of a highly individualized society where everyone is out for himself. The course of American business history, however, is marked by the successful interplay of individual and corporate, collectivist actitivities. All the businesses we have glimpsed in this chapter (all businesses everywhere) start as small entrepreneurial concerns driven by the vision and, to no small extent, the personality of the founder. In American society the founder of a business has access to the same sort of status that once went to the lord of a feudal manor in European society; indeed, in some towns in America where one business has dominated there has been something of a feudal respect for the family at the helm. American melodrama consistently records this theme, in the films of Douglas Sirk and, more recently, in the 'soaps' such as Dallas and, more relevantly in the context of *noblesse oblige*, Dynasty where Blake Carrington is the long-suffering, noble-spirited founder of the family fortunes. American managers remain inclined to rally around and give their allegiance to an entrepreneur. The modern paradigm of this phenomenon is, of course, Bill Gates at Microsoft who has created an extraordinary business full of brilliant, young millionaires whom he has galvanized around a compelling vision expressed in a working environment that fits with the 1990s, being flexible, ergonomically designed and focused on profit. The American approach to its business heroes is marked by a certain lack of irony, the principal at the heart of cynical European humour and perhaps this informs the degree to which people are prepared to follow or revere a business leader. A European, however much they might rationally applaud a particular vision, would feel that the use of the term 'vision' in the context of commerce is somehow a little inappropriate. Visions are the diet of mystics, of high cultural figures like poets and artists. This might merely betray a different sense of national identity with business. As I indicate at the head of this chapter and as we have seen in certain of the terms of the American constitution, business is entirely bound up with the origins of America's nationhood, with the identity that is conferred on all citizens. Business is a very serious business indeed and the nation and business are virtual synonyms. Of no other economy or nation could this claim be made.

But the real success of American business culture has been its ability to sustain the vision of its entrepreneurs long after those entrepreneurs have ceased to play an active role in the business they founded. The ability of American businesses to grow, to professionalize, to move well beyond the control of a founding family has been the single biggest lesson that other economies have had to learn in order to compete. Francis Fukuyama's explanation for this astounding capability is based on the capacity for Americans to form non-familial highly trusting relations, based on the numerous civil associations that developed in a culture built on an immigrant community with many shared interests and goals but without extended family networks. Similarly, America was not overly regulated by a strong state but allowed to develop its own more informal regulation networks. The Fukuyama case is extremely compelling. He does not, however, offer an explanation for the extreme cohesion of the corporate cultures. The Taylorite mechanization of production could hardly have contributed to this cohesion, being ultimately divisive. The notion that an immigrant population looks for a common source of identity has some intuitive appeal but scarcely accounts for the longevity of some corporate cultures, well beyond the lifespan of several generations of immigrants. Indeed, ironically, the extraordinary homogeneity of American corporate cultures, as exemplified by that of IBM above but also to be seen in a McKinsey or a Procter & Gamble, might derive from the uniformity of the community from which business managers are drawn, not from any shared emotional need by people of different lineage and background.

The profile of the modern Chief Executive – some clues to cultural homogeneity

The vast majority of managers in American businesses throughout the twentieth century have been white, Anglo-Saxon, Protestant – the large Catholic population, in contrast, has tended to favour politics and bureaucracy rather than business – and middle class. An analysis of the average American CEO (based on those in the Business Week top 1000) shows that in the 1990s this remains true. 92% of CEOs have an undergraduate degree, usually either in engineering, business or a closely related discipline. The first degree is typically followed by an MBA or, sometimes, by a qualification from a law school. Attendance at one of the elite American colleges (Harvard, Yale or Princeton) is almost mandatory amongst top business leaders followed by a sound business qualification. Preferred MBA schools are Harvard, Stamford and Wharton. The majority of American business leaders come from the areas around New York, Pennsylvania and Chicago (reflecting the origins of American corporate success in the élite northern states that we note above). Future surveys are unlikely to find the same northern dominance as Texas and California have developed over the last 20 years to be significant foci for business. Once inside an organization a would-be CEO will have the best chance of achieving his ambition if he is in finance and accounting, which currently supplies 31% of all US CEOs, against 27% from marketing and merchandising and 22% from engineering and technical functions. In short, a professional (middle class) qualification is a passport for success in an American culture. American Chief Executives then, the individuals who drive culture, come from similar backgrounds, have imbibed similar values to one another and the community of managers they lead. They are also loyal company men. Tenure is an interesting issue in relation to US business. The average length of service with the company of which the CEO is in charge is 22.5 years. 80% of executives, then, are lifers, loyal company men – people who have had time to inculcate the culture of a company, who have effectively taken in that culture virtually at the breast. This statistic, however, might appear to be undermined by the information that, on a year-by-year basis, there is change at the top of companies amounting to a CEO turnover of around 10% – a staggeringly high statistic. But the high level of executive mobility need not undermine cultural homogeneity. On the contrary, people of similar backgrounds moving between businesses of broadly similar type move in the expectation that they will need to absorb the culture of the new corporation to which they are switching their allegiance. Individual cultures may differ but the notion that corporate culture counts is itself a cultural value common in the US business sector.

Perhaps the most interesting angle on the homogeneity of American corporate cultures is the national, inward-looking nature of most American CEOs. Indeed, analysing this community parochialism can be seen to be endemic. Heidrick and Struggles undertook an analysis of the top 300 CEOs in corporate America, which found that only 8% of those questioned claimed to have international experience. On probing further it transpired that for most of this 8% the international arena in which they had worked was Canada, typically for a two–three year period before a return to the corporate headquarters. It does not seem likely that this situation will change for the generation coming up behind the current group of CEOs – those now in their 30s and 40s – have scarcely more international experience than their predecessors. The route to success in a US company is to stay close to home and preferably close to the kingmaker, to be noticed, to make a difference in the home market and to avoid an overseas posting, since to be out of sight is very definitely to be out of mind and then out of the running. It is a chastening thought that the competitive zeal that made the US great in the first instance is now acting as a check on the international development of its managers which, in turn, can only act as a check on the international expansion of the economy. A study of the corporate elite in *Business Week* magazine in January 1992 throws up an interesting statistic. Of the top 1000 CEOs 63 were foreign born. Of these 63 most of these were born outside the US but raised inside the US, or spent the greater part of their career inside the US as in the case of Emmanuel Kampouris, Egyptian born CEO of American Standard.

The inward-looking aspect of American business presumably has its origin in a certain complacency about the size and scale of the home market and the relatively unchallenged success of home companies overseas. The American business is relatively immune to external influence, as large companies have grown, their identities have been entrusted to loyal company men, of similar background to their predecessors, who have held that identity in trust. America has a diffuse, decentralized system of government. As a nation state it is relatively young. Despite the routinized singing in schools of *God Bless America*, the corporation may be an easier entity with which to identify than a relatively centreless state. Identity with the corporation, symbol of American success, is an expression of national allegiance. The homogeneity and longevity of American business cultures, then, must be linked to the fact that business is America's principal invention, to the fact that America is business.

The techniques that characterize American business

In this description of the birth and growth of corporate America we have not dwelt on some of the key techniques that characterize American business. The recognition of the mass market led to the development of marketing techniques and the increasing sophistication of the advertising industry. The frontier population in the latter part of the nineteenth century were reached by the catalogues of such companies as Montgomery Ward and initially advertising was, like a catalogue entry, no more than a description of an article. With increasingly sophisticated products and production techniques and a more penetrating understanding of what could motivate the consumer came more subliminal marketing and advertising techniques, which were geared at the self-image and the psychology of the potential consumer. Marketing and advertising were supported by market research and the attempts to quantify public opinion and the image of companies came under the scrutiny of public relations officials. Shakespeare might have asked 'What's in a name?' but the American business community of the twentieth century would have frowned at the bard's disregard for names. In business the name was very definitely the thing. Brand names that registered quality, and a consistency of standard had tremendous appeal in a market where there was massive freedom of choice but between products of variable standards. Company names too, often realised in pictorial form in a logo, were also important – witness Florence Nightingale Graham who changed her name to that of the company she founded – Elizabeth Arden. Names, of brands or of companies, gave the stamp of authenticity, of authority and of quality as well as being memorable tags to stick in the consumer's mind.

Since all people are potential consumers it is scarcely surprising that business encroaches on all areas of life. Marketing initiatives are obvious on every street, in every newspaper, in every shop-front and salesmanship, in the great tradition of the travelling salesman, enters the home. Companies such as Tupperware, Mary Kay, and Amway are built around notions of hospitality, of consumption as a leisure activity and those who sell are galvanized by revival-like training and motivational sessions where top performers are celebrated and company credo reinforced. In America a company, as we have seen, can and does confer identity.

Business needs are enshrined in the constitution as we have seen, but social structures also support commercial requirements. Education was geared toward the skills required by the young would-be entrepreneur. America lagged behind Europe in the provision of advanced technical education where Germany, in particular, excelled, but as early as 1820 small night schools that had been running since the early eighteenth century and teaching elementary science and book-keeping came to call themselves business colleges. The modern business school emerged in the twentieth century and institutions such as Harvard, Stanford, and Wharton have established in under a century a reputation for excellence that has not found its equal outside the United States. Harvard's first student intake was in 1908 and the pattern of learning was set in that first year. Theory was to be rigorously tied to practice and each student at the end of his course was obliged to submit a thesis that dealt with a concrete problem and demonstrated an ability through deductive reasoning to solve that problem. Early prize-winning theses bore such titles as *The Problem of the Used Car in the Automobile Industry* and *Should a Retail Grocer Buy Futures in Canned Goods* – indicating the close tie between the classroom and the board room. Despite the example from the States, Europe was slow to imitate and European business schools are a feature of the post-war period. That it took so long for business education to become acceptable in Europe, despite the presence of numerous thriving American businesses from the early part of the century onwards, is a reflection of the different cultures that are implicit in European and American society. America is, and has been since first it was colonized, a land of enterprise and the birth-place of business and so it boasts a true business culture.

A review of American business culture, past and future

In defining culture it is hard to avoid the cliché or the sweeping generalization, but from the above survey of the history of American business life certain factors emerge. In the first place the timing of American expansion was propitious; it led to a gradual migration of go-getting Europeans, well versed in the basic tenets of a market economy, to a land where dreams of plenty could be pursued. The early settlers, bound together by religious conviction, uniformity of ambition and a recognition of collective responsibility (no one could go it entirely alone) combined hard work and flexibility with an appreciation of abilities over and above origins. Success was seen to indicate Godliness and social position followed on from wealth and in an ever more secular society success is still the standard by which people are judged. A frontier and pioneering society is inevitably one that is thrown upon its own resources and the tinkerer, the self-reliant amateur who will solve a practical problem by application of thought and experiment, is a feature throughout the history of early American commercial life and one that Henry Ford, Steve Jobs, Steve Wozniak and Bill Gates embody. The prevailing trend in America has always been to try – the taste perpetually for the new, the endeavour always for excellence. Failure can be forgiven, provided it is followed up by further attempts at success – effort is all. Free enterprise has certainly created victims and while John D. Rockefeller, J.P. Morgan and Andrew Carnegie are examples of outstanding victors, such victors were created at the cost of numerous less able and less lucky individuals (indeed, one cannot overlook the fact that white America has grown great at the expense of Native Americans and imported black slaves). Still, however many losers, attention tends to focus on the winners and national business heroes are, like film stars, meat for politics – note Tony O'Reilly's invitation by George Bush to advise his administration and the speculation that, after Chrysler, only the US State itself could offer a sufficiently broad canvas for the brush of Lee Iacocca.

Money matters. In Europe we have grown sentimental about images of an impoverished aristocracy that is obliged to open up its ancestral homes for the scrutiny and pennies of the public – not so in the States. No distinctions exist between old and new money and the media have their own stately homes in Pickfair, Gracelands and Never Never Land where Michael Jackson briefly played husband to Lisa-Marie Presley – the marriage of two mighty fortunes. It is all too easy to characterize America as a greedy and rapacious society, to style any successful consumer society in such a way, but the issue is not whether America may be more materialistic than any other nation but simply that America has proven better at supplying the material needs of its population. The eagerness for branded goods amongst former Soviet states well before Perestroika testifies to a common tendency to covet what others have irrespective of the prevailing political ideologies. America, by the standards of world civilizations, is a very young continent and the focus on newness and novelty in a land where tradition and history are but recent concepts comes as no surprise. It is also a nation peopled originally by migrants, individuals with more differences than similarities who were obliged, given the necessity for collective action, to obscure differences under a common banner. That banner proved to be business, the business of wealth generation, the fulfilment of shared dreams of plenty.

From American innovation, experiment and effort came, as we have seen, one of the enduring emblems of the American Dream – Hollywood. Drawing extensively on European talent (absorbing and making best use of its immigrants) the studio system peddled dreams of plenty, myths of rags to riches and distributed these across the Western world, creating an extended market for the nation's lifestyle-enhancing products. American companies came and colonized Europe, and became for the post-war generation of Europeans the clear training ground for future business success – many European leaders today have consciously opted to gain experience of the American way of doing business. The American model has given Europe standards of performance, procedures to meet those standards and set down a blueprint for executive excellence. As America in its youth took and improved upon the commercial dynamism of Europe, so Europe in its renaissance is learning in turn from America. The lesson that Europe now has before it is the ease with which other nations can lay economic siege to one thought to be unassailable (the Japanese example is a telling one). The irony here is that the American way of doing business that made America great might now be in danger of undermining that greatness, of becoming fossilized and losing the flexibility of a living, evolving organism. In future chapters we will go on to suggest some of the social perils that America must overcome. Here we will indicate just a couple of the cultural impediments we see to continuing success. First, how suited is the parochialism of American business to an increasingly internationalizing economy? Second, how flexible can a homogeneous business culture prove when values change fast? And third, to what extent have the values of the emerging generation of business leaders remained as acute as that of their parents? In 1991 Paul Leinberger and Bruce Tucker interviewed the children of the company men who had formed the basis of William Whyte's study, *The Organization Man*. The findings, as recorded by Anthony Sampson in his study *Company Man: The Rise and Fall of Corporate Life* are fascinating:

> 'They had come of age in the sixties and seventies, and began by resisting the pressures of organisations and cultivating their private selves. They

> *looked towards self-expression, self-fulfilment or self-assertion: many had artistic aspirations, to be musicians, film-makers, actors, poets, novelists, dancers or visual artists.'*

The children proved to be very unlike their parents in motivation and in aspiration. Disenchanted and disillusioned by recession they identified less strongly with large corporate entities and had followed unorthodox careers. Sometimes this gave rise to high levels of innovation, which would equip them for fast-moving business sectors, but the writers found substantial evidence of declining loyalty to large institutions, to the huge number of multinationals on which America's greatness is based. The motivation and composition of the next generation of business leaders in America must be of critical interest to those curious to see how American business will fend off the growing overseas threat.

Europe, with an understanding now of how business might best be done and a recognition that the market place must be a global one, has a surprising advantage which is the very antithesis of that which placed America and, to a certain extent, Japan at the forefront of the business arena. That advantage is its very multiplicity of values – the palpable absence of a European way of doing business – which dictates a certain sensitivity toward other cultures and gives also an ability to sense the subtlety of different approaches, an interpretative acuity. Hollywood's fascination in recent years with dinosaurs, with *Jurassic Park* and *The Flintstones*, brings to mind all too easily a caricature of the American way of doing business as a dinosaur itself – a creature that has been great, that has ruled the world but cannot survive seismic change. Such a statement would be to condemn too harshly and to picture Europe as a flexible and adaptable chameleon would be no less of a distortion. All the same, there is a warning here somewhere and an opportunity. America may be the advocates of such ubiquitous phrases as culture change and business process re-engineering, but its own national economic culture may be too cemented for the kind of change required. Europe, then, might step into the breach and devise a culture that eludes definition, that is defined by the very imperative to be indefinable.

4

Miracle Workers: Development of the Japanese and German Economies

'... There is a vastness behind them – a past of indefinite complexity and marvel – an amazing power of absorbing and assimilating – which forces one to suspect some power in the race so different from our own that one cannot understand that power.'
Lafcadio Hearn, authority on Japan writing of the Japanese in 1891.

'... The single most important explanation of West Germany's post-war economic success may be a simple human one, hard to prove or quantify. This is the fact that Germans at all levels, from shop-floor workers to managers, just happen to be very disciplined, thorough and realistic.'
John Ardagh, *Germany and the Germans*.

The United States may be the home of business and may have enjoyed economic hegemony for the greater part of the twentieth century but that hegemony has not gone entirely unchallenged. Indeed, America provided a model, some of the money and the motivation for two major economies to develop and threaten the supremacy of the super power on the world's business stage. The development of Germany and Japan, two nations with distinct and homogeneous cultures not unlike that of the United States, is generally held to have been miraculous. Industrial capitalism in Europe and then a corporation-dominated business world in America developed over the space of half a century. Within little more than a decade Germany and Japan secured a position for themselves amongst the world's major economies, which achievement was the more miraculous given the point from which they began – in the aftermath of devastating defeat in wars in which they had been the initial aggressors. The post-war miracles of which so much is made represent something of a second coming, however, for as we shall see both economies enjoyed tremendous growth at the end of the last century, putting in place many of the foundations for the later transformation. Rapidly achieved, has the miraculous ignition of the German and Japanese economies already extinguished itself? Has innovation given way to complacency? Have other aggressive developing economies now stolen the march on the steady performance of the Japanese and German engines? It is the business of this chapter to assess the chances of Japan and Germany in a race for economic supremacy in the next century. In Chapter 5 we will consider the other runners and riders, the emerging economies of Asia. We will consider here the parallels between German and Japanese experiences of growth, charting the cycles of miraculous growth and rapid decline and will attempt to identify the contributory cultural factors at play. This chapter will draw upon analysis of different capitalist systems and close by attempting to place in context the German and Japanese experience, relating that to the United States as the exemplar of another model.

From the same stable

A strong industrial base is a prerequisite for an aggressor in war on the scale seen in 1939–45. Neither Germany nor Japan could have gone to war without substantial industrial resources behind them and both were warfaring nations from the latter part of the nineteenth century onwards. Not surprisingly, then, both also experienced an industrial revolution, a first economic miracle, which supported their militaristic and expansionist policies in the final decades of the last century. So far apart geographically and culturally, there are clear parallels between the two nation states. The shogun, warrior-style culture of the Japanese chimes with the traditions of Prussian militarism and to both can be attributed highly sophisticated bureaucratic systems. Under Bismarck a united Germany strove to preserve and extend its power against strong neighbours France and Austria–Hungary – both keen to contain or annex that power. Japan, on the other hand, was obliged to develop a modern economy and military in order to withstand the inroads of Western colonial powers, notably the United States. It is a small step from defender to aggressor and, by virtue of economic power, both states were able to lay claim to extended political power on the world stage.

The Westernization of Japan

Almost overnight Japan began to model itself on Western lines from 1870 onwards. In 1871 the old feudal structure was abolished to be replaced by a strong central bureaucracy staffed by university graduates. A peerage was created in 1884, a cabinet government in 1885 and a two-house legislature was set up in 1889. The Samurai were replaced by a conscript army in 1873, a navy was founded and modern ships built. A national education system was introduced in 1872, just two years after the same had happened in Britain. New legal codes were also introduced, borrowing heavily from French and German systems.

In terms of economic development Japan used Western styles of production and copied Western means of enabling production, principally through the development of good banking practices, but the apparent Westernization of Japan obscures the highly local and distinct manner in which the state facilitated growth. Commercial decisions were always affected by the requirements of the nation and economic magnates recognized their obligation to the state, as evidenced by a note in the house rules drawn up by the founder of the Mitsubishi fortune: 'Operate all enterprises with the national interest in mind'. With the reform of land tax in 1873 and the development of a stable source of revenue, the Japanese exchequer was able to pour a third of its taxes into the development of a strong economic base. Model factories in strategic and import-saving industries were developed, such as steel and textiles; subsidies were offered to shipbuilding and shipping industries; and quality control and training schemes were lent government support to facilitate the export trade. The state also undertook infrastructural projects in support of its burgeoning industrial base; and in this as in its focus on core industrial developments prefigures the activities in more modern East Asian economies as we shall see in Chapter 5. Japan of course has been a conscious model throughout the region.

A business is not born as a corporation. Its origin is as a family concern. Curiously, the oldest family business of all is Japanese, the Hoshi Hotel, founded in 718 and now under the management of the 46th generation. Mitsubishi and Mitsui were family concerns that developed by the shrewd use to which government subsidies were put by young entrepreneurs. Dependence on founding families lessened, but the familial aspect of the organizations remained with a prevailing patriarchal structure of reciprocal duty and respect. The influence of the family structure was important across the spectrum of Japanese commercial concerns. In addition to supporting large scale businesses Japan also championed the small businessman who operated within traditional family or artisan structures. These were modernized via the introduction of power tools and third-party distribution and marketing networks, but the emotional import of the working relationship was allowed to remain intact. A system evolved whereby large businesses would put out work to small and these large, marketing organizations would in turn be supported by a network of major economic enterprises such as banks, metallurgical and shipbuilding industries who often provided finance. Ultimately economic power, like political power, resided in a few powerful hands with considerable interplay between them as in the case of the Mitsui or the Mitsubishi families.

In the first Japanese economic miracle then, can be seen some of the factors that enabled the second. Principal amongst these is the social structure based on reciprocity and respect and a commingling of the interests of state and entrepreneurial class.

German industrialization

The close ties between industry and state in Japan are reflected in the industrial expansion of Germany from the 1870s onwards. The 'respect' culture in Japan had its fellow in the rigid class system in Germany and the popularity and mystique of the state allowed similar uniformity of development. As the small business culture in Japan was modernized so too was the network of guilds and handicrafts in Germany turned into part of the economic strength. Perhaps the most notable aspect of German economic development, however, was the elevation of management and the development of a strong, integrated research and development culture. In short, the German period of industrial development was marked by the organization of entrepreneurial zeal into efficient structures.

The excellent education system in Germany produced a cadre of skilled scientists and researchers who were immediately harnessed by developing chemical and electrical companies. The industrial research laboratory where innovation was the goal of highly skilled and extensively educated scientists emanated from Germany in this period. Innovation was seen as an integral element of an ongoing manufacturing process and the twin processes of research and development (R&D) and production were harmonized to the tremendous benefit of German industry. If the original, British-led industrial revolution was dominated by iron and steel and the invention of the first aniline dye, the Bessemer steel converter, the basic steel process and the steam turbine then the second phase (in which the US as much as Germany was a key player) was dominated by the chemical and electrical industries and such predominantly German inventions as the internal combustion engine, the diesel engine, the automobile, the electric dynamo and electric traction. (US inventions to parallel these include the ring frame, the sewing machine, the typewriter, the filament lamp and the telephone.)

The same education system that gave rise to Germany's strength in research was also the origin of the management class. The universities provided skilled administrators and bureaucrats who developed rapidly into a corps of professionals and operated the factories, firms and banking institutions. The spirit of fraternity amongst alumni facilitated the development of an organized professional elite where a leading position in the hierarchy, based on merit, was as much a reward as the wealth that accompanied entrepreneurial success. The *esprit de corps* witnessed amongst generations of graduates was later transferred to a regimental spirit when, after the war, old military hierarchies were sustained in industry.

The role of the state in the development of industry was linked, as in Japan, to the needs of defence. Indeed, commercial gain was secondary to military expedience and the government controlled the market in such a way as to give special tariffs to encourage industries that contributed to the national defence. A notable example of state intervention came in 1879 when state purchase of privately owned railways became compulsory. While commercial gain may have been a secondary consideration to military need, a by-product of this policy was the creation of a transport network that would be as efficient in the distribution of goods as of people.

The means by which German industry was financed offered a new model. Under the umbrella of the state a few private bureaucracies or 'banks' supplied extremely long-term loans to developing industrial concerns and in return demanded as a form of security a voice in the management of the businesses in which they invested. This voice usually took the form of a representative from the investor being placed on the board. There were only half a dozen or so of these organizations controlling, over time, swathes of companies in core sectors and in this structure can be found the origin of the cartel. The cartel was a vehicle that controlled the supply and sale price of a particular product so as to maximize profit and smooth some of the fluctuations that led to cycles of boom or bust. The development of the cartel gave to German industry considerable ballast and two of the greatest rank as substantial multinational corporations into the twentieth century. The electricity industry spawned the Siemens–Schuckert Group and the Allgemeine Elektrizitats Geshellschaft (AEG). Walther Rathenau, son of AEG's founder, was by 1909 on the board of 84 large companies and concerned that the fortunes of so large a nation sat in the hands of a maximum of 300 people. He resigned his presidency and went on to be Minister of Reconstruction and Foreign Minister but his apparent radicalism led to his assassination in 1922.

Running neck and neck

The emergence of Japan and Germany show striking similarities: strong state involvement; the development of a few vast, strategically important family-run businesses amongst myriad small concerns; a high value placed upon commercial endeavour among the middle classes; and, though from within different ideological frameworks, a strong respect for hierarchy. Both states developed industrial empires where there was a discernible, uniform, heterogeneous operating environment, a set of shared values which in the latter part of the twentieth century we would term 'culture'.

Those shared values which informed economic success were also critical in a spirit of national and imperial endeavour. In the latter stages of the nineteenth and the first years of the twentieth century Japan busied herself trying to secure a wider share in the east Asian markets through annexation of new territories, while Germany engaged in the diplomatic manoeuvring which led to the first world war. During the 1930s, while Hitler consolidated his power in Germany, a period of militant nationalism in Japan led to increased militarization and ultimately the downfall of democracy. Both Japan and Germany were members of the ill-starred League of Nations but Japan was the first to violate its terms via the invasion of Manchuria, which exposed to Hitler the inherent weakness of the League and of its key members Britain and France who were Hitler's clear opposition. Germany's attempts to build a European empire were matched by Japan's ambitions in south-east Asia and particularly amongst the British colonial empires. Japanese motives were dissimilar – a mixture of self-aggrandisement and the desire to develop markets which could enable Japan's self-sufficiency and put some distance between the Japanese and the increasingly antipathetic United States. As Axis allies, Japan used Germany's invasion of the USSR to launch hers upon Indo-China, which was the springboard to the war in the Pacific. Exposed on too many fronts, both powers were ultimately destined to lose their respective wars and both Japan and Germany were vanquished and occupied in 1945, although the Germans escaped the ruthless allied action of atomic destruction which was the fate of Hiroshima and Nagasaki. The broadly parallel development of Germany and Japan was still to continue.

The German economic miracle

Myths abound concerning the phoenix-like conduct of the German economy. Principal amongst them is the notion that Germany emerged from total ashes largely due to the beneficence of the allies, notably the Americans via Marshall Aid. If aid alone could generate such phenomenal recovery the global economy today would look substantially different and, while it would be wrong to underestimate the extent of the devastation to some German cities and towns, it would be equally misguided to assume that the whole of Germany's substantial territory was razed to the ground. In fact in 1945 less than half of Germany's industrial plant had been destroyed. A further 5% of plant was dismantled by the allies before Adenauer persuaded them to discontinue the policy. Clearly, there was a need for substantial rebuilding and reinvestment, and Marshall Aid was an important source to the Germans as to many Europeans. However, the Germans had some foundations on which to build and it was a combination of shrewd, perhaps inspired, economic leadership and the will of the German people themselves that gave rise to the revival of Germany as a major economic force. Perhaps the critical factors were an immense will to work, a remarkable degree of industrial peace and the decision by the Minister of Economics, Ludwig Erhard, to create opportunity and incentivize.

Erhard, as much the architect of post-war Germany as Adenauer, was the son of a Bavarian farmer turned shopkeeper who as a result of infantile paralysis suffered a deformed right foot, slight curvature of the spine and as a consequence had a short neck, slight stoop and several chins. He was also deeply introverted. A man of courage and conviction, he refused to co-operate with the Nazi regime to even the slightest extent and resigned his post at Nuremberg's Institute of Market Research rather than join the Nazi Labour Front. With the end of the war he began a rise to political eminence which was as seemingly miraculous as the economic recovery he engineered. First in charge of the economic administration of Furth, he moved to take over the role of Ministry of Economics for Bavaria, from there to six months as Professor at Munich University and then he was sent by the Americans to the Frankfurt Economic Council and put in charge of economic and financial planning. In March 1948 he became Director of the Economic Administration of the US–British Bizonal Council, which made him the most senior German administrator. In 1949 he became the Economic Minister for the CDU, which position he held for 14 years until becoming the Chancellor.

Erhard's achievements

The milestone in Germany's turnaround was the currency reform of 1948. A huge black market operation made a number of allied troops wealthy as they bartered goods like cigarettes for Reichsmarks which were then converted into dollars or sterling, yielding in some cases profits that ran into thousands. One cigarette cost 7 Reichsmarks. The Germans were familiar with currency collapses – between 1921 and 1923 the exchange rate of the mark against the dollar rose from 63 to 4,200,000,000,000. In a move of extraordinary speed and daring, and with allied support, Erhard changed the currency literally overnight from the Reichsmark to the Deutschmark, and the German people were given one Deutschmark for 10 Reichsmarks. Savings were wiped out but with them went the black market and in came true purchasing power.

To underpin the success of the currency reform Erhard dropped most of Germany's wage and price controls. Controls were first dropped on a range of consumer goods and, after six months, on food. Almost instantly food appeared on the shop shelves, unemployment reduced and within two years industrial output tripled. Erhard's incentives to the German people included interest-free loans for everything from the building of modest homes to the reconstruction of large-scale plant and huge grants to agriculture. Under Erhard's direction 12 million refugees were resettled and 7,700,000 new jobs were created. National income and purchasing power multiplied and the Deutschmark became one of the three strongest currencies in Europe.

The German worker

At whatever level in whichever sector, the German worker, manager and owner shared one thing – a tremendous will to recover from the zero hour of destruction, defeat, hunger and shame in 1945. That motivation to succeed is an immensely important factor in the recovery of German industry. As we have seen above, the organization of German society into cadres of professionalized people operating in a number of small- to medium-sized businesses provided a flexible model that lent itself to being re-used. It gave the German army its logistical edge in two wars and could then be turned to good account in the reconstruction of industry. The seeds of the second industrial revolution in Germany, then, lay in the first. This time, however, the German economy had a substantial new labour pool on which to draw, as by 1949 there were no fewer than 8 million refugees in the West; and that labour was organized in an enlightened way. A pioneering piece of legislation devised by the allies was the *Mitbestimmung* or co-partnership scheme for workers. This was part of an allied initiative to break up the cartels that dominated heavy industry. The co-partnership law of 1951 provided for trade union representation on supervisory and managerial boards. The participation of workers in the governance of enterprise has given Germany a substantial advantage over other European nations that have at times been decimated industrially by labour problems.

Germany was also fortunate in its political leadership. Konrad Adenauer was an early exponent of European integration and under his leadership Germany entered the European coal and steel community, which gave an important fillip to German industry. Exports have been an important element of German development and the increasing role of Germany in the European community has served to strengthen its export record. Also Germany has seen considerable political stability. Even when there has been a change in administration, the distinctions between political parties have not been sufficiently marked to undermine economic policy.

Industrial strengths

Germany's key strengths have been in the automobile and chemical industries. As noted earlier, the car was a largely German invention and in developing a thriving car industry Germany was again building on existing foundations. The particular niche Germany has made its own is the high-speed, high-image, high-performance car but none of the principal companies in this sector have their origins in the post-war period. Daimler Benz brought together the genius of Gottlieb Daimler, the inventor of the petrol engine, and Karl Benz, a Stuttgart engine maker in the mid 1880s. Although it would be some 80 years before the companies were formally merged in the 1960s, a long collaboration brought the Mercedes fleet into prominence. Porsche, another Stuttgart firm, was founded by an Austrian in 1931, while BMW has its origins in the First World War when it was a maker of aircraft engines. By the late 1950s the company was facing bankruptcy because of over-extension and was taken over by the Quandt family – much in the tradition of family involvement in German businesses (other families to revive their fortunes after the war included the Thyssen, Flick and Henkel families). Volkswagen has been very much the poor relation of Daimler-Benz and BMW, dependent on a low–mid-range car that was hit by substantial competition from Asia. However, it eventually extended its range and now the Golf is the most popular small car in Europe and Audi its sporty, more up-market image. The automobile industry played to Germany's original strengths in production processes and quality finish – supported by its remarkably peaceable labour relations (the car industry being a perennial source of labour unrest in other parts of Europe).

The other great post-war success story for German industry was the growth of the chemicals business. Again, this was a revival of former strength. The largest of all German companies prior to the Second World War was IG Farben. The allies, in their bid to de-cartelize and neutralize the power of Germany's huge corporations, split IG Farben into three parts: Bayer, BASF and Hoechst. All three are now larger independent entities than the body from which they sprang and are only outpaced by the UK's ICI. The allied action in splitting the three companies was probably a major contributory factor to their growth as it gave impetus to competition.

While the top 30 companies in Germany account for 40% of manufacturing output the remainder is accounted for by the *Mittelstand* – small- to medium-sized businesses – and the *Handwerker*, 500,000 or so handicraft businesses. Again this continues the nineteenth-century traditions. Thus German economic growth has depended upon a few large, highly organized corporations that take a long-term view of the market they occupy and myriad smaller concerns driven by hardworking entrepreneurs who plough their profits back into the businesses they run. In that spread of risk alone may lie some of the secrets of Germany's growth from a devastated nation, both in terms of its morale and its economy, to the largest, strongest economy in Europe with GNP that is broadly that of England and France combined, the highest export quota in Europe, rivalled only by the United States which can draw upon three times the population. We shall save an analysis of the shortcomings of the German model until later in the chapter but there is little doubt that it has developed a nation with the most affluent living standard in Europe, much as Japan has achieved the same in Asia.

The Japanese economic miracle

Although there are numerous parallels between the German and Japanese experience of economic turnaround the two were separated somewhat in time. Japanese expansion, although motivated by changes made in the immediate post-war period, did not accelerate until the 1950s and it was primarily in the 1980s that the rest of the advanced industrialized world awoke to the competitive threat posed by Japanese business, although the scaremongering began as early as 1970.

The American occupation

While the responsibility for German occupation was shared amongst the allies (however much the financial burden may ultimately have rested with the

Americans), in Japan the occupation force was entirely American, led by General MacArthur. The actions of the occupying force, then, were subject to the vicissitudes of just one government and one set of taxpayers. Choices made in Japan reflect the ideology of the US government and a need by Washington to appease the electorate.

The initial intention of the US occupying force was to implement a mixture of punitive measures and democratizing reforms. This gave an agenda which included the demobilization of all Japanese forces, the carrying out of war crimes trials, the purge of all public figures known to have sympathised with the wartime military regime and, of most relevance in this context, the disabling of the *Zaibatsu*, the huge trading, industrial and financial conglomerates that had dominated the pre-war economy, such as Matsui and Mitsubishi.

The Zaibatsu were antithetical to US principles of competition. Before the outbreak of war some 10 major corporations accounted for 75% of commercial, industrial and financial activities, operating through some 75 subsidiaries. Initially the US force took a strong line on the break-up of the Zaibatsu, and succeeded in passing a harsh anti-monopoly law preventing any trusts or interlocking corporate controls; in addition, a deconcentration law designated over 300 companies to be dismantled. However, some businesses at home in the US were averse to the prospect of losing altogether previously lucrative trading partners and, ideologically, there was considerable alarm at the ineffectiveness of the nationalist party in Taiwan and fear of the scourge of communism. It became increasingly important to prevent the Japanese economy from foundering further (in the spring of 1946 some 800,000 tonnes of grain had to be imported to alleviate a serious food crisis) if the country and thus south-east Asia were to be preserved from the spread of communism. After all, MacArthur himself in a radio address in 1945 noted that: 'Today freedom is on the offensive, democracy is on the march. Today in Asia as well as in Europe, unshackled peoples are tasting the full sweetness of liberty, the relief from fear.' A further pressing reason to open up rather than foreclose on the Japanese economy was the simple need to relieve the US taxpayer of the burden of supporting a starving nation. By 1949 the cost of the occupation had already risen to $900 million.

So the Zaibatsu were somewhat disabled but not dismembered as originally planned. The original 300 target closures were refined to 83 and 5000 corporations were forced to reorganize rather than cease operating altogether. After the departure of the occupying forces many of the 83 regrouped, but in subtly different ways. Instead of the dominance of the family members, the professional, highly skilled university graduate came to prominence in the management of corporations that were in essence not so very different from the vehicles of the late nineteenth century.

The need to keep the Japanese economy afloat, if not buoyant, motivated the Economic Recovery in Occupied Areas programme, which gave substantial aid and also created the seeds for a developing textile industry, through generous loan facilities to be repaid through finished product.

The labour problem

Japan is usually represented as a nation of abiding hierarchies and cross-generational, cross-status respect between individuals. Until 1949, however, it was bedevilled by labour problems. In 1945 labour laws were passed giving considerable new rights to workers, in an enlightened effort to liberalize labour relations. In September 1945 there were just two unions with a membership of just over 1000. By February 1947 this figure had risen to an astonishing 18,929 unions with a membership of around 5 million (over 40% of the work-force). A wave of strikes, some violent, and the fear on the part of an American administration with changing political priorities that a radical labour force could render Japan vulnerable to socialist revolution, led to a clampdown and reversal of laws (strongly supported by the Japanese subject, but actually highly empowered, government). As in Germany many of the economic drivers that enabled post-war success were latent in pre-war circumstances, so the alternative found to the strong Japanese unions looked uncannily like a pre-war institution, the Patriotic Industrial Unions (Sanpo). As legislation was passed to prevent strike action, 'enterprise unions' began to emerge which comprised both blue and white collar workers, managers and bosses aping the pre-war models that allowed the head of the union to be the head of the enterprise, so ensuring that the corporatist ideals were inculcated in the work-force.

The Ministry of International Trade and Industry (MITI)

As the labour issues of the 1940s were resolved so was one of the most important steps towards economic recovery taken in 1949 when the Ministry of International Trade and Industry (MITI) was established. Again, this was a thinly disguised revival of a pre-war organization. The Ministry of Commerce and Industry had been established in 1925 and the MITI drew extensively on personnel from the Ministry's previous incarnation, and both borrowed and took further certain of the original ministry's guiding principles such as that of industrial rationalization – the notion of co-operation rather than competition in key industries. The MITI also took on all the responsibilities for foreign trade that had lain with the occupation forces. In the post-war period the MITI has been one stable element in a polity which has seen tremendous factionalism and corruption. All parties unite behind a fundamental belief in the importance of industry and a degree of state control over that industry. With MITI's support, Japanese business has been able to achieve long-term, co-ordinated planning in selected industries and to show enhanced technological innovation – in 1992 Japanese companies filed more patent applications than the USA and the UK combined. As in the late nineteenth century there was a traditional link between the people in government and those in industry. Similar links developed in the post-war period (and a curious aside here is that Yoshida Shigeru, five times prime minister between 1946 and 1954, was linked by marriage to the Mitsubishi Zaibatsu). It became common place for bureaucrats retiring from the MITI to move into business enterprises and the partnership between bureaucrats and business has been seen as one of the key factors in Japan's success. Certainly, the MITI has played a very powerful role. For the greater part of the post-war period the MITI backed a strategic or goal-orientated policy towards the economy. Through its control of the Japan Development Bank (founded in 1951) the MITI could manage industrial policy through loan application screening. Between 1953 and 1955 83% of funding from the Bank was channelled into electric power, shipbuilding, coal and steel. More recently the tight control has been relaxed within the private sector, notably in consumer electronics, textiles and petro-chemicals, having greater economic say in the definition of long-term strategic goals and on market competition. Nevertheless the MITI has had extraordinary influence. That influence has included a strong say through the Industrial Rationalization Council in issues such as management reform, lifetime employment and worker productivity with committees devising standards in each of these areas. The MITI was behind the recombining in new form of the old Zaibatsu, offering tax write-offs and contingency funds in key supported industries (notably textiles).

The MITI, indeed the civil service in Japan in general, attracts some of the nation's ablest graduates. Japan is a nation of able graduates and the emphasis on education, mirrored – although taking a different form – in Germany has been a critical element in the country's economic fortunes.

The impact of trading relationships with other nations

The issue of rearmament was fraught within Japan and had implications for the development of industry. Curiously, the effects were largely beneficial, obliging Japan to go ahead and develop strong export markets rather than relying upon fail-safe government orders. On the other hand, defence of another nation was to play a major part in the development of Japanese business. The United States became embroiled in the Korean War in 1950 which gave a tremendous kick-start to Japan's economy. US procurements in Japan injected $5.5 billion into the economy between 1951 and 1960, the US contribution in 1951 representing some 38% of total foreign earnings.

It is ironic that the Americans should have ended up giving such a boost to Japanese foreign earnings, the more so since they had envisaged those earnings coming from the other nations of south-east Asia. However, development in south-east Asia, as we shall see in Chapter 5, was much slower, so Japan suffered a tremendous trade deficit, some $400 million in 1953, and from 1946 to 1964 Japan's imports regularly exceeded its exports – on three occasions Japan was obliged to borrow from the International Monetary Fund (IMF) to finance exports.

However, the nations of south-east Asia did make a contribution to Japanese economic revival although not in a manner that might have been foreseen. The Japanese were committed to paying reparations to other countries in the region. Over the 20 years from 1954 to 1974 Japan paid $1012 million to Burma, Indonesia, the Philippines, South Vietnam, Laos, Cambodia, South

Korea and Malaysia. Some of this took the form of economic aid and that often involved the purchase of Japanese manufactures. The various agreements had the side-effect of stimulating the Japanese steel, shipbuilding and electrical industries.

Japan takes the lead

If during the 1940s and 1950s Japan lagged behind, she found her form in the 1960s and started to lead the field. The statistics are compelling. Throughout the decade real annual GNP increased by an average above 11%, Japan's share of world exports increased from 2.1% in 1955 to over 7% in the early 1970s and the GNP in 1970 was the third largest in the world. Industrial production between 1951 and 1973 grew by a factor of 14, focusing on shipbuilding, chemicals, steel and automobiles. To take the latter example: in 1950 Japan produced 1600 cars, by 1980 it was producing 11 million. Living standards grew accordingly and by the early 1970s most of the Japanese population referred to themselves as middle class. Educational attainments demonstrate the validity of that claim. By 1980 some 37.9% of the population in the age range to attend higher education were engaged in some form of tertiary education. Moreover, 94.3% of junior high-school graduates moved on to senior high. Birth rates fell and life expectancy rates rose to the highest in the world from 54 and 50 for men and women, respectively, in 1947 to 80 for women and 75 for men in 1980 – a triumph for successive administrations, a potential time bomb for future governments needing to support an ageing population.

Japan's success does not merely resonate on home territory – she has taken production overseas to the United States and to Europe where the Japanese have quite simply been beating the local, old established economies at their own game. Honda's Accord model, for instance, became the biggest selling model in the US, entirely built in Ohio. Innovative means of production, high quality standards and good labour relations have contributed to substantial Japanese success overseas.

The Japanese formula for success

A number of contributory factors to Japanese success have been noted above. The fact that there were established patterns from the nineteenth century to provide a template; the impact of the US occupation force and the varying needs of the US administration both in practical and ideological terms – all have been important. As early as 1962 *The Economist* referred to the Japanese economic miracle and attributed it to high productivity, harmonious labour relations and a high rate of savings. Much of what has been written, however, focuses on the cultural dimension – often straying perilously close to certain racist assumptions, or betraying at least cultural suspicion.

Japan undoubtedly has a militarist background. As we have seen, American businessmen are often seen in the tradition of the great frontiersman, pioneers, extending boundaries and developing new territories into which the less intrepid can follow. All in all, the American businessman is consistent with American history, the product and expression of it (see Chapter 3). In a similar way the militarism of Japanese history, the Shogun tradition, is somehow seen to characterize Japanese development. Some commentators note the importance of Sun Tzu, an authority on warfare some 2500 years ago and indicate that his military wisdom was a primary guide to company chairmen in Japan:

- All warfare is based on deception.
- If you know the enemy and know yourself, you need not fear the result of a thousand battles.
- Energy may be likened to the bending of a crossbow; decision to the releasing of a trigger.
- The clever combatant looks to the effect of a combined energy and does not require too much from individuals.
- Regard your soldiers as your children, and they will follow you into the deepest valleys.
- Keep your army continually on the move, and devise unfathomable plans.
- Be subtle! Be subtle! And use your spies for every kind of business.

From these adages can be found the confirmation, for those who seek it, of certain perceived traits in the Asian character: dishonesty, shiftiness, aggression, inscrutability and a tendency to follow a leader slavishly and to absorb the interests of the individual in collective action. Japan's economic strength can be glibly attributed to a nation of unpleasant aggressors, duping its populace into unethical practices in relation to competitors. A less sinister but no more flattering interpretation is that of a nation of brainwashed automatons. In 1979 an EEC report described the Japanese as 'workaholics living in rabbit hutches', while 9 years previously a much-quoted book, *The Emerging Japanese Superstate: Challenge and Response*, revealed the Matsushita Electric Company Song:

> 'For the building of a new Japan,
> Let's put our strength and mind together
> Doing our best to promote production,
> Sending our goods to the people of the world.
> Endlessly and continuously,
> Like water gushing out of a fountain,
> Grow industry, grow! grow! grow!
> Harmony and sincerity,
> Matsushita Electric.'

Hard to envisage the staff of Unilever or General Motors beginning the day with a burst of a company song, certainly, but no real indicator of a nation of simpletons in Japan. Indeed, the mission statements routinely distributed in many modern corporations in the West are not so very far away from the spirit of the above, if not the style.

However, some of the features highlighted above merit closer consideration. Certainly it is a truth universally acknowledged that the Japanese economic miracle derives, in part, from collective action and strong paternalist patterns. We will consider some of these elements further in Chapter 5 in the wider context of Asia. The Japanese pattern of paternalism could be seen to be deeply embedded in the national psyche. However, while there is every truth in the fact that paternalism has been a significant factor in Japanese growth, there is a case to be made for that paternalism being a relatively recent construct rather than something instinctively Japanese. Indeed, in the late nineteenth century the conditions of the labouring masses were extremely poor and there was considerable labour unrest, denied by Japanese leaders who pointed to the in fact mythical existence of traditional paternalist structures as an argument against laws to protect labour. By the 1920s and 1930s the labour unrest had become considerable and it is from that era that the pattern can be traced of lifetime employment, advancement based on seniority and loyalty bonus schemes – measures introduced to secure labour stability. Institutionalized paternalism can be seen as evidence of Japanese pragmatism and flexibility rather than of some innate cultural heritage.

Another myth about Japanese development is that it depends on huge organizations, the scions of the Zaibatsu, where large numbers of workers come together and in the structures outlined above bend their wills to that of the company, which in turn owes its allegiance to the State, demonstrated by the good will shown via the MITI. Unfortunately, this neat formula disregards the role of small- to medium-sized businesses in the development of Japan. In 1965 53% of all wage earners were employed in businesses with fewer than 100 people. In 1981 74.3% of all wage earners were employed in businesses with fewer than 300 people. Between 1954 and 1977 the contribution of small- to medium-sized businesses (those employing under 300 people) to total manufacturing rose from 49 to 58%. A clear parallel emerges with the German model of the Mittelstand and the Handwerker and it seems, from the figures at any rate, undeniable that Japan has a dual economy, spreading its risk across large and small businesses, not depending exclusively on economies of scale. These flexible small business units have been the source of considerable innovation, not least in terms of manufacturing processes. In the machinery industry where the MITI tried to build up cartels, the market in fact prevailed and new entrants flooded the high-tech sector, generating increased competition and spiralling innovation.

The large company image of Japan is no less relevant. In his case study of Toyota, however, Anthony Sampson in *Company Man* dispels the myth of the brainwashed automaton. He demonstrates that novel production techniques introduced into the factories were based on a desire to harness worker skills and responsibility, and maximize an artisan and craft tradition. Thus at each step of the process, workers would have considerable autonomy and responsibility for quality. From Toyota came the *kanban* or 'just in time' system, designed to trim costs and so better serve the customer. Far from fitting Edith

Cresson's analogy to ants (made as late as 1991), Toyota's success derived from recognizing the skills and requirements of individuals (customers and labour) within a collective construction.

Japanese success then, depends on a range of factors, some historically specific, others deriving from certain existing commercial traditions and still more from the intangibles like pragmatism and, as in the case of the Germans, a passionate need to rebuild confidence and living standards. Before comparing German and Japanese models more closely we will see the extent to which these two economic miracles have been sustained.

The German economy loses pace

At the time of writing the German economy seems to have slowed almost to a stop. Economic growth in 1996 was, at best, sluggish with GDP growth slowing to 1.4% from 1.9% in the previous year. Unemployment is growing by 10.8% and the mark has tumbled against the dollar. Chancellor Kohl blames slow growth on huge costs related to reunification with East Germany. But are there other factors, the obverse of some of the strengths seen above, that merit consideration? Certainly, Germany has had considerable problems keeping up with its old stable mate Japan and is increasingly threatened by the tiger economies. We shall briefly chart some of the possible factors mitigating against Germany.

Education systems

Germany has been remarkably slow to embrace the high technology industries, its share of the market falling from 26 to 17% since 1972 in the face of Japanese competition – some point to the conservative education system which has not, as elsewhere in the world, integrated computers into the curriculum. Germany is comparatively computer illiterate and, perhaps influenced by its green politics, increasingly disarmed by the technology revolution.

A general trend towards egalitarianism in Germany has been reflected in schools where there has been a move away from specialism towards generalism.

This factor is thought by some to have played a part in the declining technical innovation emerging from the universities. Few Germans working in Germany have won Nobel prizes since the war – although German émigrés continue to succeed in other cultures. The loss of Jewish talent is a possible factor as is the status accruing to the university professor. The professor in Germany has attained such an elevated status that the young research scientist is less likely – especially in a culture with some veneration of age – to question the thesis of a senior professor – and German research is dominated by older men. Some of this is simply generational. Those who came to prominence in the post-war period and were innovative in their youth remain in senior positions today, but that innovation has turned with increasing age to orthodoxy and conservatism. Perhaps the pendulum will swing back again. Certainly, German business enterprises have shown better R&D records than the universities; all the same there needs to be cross-fertilization between the two.

Business education

While America pioneered business education and the rest of the world has followed on, Germany has resisted forays into the world of management science. German executives remain among some of the most highly educated in the world, with doctorates and enviable language skills, but the emphasis on education is technical rather than broad. Germans who attend business schools outside their native country tend to return and enter management consultancy – the culture of the business school graduate has simply not taken root. Large companies recruit from universities and then train in their own administrative methods. So staff roles in German companies are likely to be held by people with qualifications equivalent to those of people in the line. To be simplistic, the absence of business education may be delivering a population of managers who think in detail rather than of leaders who can conceive a vision. Further, some of the most highly trained managers from the largest companies will have imbibed a methodology and way of being that is particular to that large company. This cannot serve the interests of smaller organizations, which are often the source of innovation.

Finance

As small- to medium-sized companies may be losing out in relation to a skilled pool of workers, so may they be losing out in relation to finance. The inadequate supply of venture capital and the extraordinary power of cautious, large banks may be stifling some innovation. Typically large banks are only prepared to put finance into ventures that are water-tight, put forward by people with sound credentials. Thus capital is available, effectively, only for those who do not have need of it. Some private sources of funding are closed to those needing risk capital because of a certain risk aversion on the part of family trusts and individuals of high net worth who have more than once seen fortunes eroded in the course of this century. Political upheaval in Eastern Europe and the reunification of Germany will only have exacerbated fears of inflation and volatility in the markets.

Changing values

In 50 years the values of Germans have been turned entirely on their head. The tyranny of Nazism has been replaced by one of the most enlightened, liberal democracies in the developed world. The German welfare system, providing health care, unemployment benefits and pensions, is both generous and humane and workers receive excellent perks with long holidays and bonuses. The consequences of this, however, are huge welfare bills putting a strain on a society that is ageing and where there is a falling birth rate.

A considerable concern in Germany is the perceived declining work ethic. Germany now has the shortest working week in Europe and, as successive generations acquire increasing wealth, materialism in younger people declines. Respect for money making is lower on the agenda of the young than of the old – perhaps because the young are born into its security. The advent of green politics and the concern with environmental issues might have had some impact on the negative attitudes on the part of youth towards the traditional industries that have made Germany successful. Possibly, again, the increasing age of those at the helm of German businesses is a deterrent to young would-be executives. Perhaps the parlous state of the German economy (if one in growth mode can ever be seen as entirely parlous) merely reflects the vicissitudes of the life cycle, with Germany in late middle-age, finding itself with a new child to look after (in the shape of East Germany) and without the speed and resources of some younger neighbours. Possibly, economic fortune is simply cyclical, tied to the clock and the swing of the pendulum.

Japan falls behind

The 1996 Global Competitiveness Report of the World Economic Forum based in Geneva makes worrying reading for the Japanese. Once one of the most competitive of all major economies it has now slipped to 13th place – an inauspicious ranking even if fortunes were ascending rather than descending. How could global leadership have slipped so quickly? The report attributes Japan's plight to a combination of a deteriorating fiscal system, a banking crisis and the domestic nature of many businesses.

Although it is still too early to stand back and analyse the reasons for the current appearance of decline there are some clear indicators. The rot set in during the boom period of the 1980s which could only end in the bursting of the investment bubble, leaving many companies burdened with bad loans and valueless collateral. The economic growth rate fell to 1.5% in 1992 and the following year Nissan shut down one of its plants near Tokyo, the first closure of a car-making plant in the post-war period. Political and commercial scandals, mixed with a soaring yen and a stock market plunge, have combined to hold Japan in a state of recession. The rapid development of competition from the south-eastern nations plus a trading battle with the United States has done little to improve either morale or trading conditions.

Ironically, but not surprisingly, some of Japan's decline can be accounted for by the very factors that led to its growth – in particular, the high degree of state intervention and controls. Once regarded as having the best civil service in the world, a laboratory for government, Japan has been rocked by bureaucratic scandal and there is little faith in the honesty and efficiency of public servants. The Ministry of Finance enjoys a stranglehold over the economy which is believed to have led to the bubble economy in the late 1980s and has proven utterly unequal to the regulatory tasks that might have prevented the massive losses suffered by Daiwa Bank and Sumitomo Corp. If Japan is to recover some of its competitive edge then it needs drastically to cut back the powers of the state and give increasing power to industry. Certainly 1997 appears to be a time when banking reform will go ahead, with the Bank of Japan being given significantly more control over monetary policy. Some of the red tape that binds the Tokyo market is also to be loosened so that Tokyo can achieve something of its former status and compete, once more, with New York and London.

Complacency in governance has become a by-word in Japan. The practice of *amakudari* – leaving government service for a high-ranking job in business – once an asset because it strengthened ties between commerce and government and allowed government access to commercial needs, has now become a considerable problem. The fat cat syndrome, the issues of croneyism and stifling of innovation and challenge all accompany the practice.

Japan's international growth and development of off-shore manufacturing facilities leaves the domestic market with a problem of overcapacity. Once companies are given greater rein to control their own destinies they will start to restructure, to close sites and to lay off staff. Unemployment will then, as in Germany, become a considerable concern, made worse by the challenge to the accepted wisdom that big company membership is a lifetime, two-way commitment. Practical problems will combine with attitudinal ones and there will need to be considerable administrative and social dexterity to cope with the implications. Like Germany, Japan has an ageing population, which is not one that is best geared to change.

The German and Japanese model versus the American and British model

Throughout this chapter comparisons have been drawn between Germany and Japan and implicit in the text is the assumption that both found a way of doing business that differed from that of other, broadly Anglo-Saxon powers like the US and Britain. In his book *Capitalism Against Capitalism*, M. Albert draws the distinction between the two models, which can be illuminating. The German/Japanese model he calls the Rhine model and associates it with Switzerland, the Netherlands and Scandinavia as well as our two paradigms of economic powers. He pitches this against the neo-American model, which is broadly Anglo-Saxon and followed in the US and Britain.

Rhine model	Neo-American model
Emphasis on collective success, co-operation and long-term planning	Emphasis on individual success, competition and short-term financial gain
Great emphasis on thrift and saving	Great emphasis on consumption and spending
Strong training ethic higher	Declining training and education, incidence of entrepreneurialism
Reliance on finance from banks with long-term close relationships	Dependence on capital raised in stock markets
Better income distribution	Less equal income distribution
Better state welfare provision (not Japan)	Limited state welfare (Britain excepted)

Albert would appear to put a value judgement on the two systems and certainly, from the perspective of 1993, thought that the Rhine model would outperform the neo-American one. In 1997 it might be safer to predict that the two models will fit different points of the cycle.

A nightmarish vision of American society can be conjured quite easily. The nation is the world's biggest debtor, suffers extraordinary urban decay and social deprivation and is underperforming educationally with more than half of all American adults unable to locate Britain, France or Japan on a world map. Adult illiteracy is higher in the US than in Poland. Salary differentials are pernicious, with captains of industry in the US paying themselves 110 times as much as their employees, compared with the modest multipliers in Germany of 23 and Japan of 17. The Americans and British speculate. Over the 10 years from 1980 to 1990 savings in the US fell from 19 to 13% of GDP. Over the same period they rose from 22 to 26% in Germany and from 31 to 35% in Japan. The culture in the neo-American model of short returns and reliance on the stock market makes for a climate of volatility in which companies can move their shares with devastating effect overnight to others. Contrast this with the stability of German businesses and the emotional security that gives to its work-force.

The US has tremendous advantages, a legacy of huge capital investment from the past, reserves of raw materials and energy, some of the best brains in the world and the considerable advantage of operating in the world language of business, English, and having a world reserve currency. Despite these massive assets, from a 1993 perspective, the US was seen to be in decline, the neo-American model with it.

However, the Rhine model is not without substantial disadvantages, which the Neo-American exponents have been able to exploit. With the introduction of new communications technologies and the invention of new financial instruments, the emphasis in global trading has gone the way of the neo-Americans, towards an increasing reliance on stock market trading. The strength, then, of London and New York has won out to some extent against that of Tokyo and Frankfurt. Certainly, as seen above, both Germany and Japan must free up their financial systems if they are to maintain competitiveness.

Further, the Rhine model is a high-cost system and lacks the flexibility to compete with emerging markets with low welfare provision. Second, the Rhine model has flourished in states where there has been a tradition of conservatism and an intolerance of individual diversity. The neo-American model has given much greater credence to difference. This can be seen simply in the different attitudes to immigration. Britain and the US have been receptive to immigration and despite, at times, intolerable racism have, nevertheless, given citizenship to people from other states, whereas Germany remains unusually unenlightened towards its Turkish immigrant community to whom it will not grant even basic civil rights. The ghetto is, it would seem, an acceptable aspect of German life.

The neo-American model fits a broadly liberal pattern, hence there is tremendous resistance to such infringements on liberty as identity cards and conscription. Countries that follow the Rhine model seem to encourage such measures. On the one hand, taken to extremes, the neo-American model can lead to anarchy, the Rhine model to sterile conformity.

The neo-Americans today

While the principal exponents of the Rhine model grapple with substantial structural and cultural issues those of the neo-American style are forging ahead. British industry is stronger than it has been for years. Over the last decade output per person has risen by 43% and Britain has closed the gap in productivity in terms of her main rivals. In particular, Germany's productivity lead of 51% in 1979 was down to 14% in 1994 and is set to be lower still by the end of the 1990s. The US advantage remains substantial at 50%, but considerably better than the 86% lead of 1979. Britain is prospering with the advent of the single market, giving access to economies of scale that Japan and America with huge internal markets have long enjoyed. While benefiting from exports Britain is also a magnet for foreign investment, with some of the lowest labour costs in Europe. Non-wage costs for every £100 spent in the UK total £18, compared with figures of £44 for France, £34 for Spain and £32 for Germany. Corporation tax at 33% is also lower than continental rivals. Eighteen years of political stability may end with a change of administration in the middle of the year – however, the gulf between political parties is far narrower than was the case in 1979 so the UK should be shielded from some of that potential volatility – one instance of the neo-American model proving robust.

The scenario in America itself, written off at the turn of the decade, is almost spellbinding. The US has enjoyed no less than five years of uninterrupted growth and is close to full employment yet without any inflation pressures. The economy is remarkably flexible, able to create new employment and re-allocate resource with a speed unmatched elsewhere. Since 1980 the US has lost 42 million jobs but created 67 million. Europe in contrast has a net yield of new jobs of a mere four million. Few commentators expect the US to improve dramatically on current conditions, but even stability gives America a substantial lead on any other world economy. The stamina of the neo-American model should not be underestimated.

Conclusion

So where does this take us? We have studied in depth two key economies which have moved through the cycle of development, destruction, miraculous recovery and sustained recession. We have traced a pattern and found cultural explanations for events and, borrowing from social theory, have found a model that fits the scenario. Against this we have, briefly, looked at the two economies on the alternative axis and seen, on the basis of current showing at least, that the two models are in competition with one another and while one is in the ascendant position the other must be in decline. We have confined ourselves, however, to single economies based on the nation state. Whatever one thinks concerning the nation state and its future, increasing internationalism is a reality and to study economies in isolation, although interesting, offers only a partial understanding. The thesis at the heart of this book is that the world is a series of trading blocs within which individual economies have alliances and relationships based on a combination of common cultural experiences and adjacent geographies.

Seen in this context the above analysis of particular economies and definition of models of economic conduct throw up a new set of questions and interesting choices for the constituent parts of the various trading blocs. The three trading blocs to which reference is typically made are the US, Asia and Europe. Clearly, the latter two are blocs – groups of different nations with distinct traits and models at variance with one another. The UK and Germany, for instance, sit within one bloc but display very different characteristics in terms of their approach to the economy. To call the US a bloc is something of a misnomer. However large the internal market in the US, it remains a single economy, subject to the vicissitudes of various market forces with consequent high risk exposure. A united Europe spreads its risks by having a mix of styles. However, the US has an option on being an integral part of a bloc – that of the Pacific Rim, a re-working of the Asia bloc. Similarly, Japan can either continue as a lone economy, maintain its uncomfortable but established links with the US and focus on APEC or throw in its lot with south-east Asia. APEC and the ASEAN are not mutually exclusive but Japan will need to prioritize some trading relationships over others; thus it is not entirely absurd to posit such a choice. It remains to be seen how the economies of many Asian nations will stabilize; similarly the polity. Here Europe has the edge. Despite war in eastern Europe and the integration of East and West Germany the European Community comprises a group of nations with by and large high levels of political stability.

There are other measures than single economies or groups of economies, growth rates in GDP, employment or levels of inflation. The increasing role of the corporation should not be neglected. How do our trading blocs emerge from a calibration of this type? Taken in isolation we find that the US economy boasts 422 companies in the *Business Week* top 100 most valuable companies. Japan has some 227, whereas the UK has a mere 97 and Germany just 35. If we look at Europe as a whole (or, at least, EU members) then we find 265 world-class companies, still many fewer than the US. The position changes only very slightly if we look at composite values (of companies within the particular regions) with the country composite – that is, the total value of all companies represented – for the US at $5,108,144, for Japan at $2,616,814 and then the European Community at $2,520,763. A Pacific Rim trading bloc that united aspects of the Japanese and the US economies could clearly be formidable, with a huge array of global companies and potentially complementary (although apparently conflicting) models for economic conduct. A Pacific Rim bloc would have substantial muscle and risk less exposure by uniting different regimes. But does it, as a trading bloc, have sufficient geographical and cultural unity to enable it to function? Common interests perhaps, but a much wider cultural and geographical gulf to be spanned than in Europe. Of course, a measure that looks at corporations is unreliable when it is so hard to quantify the corporations in the emerging markets, which will have substantial impact on both the European and the Asian blocs, and potentially North America if Latin America can develop from its current shaky base.

It might seem as if the only conclusion we can reach is that we cannot even begin to look at the subject because definition is so elusive. One thing emerges, however: from whichever set of measures one uses Europe can be seen in a strong position, not necessarily in the lead but very much a front runner. The nations that comprise the EU have a strong list of global companies, stable political regimes, economies which, if not all growing, are nevertheless robust and a spread of styles which can give ballast to the community at any stage in the economic cycle. There are no dead certs in the race for economic supremacy in the next century – the hurdles are too many – but if stability, longevity, flexibility and corporate quality count for anything Europe must be at least a safe bet.

5

Knowing the Field: the Asian Runners and Riders

'The Chinese bloody invented nerve-splicing. Give me the mainland for a nerve job anyday ... The Japanese had already forgotten more neurosurgery than the Chinese had ever known.'
Neuromancer, William Gibson.

Tokyo, almost destroyed by a stupendous earthquake and now recreated, has become subtly different. Ghosts are everywhere in its all-pervasive neon fog, between the towers and amidst the buildings that seem to change shape as you look at them. The very nature of reality seems different here.'
Flier to Idoru, William Gibson.

Threats to Western security

Science fiction, the projection of a new world reflecting elements of the old, is a fitting genre to dominate popular culture as the 1990s come to a close. The turn of the century – a period even given a name, *fin de siècle* – is of minimal importance set against the mighty turn of the millennium which appears to exert a strong pull on the imagination of the West, assisted by an interested media machine. Certainly, this is a period of reflection upon the horror and change of the twentieth century and a projection of current fears onto the next. Science fiction, as it did in the Hollywood B Movies of the 1950s at the height of the Cold War, takes those fears and expresses them in a vision of a fearful new world. William Gibson, a product of post-war America, now resident in Canada, is the pre-eminent observer and commentator on these fears and translates them into the most consistently and stylishly conceived world. That world is dubbed the matrix (borrowing a term from the business lexicon), a world within a world, a graphic representation of the databanks of every computer in the human system ...

The fears Gibson's work projects are illuminating. Fear of the Asian influence can be seen to be paramount. Is it the Chinese or the Japanese who have the superior technology for maiming the nervous system? Even when a fantasy is realized and a threat neutralized by natural disaster, reality is still not comprehensible. In Chapter 1 we noted Gibson's identification of the global corporation as a sinister entity. The combination of big business and Asian powerhouses in an information-driven world can be seen as ultimately threatening to Western security. Gibson's world knows no barriers, people move fluidly from place to place and yet in this futuristic place those with power are recognizable in the garb of a businessman of the 1990s, not some far-fetched fashion for the next millennium: 'he wore his dark suit, his Rolex watch, a galaxy of small fraternal devices in his worsted label'. Whatever else will be of importance in the next century, if not the next millennium, there can be little doubt that business holds a commanding position, Asian business especially so.

So an Asian global corporation represents twice the fear. At the end of the twentieth century there is little doubt that the potential economic dominance of Asian nations is an unsettling notion for the average complacent Westerner. A number of the nations involved have only relatively recently freed themselves from Colonial rule by Western empires and citizens of those former empires adjust slowly to the dramatic shift in relations. Racial and cultural differences are profound and the emotional distance between west Europeans and Americans and those who live in south-east Asia can seem unbridgeable. Asian peoples are frequently dubbed 'inscrutable' and the word itself is telling – it suggests the unknown and the unknowable and, by extension, the uncontrollable. Humankind is at its most comfortable with sameness; to many Westerners, Asian peoples are the very epitome of difference, of the threatening other. Fear of Asian economic dominance in the next century is a twofold fear: a fear of lost status and a fear of the ascendancy of alien values.

The intention of this chapter is certainly not to defend the validity of these fears; merely to acknowledge their existence. Once we understand that these fears are a form of currency, especially in Western cultures, demonstrated or expressed allegorically in all manner of media artefacts, then the oft-repeated prophecies that Asian businesses will dominate the world in the next century take on a new significance. They cease to be reasoned analyses of a live economic situation and become mere prophecies of doom – scaremongering. It is as if by expressing our worst fear we neutralize and nullify it.

Assembling the runners and riders, eliminating the non-starters and also-rans

Yet there would seem to be little doubt that there is a geographical shift in economic power away from the West towards the East. Certainly, economic seers point to the Pacific Rim as the powerhouse of the twenty-first century – a comforting notion because it embraces the west coast of the United States and, technically, the commonwealth strongholds Australia and the west coast of Canada. It should also, technically, include the Asian states of Russia and parts of Latin America. The actual intention of this chapter is to assess the runners and riders in the race for economic/business supremacy in the twenty-first century and we can probably write off from our race card the latter two regions as non-starters. Political turmoil will probably inhibit progress for a number of years to come, although Mexico is industrializing fast. Australia and Canada are probably mere also-rans. Canada is too tied to the US and riven by internal difference. Australia simply lacks the numbers in terms of population to grow and has improved its weak industrial base only very recently. In practice, therefore, the Pacific Rim still means largely west coast America and the Asian regions.

In considering the long list of runners and riders I consulted the *Business Week* Global 1000 published in July 1996 which measures the world's most valuable companies and also offers a country by country analysis. To extrapolate from the information the following table represents the card of runners and riders as defined by Business Week:

	Number of companies in top 1000	Composite value of companies ($ million)	Value as a percentage of global composite figure
Japan	227	2,616,814	23.36%
US	422	5,108,144	45.5%
UK	97	983,815	8.78%
France	43	342,524	3.06%
Germany	35	406,574	3.63%
Canada	25	170,065	1.5%
Sweden	19	133,204	1.18%
Switzerland	18	318,312	2.84%
Netherlands	18	264,095	2.36%
Hong Kong	17	194,733	1.7%
Italy	17	168,707	1.5%
Australia	16	128,009	1.14%
Singapore	13	123,284	1.10%
Spain	12	96,702	0.86%
Belgium	11	59,500	0.53%
Denmark	7	31,284	0.27%
Ireland	3	10,420	0.09%
Finland	2	18,154	0.16%
New Zealand	2	11,451	0.1%
Norway	1	10,854	0.09%
Austria	1	5,784	0.05%

Featuring largely established nations we find America still in the lead (but the whole is measured in dollars and a bull market and strong currency gives US companies edge in the calculations). Japan and Europe (if we take Europe as a composite) feature well ahead of Asia, which is represented only by Singapore and Hong Kong. However, the same publication offers us some insight into the top 200 companies in emerging markets and here we find that six out of ten countries with a strong presence in the top 200 companies by market value in emerging markets are from Asia.

Country	Number of companies in listing
South Africa	33
Taiwan	25
Thailand	21
Malaysia	20
Brazil	18
Mexico	13
Korea	13
India	13
Philippines	10
Chile	7
Argentina	5
Israel	4
Greece	2
Turkey	2
Peru	1
Portugal	1
Pakistan	1

For the purposes of this chapter we need to narrow the field a little, or run the risk of one that more closely approximates the Caesarewitch than the Kentucky. Clearly, the US, Japan and the countries of Europe must feature prominently on our race card and we shall study their form separately – indeed, this volume is in large measure a study of European form. From our survey of emerging markets South Africa would appear to be worthy of study from its number of entries but is unlikely as a lone trading nation to gain the muscle of those that form inter-regional alliances. Part of the thrust of this book is that the go-it-alone nation, which does not enmesh itself in global alliances, will have little chance of business supremacy in a global environment, hence the need for increasing integration. Thus it would run counter to our argument to focus on South Africa. The volatility of the markets in Latin America, as we have seen, reduces our real interest in Brazil and Mexico, thus leaving us with our core group of south Asian territories.

One of the problems in any study of form is that very little time need elapse for situations to alter and non-starters in the 1990s could in 30 years be in pole position. Just 30 years ago there was little differentiation between Ghana and South Korea at least when measured in terms of gross national product (GNP), which *per capita* was identical. Moreover, both shared an agrarian economy and had only recently emerged from colonial rule. In just 30 years the situation could not be more different. South Korea is one of the runners in the race for economic supremacy while Ghana, along with other west African states, remains one of the world's poorest. The GNP of South Korea is now 10 or 12 times that of Ghana. Writing in the late 1990s, already the perspective we bring to bear on the economies of Asia differs from that which would have dominated in the early 1990s. So I must issue the caveat that any tips included in this chapter are necessarily flawed and cannot take into account the numerous contingencies that will affect performance in the coming years. What, more positively, this chapter should offer are some pointers to the much-discussed geographical shift in economic power. It will comprise:

(1) A case by case summary of the emerging Asian economies (both founding members of the Association of South East Asian Nations and the little tigers) including a brief analysis of each, putting the case both for and against their likely success in the race for economic supremacy.
(2) A separate consideration of China.
(3) A brief summary of other areas that merit observation in the coming decades.
(4) An assessment of some of the factors, both cultural and practical, that these different economies hold in common, and equally those which are at variance and perhaps threaten or inhibit development.

Case studies of the Asian economies

Some definitions

Any study of the Asian economies will make reference to particular groupings, as given below.

APEC

The Asia Pacific Economic Co-operation forum is the largest single trade initiative in history. Currently numbering 18 nations, it was founded in 1989 on a proposal by Australia as an informal forum for the discussion of matters of common interest. Its original members were Brunei, Canada, Indonesia, Japan, Malaysia, New Zealand, the Philippines, Singapore, South Korea, Thailand and the US. This has been extended to include China, Hong Kong, Taiwan, Papua New Guinea and Chile.

Seen as a vehicle for promoting open trade and economic co-operation in the region, its members are concerned not to allow it to become just another elite trading bloc. Instead it is concerned with issues such as the simplification of customs procedures and the foundation of region-wide product standards – a practical aid to the region's business operators.

However laudable the intentions behind APEC in practice, some members are resistant to it, particularly given the presence of strong established nations such as Japan and the US. There has been a perception that the US has sought to dominate proceedings leading to some of the emerging economies preferring to focus on building ASEAN.

ASEAN

The Association of South East Asian Nations was founded in 1967 by the five states of Indonesia, Malaysia, Thailand, the Philippines and Singapore. Brunei joined in 1984, Papua New Guinea has observer status, South Korea special status and Vietnam, Laos and China are in the process of joining. The object of the association was originally to promote the co-operation of member states in the economic, social and cultural realms in order to secure peace in south-east Asia. Although the political element remains important, with conflicts between member states restrained by ASEAN-sponsored co-operative efforts, it is as a trading bloc that the grouping is now more important. In 1992 the member states agreed to create a free trade zone to be fully operational within 15 years.

NIEs

This stands for Newly Industrializing Economies, principal among them Singapore, Hong Kong, Taiwan and South Korea. They are also often dubbed the little tigers or dragons, with China as the big tiger or dragon.

Taiwan

With 25 companies listed in the top 200 Taiwan is clearly a force to be reckoned with. It occupies an unusual position politically as an official pariah because China will not entertain diplomatic relations with countries who recognize the island, which has been governed by the Kuomintang (KMT) – breakaway Chinese nationalists – since 1949, first under martial law and subsequently via democratic elections. Britain broke off relations in 1950, the US in 1979 and South Korea in 1992. Taiwan remains a considerable irritant to the Chinese government, which will not recognize its independent status and covets the considerable economic success it has enjoyed. Similarly, until 1991 Taiwan refused to accept the validity of the Communist regime in China, claiming sovereignty over the whole of China. Small wonder that Taiwanese success irks the Chinese authorities – it was achieved in reaction to Communism via the considerable support of successive US governments who sought to build a trading empire around the Pacific Rim to the exclusion of Communist China. Highly successful economic policies have also ensured a smooth transition to democratic elections, with the KMT gaining a 70% lead in the 1991 elections.

Relations remain officially frosty but unofficially there is increasing co-operation. Taiwanese citizens are now allowed to visit China but only via Hong Kong and passports are not used. Instead an identity card is issued to be handed over upon departure. Taiwan and China conduct trade through the back door via Hong Kong and Taiwan invests heavily in the mainland. China's show of force in 1996 with missiles fired close to the island to scare the KMT leaders ahead of the first free presidential elections have renewed fear of actual invasion.

Taiwan's economic growth began early, and as a consequence is advanced and *per capita* GNP is high ($7512 in 1990). Production focuses on heavy industrial goods along with textiles and electronic goods. The island exports 28% of its goods to the US, 28% to Hong Kong, 15% to the EU and 10% to Japan. Exports are valued at around US$ 100 billion (1995).

Taiwan is currently a stable rather than a growth prospect. On the positive side it has a highly skilled work-force (the literacy rate is 86%) and can boast superior engineering and managerial talent. There is little doubt that the island will be able to maintain its edge in computer, telecommunications and multimedia equipment. However, costs are high, space is at a premium and there is considerable traffic congestion and restrictions on expatriates and this will deter major multinationals from developing Taipei as a hub. The unresolved situation and dubious trading arrangements with China are increasing deterrents to other trading nations who need to maintain relations with the Chinese administration.

Thailand

Not in the first wave of Asian economies to industrialize, Thailand has undergone extremely rapid growth and boasts 21 companies in the top 200. Growth has been focused on the last decade – indeed, the capital city Bangkok has seen more buildings constructed in the last decade than in the preceding 300 years. A massive export drive in the late 1980s and the ascendancy of manufacturing over agriculture has created a new and wealthy entrepreneurial class that has fuelled the property boom. Success was originally built upon the export of machinery, foodstuffs and fisheries products through the reliance on cheap labour and abundant resources. One of the primary challenges the country faces is the need to move from a largely unskilled economic success story to achieving a high-tech, high-skill economy. With one of the most advanced production bases for cars, sophisticated private telecommunications companies, strong relations with Japanese multinationals and a free press which could prove attractive in the growing media sector, Thailand could well achieve this transition and might therefore fulfil the *Economist* projection, based on World Bank figures that by 2020 it could be among the world's top ten economies. Mitigating against this, however, is the corrupt and unstable political system, which makes it hard to resolve some of the infrastructural and educational problems currently facing the nation, and with rising wages restricting labour-intensive industries the shortage of trained managers and technicians is a brake upon further growth. Recent economic trends have been discouraging: sagging exports, a downgrading of the country's credit rating and the stock market's worst showing in 1996 for three years. But as observed above, to draw any long-term inferences from one year's poor economic showing would be folly in the context of an economy that has taken such a high leap even against the other Asian tigers. Analysts still anticipate a growth rate of 7 or 8% until the end of the century.

Thailand has a constitutional monarchy based on the British model. King Bhumibol, who celebrated his 50th year of rule in 1996, is an important figurehead who provides continuity in a region which, since the absolute monarchy turned into a constitutional one in 1932, has seen no less than 18 army take-overs. The last military regime stepped down as late as 1992 to be replaced by weak civilian governments characterized by multi-party coalitions and allegations of corruption. The most recent political upheaval came in the autumn of 1996 with the resignation of the Prime Minister – but at least the nation was spared military take-over and bloodshed. The inadequacy of Thailand's political institutions is probably the biggest brake on progress.

Malaysia

With steady growth rates of around 8% per annum Malaysia appears a more stable economy than Thailand, but its close ties with Singapore represent a local dependency the country is keen to reduce. The world's largest exporter of rubber since the nineteenth century – part of the colonial legacy – Malaysia has built up re-processing and electronics industries together with a financial services sector which led to the opening of a stock exchange in Kuala Lumpur. The official religion in Malaysia is Islam and government policy closely follows Islamic teachings, which has resulted in a drive for better education and increasing value being placed on hard work. This cultural factor has led to Malaysia's status as south-east Asia's favoured manufacturing and design hub for multinationals who have been able to take advantage of a highly skilled and motivated work-force. While attractive to inward investors the country has failed to develop any truly globally competitive manufacturing industries and now suffers costs rising at twice the rate of productivity and acute shortages of production workers and engineers, which will further impede development of global businesses.

South Korea

As noted earlier, just 30 years ago South Korea was one of the world's poorest nations. Since the 1960s it has transformed itself and is, arguably, the most successful of the little tigers. It is at first easier to understand its former poverty than its extraordinary recent success. Richest natural resources are in the north rather than the mountainous south which has little land suitable for cultivation. The peninsula (i.e. both North and South Korea) has known little independent rule, having been governed by China for centuries and then for the first half of the twentieth century by Japan. To its later advantage no strong landed interest developed in the country so when, under the dictatorship of General Park Chung Lee in the 1960s, moves were taken to modernize South

Korea, there was no interest group to offer impediment. So it was that military spending was cut, foreign investment welcomed, import tariffs on raw materials and industrial machinery cut, the currency devalued and relations with the Japanese restored. A strong government line coupled with a clear-sighted strategy that focused on added value exports led to a consistent annual growth rate of around 10% between 1962 and 1990. Originally focusing on low-tech products with high labour content (Korea has a greatly underemployed population on which to draw), the state successfully managed the transition to goods with a high technology content.

Government intervention in the 1970s brought into being the current economic structure by offering direct support to key industries with high export potential. As a consequence of this policy Korean economic success depends heavily on the fortunes of a small number of hugely successful conglomerates known as the *Chaebols*. The four primary companies are Hyundai, Daewoo, Samsung and Lucky Goldstar and in 1985, some 6 years after the reversal of government policy, they still between them accounted for 50% of GNP. They remain a key source of Korean strength, offering the capital, critical mass and engineering expertise to compete globally in their respective sectors. Critics, however, point to the slowness to turn of such vast engines as a potential disadvantage in a fast-moving world.

Another factor in Korea's favour is the strength of its reformed civil service, now rated as one of the most efficient bureaucracies in the world. A more liberal constitution was introduced in 1988 and a free and fair presidential election followed in 1992, but there have been corruption scandals in politics if not in administration and there have also been substantial labour problems, which are causing clashes with the authorities even at the time of writing. Nonetheless, Korea has importantly proven that a successful economy can coexist with a democratic regime. The relationship between North and South Korea, with the possibilities either of invasion or reunification carrying substantial costs, is an ongoing problem. So too is South Korea's dependence for economic success on high levels of borrowing and investment, and the continuing growth of export markets in view of the relatively small domestic market.

Not currently the fastest-growing or most dynamic of the Asian economies, South Korea has a 30-year legacy of stability and success, which in a volatile region is a substantial asset. A measure of South Korea's success has been its graduation to OECD membership.

Philippines

The focus of considerable attention amongst Asian economies as the one state to accelerate its growth in the last year from 4.8 to 6%, the Philippines are not dissimilar to South Korea in that the country enjoys both growth and a democratic government. Had this been written five years ago, however, it would have been tempting to focus on the substantial unrest of the preceding years with struggles for power within the land-owning elite and guerrilla warfare amongst Muslim and Communist factions on the outer islands. Then it would have been accurate to record the Philippines as having the lowest economic growth rate amongst ASEAN members and as the most unstable state amongst the members. This serves simply to underline the impossibility of making a hard and fast judgement about growth or decline, stability or volatility in a region where the only certainty is the certainty of continual change.

The resurgence of the Philippines has been based upon the bold economic reform initiatives introduced by President Ramos since his ascent to power in 1992 and the political stability which has enabled them to take effect. The outlook for political stability is good, with Ramos due to stand down in 1998 and his two key potential successors unlikely to renege on the reforms. Concerns about Ramos' health have been unsettling but fears of a return to authoritarianism are probably not well founded. Economic auguries are good. The government has enjoyed four consecutive years of fiscal surplus, inflation is declining and exports and investment growing. Set against this some concerns that growth is being fuelled from external factors, which makes the state's image abroad of paramount importance and underlines the need for continued stability. Foreign investment seems set to continue given the surplus of literate, English-speaking workers and engineers. Cheap land is an additional incentive and the nation is rich in creative talent to drive marketing. Much work needs to be done to improve the infrastructure outside Manila and to upgrade the scientific capability of the work-force if the country is to be attractive from an R&D perspective.

Indonesia

As with the Philippines, Indonesia has made extraordinarily rapid progress towards becoming a major power and is accordingly dubbed a young tiger, whereas the Philippines have been called Asia's tiger cub. A recent *AsiaMoney* poll amongst institutional investors to identify Asia's best-managed companies on a country-by-country basis shows interesting results. No fewer than six out of ten of the companies listed in connection with Indonesia are new entrants to the table, evidence of startlingly fast change. Since 1988 exports of manufactured goods have jumped more than 20% annually. GDP *per capita* has risen from $50 in 1967 to $650 in 1992 to a current level (1997) of $1210. Although this is still one of the region's lowest – only the Philippines and China have a lower figure amongst the developing nations – a growth rate of approximately 9% looks likely to be sustained.

Formerly a Dutch colony, Indonesia gained independence in 1949 and in 1965, after a *coup d'état*, General Suharto came to power, ushering in an era of greater economic flexibility with the acceptance of private sector and market mechanisms. Indonesia enjoyed average annual growth of nearly 8% in the 1970s and 1980s but then the economy ran out of steam as others in the region gathered pace. This led to the adoption of new export-oriented policies in 1986, which accordingly raised the levels of foreign and domestic investment sharply. In 1993 Indonesia relaxed its conditions for foreign capital investment so giving a further boost to growth. Generous development aid from the West and from Japan has additionally fuelled growth – although Indonesia has been the focus of international outcry over its deforestation of tropical rain forest, its occupation of western New Guinea and its annexation of Timor. Rich in natural resources and having a vast population on which to draw, Indonesia has developed a strong base in labour-intensive light industry and has an edge in oil and timber. The state's largest potential drawback is the political regime. This has adopted protectionist policies towards cars and electronics which hinder freer trade and, perhaps more importantly, is seen to be innately corrupt with high evidence of cronyism and nepotism with Suharto's family holding key positions. Indeed, Indonesia is a good example of the type of autocratically led economy of which Western observers have been especially critical. In addition to corruption and red tape, which undermines some of the economic advantages of the region, there is considerable uncertainty surrounding the presidential succession. Suharto is an old man and a scare concerning his health in 1996 triggered a scare on the markets. The 1997 parliamentary election and the 1998 presidential election will both contribute to turbulent times economically for Indonesia.

Singapore

The smallest of the little tigers but one of the longest-established trading communities, Singapore, along with Hong Kong, is included in *Business Week's* analysis of most valued companies not under the emerging markets section but in the lead section. Established as a trading post by the British in 1867 the island has had well over a century in which to develop, but much of its success can be attributed to former Prime Minister Lee Kyan Yew who was elected in 1959 and ruled the province in the now familiar autocratic style, being demonized by the West as a consequence. In direct power no longer, but widely held to be the power behind the throne, a hospital stay during the course of 1996 with chest pains was sufficient to send the market into some frenzy. His philosophy of rapid economic advance and democratic gradualism resulted in policies which, with minimal tolerance of opposition, redirected the economy towards exports, nationalized the major banks and industrial companies and introduced close regulation of everyday life.

The consequences of his policies are evident in the affluence of the island with GDP *per capita* standing at $32,878, and the growth rate in GDP being 8%. One of the successes of Singapore has been the development, by the region's standards, of outstanding infrastructure to support the economic growth. The high standard of facilities has enabled it to play a major role as an international hub. A skilled work-force, good training institutes and the lack of corruption have further enhanced the status of the island for multinationals. The skilled work-force carries the disadvantage of costing more and so Singapore is losing some of its attractiveness to foreign investors compared with cheaper markets elsewhere. The government has given considerable support to technical education, which gives the island scope to extend an R&D capability. A budget surplus is leading to spending on housing and other welfare issues which, ironically, may inhibit some of the free market principles which have been a driver behind the success.

The checks upon Singapore's development derive partly from geography. It is a small island and therefore has a small domestic market but it has, currently, a good balance of industries with strength in high added value industries like electronics and a growing financial services orientation. With a downturn in the electronics sector, however, and the global focus on the media and entertainment industries, Singapore will find that the strong social controls (for example, considerable checks upon the media) might hamper development.

Hong Kong

At the time of writing, Hong Kong is on the very brink of handover from Britain to China, an event which should on the face of it be the most unsettling in the region. Certainly in the run-up Hong Kong has seen a slump in consumer spending, which has led to a slow-down in growth, but the Chinese show strong signs of leaving Hong Kong much as it is and consumer confidence is already improving. China has every reason for showing a conciliatory face to Hong Kong for it is one of the foremost trading centres, not just in Asia but in the world, and of more value to China as it stands than in the throes of change to another system. However much scepticism is felt about Deng Xiaoping's much vaunted 'one nation two systems' philosophy, it seems reasonably certain that it is in China's interests to pursue precisely such a policy, especially in view of their desire to bring Taiwan into a similar relation to the mainland. Hong Kong's economic record is impressive, less for any evidence of sustained growth but for an ability to transform itself in response to changing regional and economic circumstances. After Tokyo, Hong Kong has the most important stock exchange in Asia and the successful transition from an economy based on low-cost manufacturing to a sophisticated financial centre offers a paradigm for other parts of the region, not least Singapore. Hong Kong remains one of the world leaders in the production of toys, textiles, radios and televisions, but no longer manufactures them on the island but on the mainland in Guangdong. Its principle role is as a trading, financial and management centre and, as such, it will remain a critical centre for Greater China.

And then there is China ...

For some 15 years China has averaged annual GNP growth in the region of 9% (often considerably above that), which achievement is unmatched anywhere else in the world or in history. Its emergence onto the world stage is unarguably, in economic terms, the most significant event of the 1990s (as a potential market it is bigger than all the OECD countries combined) and, in a study of form for a race for global competitiveness, China has to be the object of close scrutiny for any tipster. Unfortunately the situation in China is so full of anomalies and paradoxes that it scarcely repays such cursory study as I have space for here. For instance, in 1993 China was already being accorded the status of a leading world economy by the World Bank while China herself argued that she is still a developing nation. And there is right on both sides. In terms of *per capita* income China ranks amongst the poorest of developing nations. However, in terms of purchasing power the country clearly accords with the judgement of the World Bank. The apparent paradox of Deng Xiaoping's 'one nation two systems' philosophy as applied to Hong Kong is echoed in the philosophy that has underpinned economic reform – a combination of command and market economy approaches. The path to reform has also been a series of great leaps amongst a generally slow march. Geographically as big as Europe and considerably more mountainous, a popular conception has been that growth is focused on the coastal regions while the interior has declined. Not true – six out of ten of the fastest-growing provinces are in the interior. The pattern of Chinese reform is not easily understood. However, the following is an attempt to chart its course.

Reform officially started in 1978, a late start by the standards of the Soviet Union. The early reform programme covered agriculture, international trade and foreign investment and outstanding success areas proved to be economic growth, protection of the population from deprivation and foreign trade and investment, achieved by a mix of some radical reforms alongside features of a command economy such as output planning and state ownership. China's growth rates from 1978 onwards could easily be mistaken for those of the tiger economies, but the comparison underplays their extraordinary nature. The principal tiger economies – Hong Kong, Singapore, Taiwan and South Korea – have the advantage of being small in terms of population and relatively homogeneous. Neither of these factors feature with China and a more just comparison would be one between the tigers and a key region in China such as Guangdong. Here we find a growth in gross product between 1980 and 1991 at an average of 12.4% – easily equivalent to the highest performing of the tigers. If Chinese growth rates are sustained at an annual rate of just 6% the impact on the global poverty rates will be substantial with a move from a low-income status nation to a middle-income status one. Currently 37% of the world's poor are in China. The global economic implications and the domestic implications are clear. China is, after all, the world's largest internal market.

This extraordinary pattern of growth has been achieved without the massive deprivation seen in Eastern Europe and the former Soviet Union. On the contrary there has been a record rise in income and living standards for both the rural and the urban population. Indeed, it is the concern with social protection which has, in part, marked out the development of the Chinese economy from its East Asian neighbours. China has managed a programme whereby exports have grown consistently and significantly, as has foreign investment. One of the more radical ideological reforms has been China's departure from its earlier stance of self-reliance and subsequent success in gaining loans from international agencies and governments, and in attracting direct inward investment.

The reform programme has not been an unmitigated success. Attempts at reforming state-owned industries have been largely unsuccessful and the reform of the financial system has been sluggish. The States Economic and Trade Commission and the People's Bank of China have put pressure on state-owned enterprises to improve their performance or face bankruptcy, and funds have been promised to ease the pain of redeploying those who will lose their jobs. The banking system is being changed and the insurance market, previously monopolized by the People's Insurance Company of China is being opened up to competition. The Shanghai stock market has been reopened and a new stock exchange established in Shenzen. Against these positive factors, many state-owned enterprises remain loss making, subject to government intervention and, on the financial side, the lending operations of banks are driven more by administrative than commercial considerations and a significant percentage of bank loans are write-offs.

Aside from having the world's largest internal market, China is also rich in natural resources with plentiful coal, iron ore, tin and other minerals. Large parts of the country remain unexplored and it is probable that levels of natural resources are much higher than generally estimated. The country boasts a pool of engineering talent and so its domination of light and medium-tech industries, given the scale of the labour force, is likely to continue. The government is investing substantially in an upgrade of China's infrastructure, which can only facilitate growth and improve foreign investment opportunities, and perhaps carry some of the burden of potential unemployment from increasing reform of state enterprises. The auguries are good for continued economic growth but high levels of inflation and demographic issues, a continuing rise in the population and the development of an ageing population remain substantial challenges for the government.

... Not to mention the emerging growth circles in Asia

As we have suggested earlier it is unwise to view economic growth purely in the context of particular states. Increasingly alliances are being formed which are cross-border but which take advantage of old trading routes, cultural ties and complementary markets. *Asia Inc.*, one of the leading publications for the region has identified a number of 'growth circles', which show overlapping interests between areas not united by a common national interest. They can be summarized as follows:

The border country around south-west China
This region covers south-west China, Burma, Thailand and Laos and has a potential market of some 325 million consumers. The links are geographical – for instance Burmese and Thai ports are more accessible to south-west China than are those of Guangzhou or Shanghai and historically this region formed a subsilk route with strong trade for some 2000 years. Culturally the links are forged by the overseas Chinese and Tai, which communities foster cultural understanding and, critically, linguistic links. The infrastructure is extremely poor and is the main inhibition on development, but Burma and Laos need China's cheap goods and an affluent Chinese population want the higher-quality produce from Thailand, which needs some of the natural resources and cheap labour it can find in Burma and Laos.

Maritime China
China's development has focused to a great extent (but not exclusively) on the coastal regions that extend from the Siberian border to the tropical frontier with Vietnam, inland along the Yangtze River to the central city of Wuhan. However, around this core area are a group of subregions or geo-economic zones. These include:

- Hong Kong–Guangdong province–Macau;
- the Yellow Sea economic zone of the two Koreas and north-east China;
- the Japan Sea economic zone of Japan, the Koreas, north-east China and Asiatic Russia;
- Zhoushan – an island south-east of Shanghai;
- Fujian province and Taiwan;
- Shanghai and the provinces of Jiangsu, Zheijang and Hubei.

Indo-China

An extraordinary tribute to the economic aspirations of the region is this apparent growth circle which incorporates Vietnam, Cambodia, Laos, Southern China and Thailand. Long-standing ideological and historical enmities appear to be being forsaken in the interests of economic co-operation and in 1991 Beijing and Hanoi opened their common frontier to trade. Vietnam has a large pool of cheap, literate labour but is dogged by the Communist Party's failure to reform. Competition from China should spur improvements in the reform of state industry. Underused ports in Vietnam hold considerable appeal for some Thai businesses who are closer to Vietnam than to the overcrowded Bangkok. As elsewhere in the region, old trading routes are re-emerging. Hoi An in central Vietnam was once a magnet for traders from southern China, Japan, Thailand, Malaysia and the Philippines. No longer a viable port, Danang to the north can exploit precisely the same trade opportunities that had been neglected during the colonial period when the market economy was not a dominant consideration. The Mekong River provides a natural route through the region, which strife in Cambodia has left underused. Factors to overcome in this area remain corruption and political ineffectiveness, a considerable smuggling problem and the ubiquitous infrastructural issues.

The Straits circle

This growth circle links Singapore with Malaysia's Johor state and Indonesia's Riau province and is already a formal trading unit, with the respective governments taking action to cement informal business ties. The links between the areas are historical. From the sixteenth until the nineteenth century it comprised the Johor–Riau empire at the centre of Malay civilization. In 1989 Singaporean Minister Goh Chok Tong called for a triangle of growth in the region to exploit complementary needs. Singapore had high-tech expertise, outstanding infrastructure, good communications links and a world-wide reputation as a commercial centre, but needed access to the cheaper labour force available in Batam, one of the islands that comprises Indonesia and Johor in Malaysia. If in practice this so-called triangle is two separate agreements with Singapore, the gap between perception and reality does not seem to have hindered co-operation between the two satellite territories. Batam and Johor have both experienced substantial growth and are now spawning their own growing hinterlands, which give rise to new circles of growth in turn.

An overview: the common factors, the common threats

The preceding pages represent a summary of the potential Asian runners and riders in a race for business competitiveness in the twenty-first century. That I have included in this summary some of the regions which are not defined by national boundaries is perhaps a bit of a red herring, but as we have seen in the parallel between South Korea and Ghana, or in the almost overnight development of the Philippines a very few years can transform a non-starter into a champion, so it is circumspect to consider the new areas of economic activity. More importantly, it would be foolish to neglect non-national alliances in a region where the nation state as an entity is perhaps a false form of definition in the first place. Many of the regions considered above have been subject nations, colonies of other powers within which process national identities – and indeed boundaries – have been obscured. To apply Western priorities such as the nation state as a key parameter is a potential mistake. Alternatively, to reduce greatly disparate regions to a single mass would be an oversimplification of the grossest kind. What we see in Asia, however, has a strong parallel with what can be seen in a summary of European development (see Chapter 2), a land mass wherein there are substantial differences but complementary needs and common historical and cultural links. The unifying factor amongst the various economies we have studied is aspiration – a burning ambition to develop and participate in the spoils of capitalism. Part of the realisation of this aspiration has been the recognition that a pooling of interests and a suppression of local interests might be a necessary factor in success. Hence we see agreements such as those between the APEC and the ASEAN nations and must note the preference amongst some in Asia to focus on the ASEAN rather than the APEC community as better representing a common interest. These groupings rival the European Community in intent and certainly in terms of economic growth. Whether that growth can be turned into a stable and continuing economic success remains to be seen and in the remainder of this chapter we will consider some of the strengths and weaknesses that will influence the fortunes of these Asian economies.

The Asian economies considered above exhibit significant differences. Populations vary enormously; South Korea has a population of some 45.6 million; Singapore's is just 3.1 million. The structures of business differ substantially; Taiwan's economic success depends on myriad small business enterprises whereas South Korea's wealth focuses on a few huge concerns. Geographies, ethnic composition, dominant languages – there is huge variation from one place to another. However, there are some notable trends which are common and which have influenced growth to date.

Perhaps the most obvious factor these markets hold in common is proximity to a startlingly successful model. Japan has been of tremendous influence in the region, not simply in terms of the direct opportunities Japanese economic development has demanded (for instance, sources of cheaper labour and raw materials) but in terms of providing a model for economic growth that depends to some extent on Western powers and traditions but subtly and highly successfully modified to an Eastern perspective. The potency of that model both in practical and psychological terms should not be underestimated. There are several other fixed elements in the development of Asian economies. One of the most notable similarities is the high level of skilled workers in the various markets studied. This reflects an equally high and consistent level of educational attainment, a feature of the Asian territories considered. By 1980 Korea numbered more engineering graduates than the UK, West Germany and Sweden combined. A second feature that has clearly influenced growth – as its absence has influenced the sharp decline of other trading empires (notably the Spanish and the British) – has been the high level of national savings. Government intervention by way of taxes and import controls to encourage investment in industry has been a common theme in east Asia and, while with increasing success increasing consumption has been seen, the tendency to maintain high national savings rates remains noticeable. The strength of government intervention reflects the generally strong, perhaps authoritarian, political frameworks that have dominated. The West, in the grip and aftermath of cold war politics, has long had a horror of autocracy and fear of Asian economies may reside in a mistrust of the strongman leadership that has prevailed – although democracy is taking a firmer hold. It is undeniable that the single-minded focus of government on the achievement of specific economic goals without tolerance of opposition has played a major part in the success of the tiger economies. The fourth unifying feature of the tiger economies has been the commitment to exports (as opposed, for example, to the consumer-driven policies of the US). The labour force has had to be trained to supply what has been demanded by the market and the economies have, effectively, been developed in response to need rather than by defining that need in the first place. This betrays a marked cultural dexterity, a willingness to suppress identity in the short term in the interests of acquiring the strength to express that identity with more force and effectiveness in the longer term – a suppression of national ego, perhaps.

This long-term view lies at the heart of what has made Asian economies great. It derives from different systems of thinking, different value systems from those that have dominated in the West. As in Chapter 2 we noted the links that have been charted between Protestantism and the growth of capitalism, so here we will consider the links between the Confucian tradition and the development of Asian economies.

Confucius was a Chinese intellectual who lived around 500 BC, about 80 years before Socrates. His teachings concern practical ethics, ways of conducting oneself, without any religious/spiritual implications. His primary concern – the difference between the practical and the spiritual – is with virtue rather than truth. The main teachings can be distilled as:

- *Stable society derives from unequal relationships.* Confucius defined the primary relationships that define social interaction in terms of senior and junior partners. These relations are based on mutual respect and obligations. The junior partner will respect and obey the senior who will in return offer protection and consideration.
- *The family is the paradigm of all social organization.* This principle is one of collectivism against individualism – the virtue of suppressing the desire of the individual to the greater good of the collective.
- *Virtuous conduct is to be found in not doing to others what you would not have done to yourself.* Stopping well short of the Christian injunction to love one's neighbours, this nevertheless acknowledges a certain pragmatic benevolence in human relations.
- *Virtue derives from restraint and self improvement, from trying to acquire more skills, working hard, not spending more than necessary, being patient and persevering.* Education, thrift, moderation and the ability to take a long-term rather than a short-term view are the key virtues.

The temporal teachings of Confucius, which spread, presumably with the spread of the Chinese peoples, widely across Asia, have an interesting spiritual parallel. Eastern religions can be seen as very distinct from Western ones. The key Eastern religions are Hinduism, Buddhism, Shintoism and Taoism, the Western are Judaism, Christianity and Islam. Western religions derive from the same root and are based on a belief in truth which is enshrined in a book as laws. Eastern religions, in contrast, are concerned with self-improvement, with a process of continual improvement to the point of unification with God or Gods. To simplify dramatically, the Western concern with laws and truth drove discovery and technological development. Eastern concerns with virtue and acceptance of the possibility that A and B can both be true and lead to C – a better way still – gives rise to enormous emotional and intellectual flexibility and the ability to synthesize and transmogrify the given.

It is a small step to see these tenets in application in the east Asian economies we have looked at. The focus on education reflects the concern with self-improvement; the incidence of high national savings reflects the concern with thrift; the strength of political regimes, the low levels of resistance and high levels of compliance demonstrate a respect for levels of hierarchy; patience and perseverance and the high export drive conforms with the notion of a people who are minded to be flexible and make short-term sacrifices in pride for long-term gains in status. The ability to synthesize and to suppress immediate self-interest plays a part in the willingness of the Asian nations to pull together in trading alliances. Some of the criticisms that people in the West might level at the Eastern nations also correspond to these variations in outlook. The West is suspicious of the corruption it sees in the East. Corruption is perhaps tolerated on the basis that it is part of a greater good (for instance in the acceptance of cronyism in the interests of maintaining an effective government) but also because there is less obsessive concern with the absolutes of right and wrong, with a single evident truth. Similarly, tolerance of sometimes inhumane practices can be seen in the same light.

There are numerous other factors that have influenced the development of these economies over the last 30 years – political, historical, geographical, and it would be wrong to overemphasize the cultural factors, but equally to ignore them, especially when the parallels between some of the known cultural beliefs – and the manner in which success has been achieved is striking. There are also, it must be said, clear anomalies. Indonesia, for instance, is the largest Islamic nation in the world with 87% of its population Muslim, whereas 85% of the Philippine population is Catholic – in both cases there is a stronger influence from Western than Eastern religions but factors will vary in their impact and the exceptions do not disprove the rule.

So far we have focused on common factors in Asian success. Are there common threats, possibly also influenced by the above factors? If current commentators are to be believed then certainly there are. Indeed, there has been an almost gleeful tendency in the Western press to deliver the news that the east Asian bubble has burst or is in the process of slowly deflating; and the reports are not without some foundation. It is certainly true that, with the exception of the Philippines, all the economies considered above have posted lower growth rates for 1996 than for 1994. This might be merely cyclical, driven by a slow-down in export growth that derived from a slow-down in demand for semiconductors and steel, reduced demand from the US and a strong dollar. Conversely, falling growth rates might indicate more deep-seated structural issues. From the above summary of the various economies certain common weaknesses are apparent. Rising costs, poor infrastructure and corruption recur. However, what did not emerge earlier is the possibility that Asia has simply over-reached and is now guilty of overcapacity in key industries such as automobiles, semiconductors and consumer electronics. Government protectionism is in some cases now an impediment where once the focus and support to key industries was a major strength. Demand may pick up with the recovery of European, Japanese and American markets, but in some critical markets, such as petro-chemicals and automobiles, overcapacity is such that observers predict a bloodbath in the next few years. Education systems that have produced droves of well-qualified engineers are now failing to deliver students with the capability for innovative thought as teaching techniques rely strongly on rote; hence in economies that are required to change direction and to move from low to high added value goods there is a marked skill shortage.

Politically, many of these economies are wrestling with democracy and striving to find a new identity; others are in need of secure successors to current governments. Playing on a world stage to an audience of key consumers, world opinion counts. As they mature, a number of Asian economies are obliged to flex their identities and there is conflict between the Western values, which have dominated via the influence of the US and those we note above. With the increasing role of Asian nations in the global economy there is diminishing tolerance of practices seen by Western nations as unethical, inhumane or undemocratic. Asian economies have perhaps reached that most uncomfortable period of development, adolescence. They must strive to find a suitable synthesis of a host of different influences and the decisions made now can influence the entire course of life. It is timely, at this point, to recall the thesis of Francis Fukuyama. He predicts considerable problems in making a transition from small- to large-scale professionally managed, potentially global businesses in those cultures that have a tradition deriving from a Chinese model (the premise being that these are low-trust societies without the cultural custom of forming allegiances and networking with non-kin or without the intervention of a higher authority in the form of the state). Subject to the continued importance of large-scale enterprises in economic success, this consideration could have a marked effect on the development of China, Hong Kong, Taiwan and Singapore, even leaving aside some of the political upheavals that confront these areas.

Are the fears that surface in the West concerning the future success of Eastern nations justified – the fears with which this chapter began? The racist terms in which they find expression are clearly unacceptable but the fears themselves inevitably have some foundation. In the course of this chapter I have charted extraordinary patterns of growth in a very short space of time, which encompass a huge percentage of the global population. While commentators point to declining growth rates, these rates would still be received with rapture in many of the economies from which the same commentators hail. It would certainly seem premature to write off the Asian economies. But these Asian economies work in a network of relations – with each other and with the more developed economies where there is not the same level of volatility, particularly in the political sphere. They cannot be judged in isolation, any more than can the fortunes of Europe or North America or the more stable economy in Japan. There can be no question that they are under starters orders in the race for business and economic supremacy in the next century, but several more seasons are required before I could place a confident bet based on a mature assessment of form.

6

Towards a Definition of a European Company

> *'This new "corporation", this new "Société Anonyme", this new "Aktiengesellschaft" ... was a genuine innovation ... It was the first new autonomous institution in hundreds of years, the first to create a power centre that was within society yet independent of the central government of the nation state.'*
> Peter Drucker on the birth in Europe of the limited company.

In 1992, 500 years after the discovery of the Americas by Columbus, European governments combined to create, in trading terms, another new continent – one that could compete more efficiently with the economically superior and sovereign states, America and Japan. At the heart of this new supra-national initiative is the corporation, itself a relatively new supra-national institution. The establishing of the common market and the happy accident of an impending anniversary of which we metaphorically-minded Europeans were able to make good use was just one of the events that have given such a charge to this *fin de siècle* period. The other event, on the eve of the 1990s – on the night, to be precise, of 9 November 1989 – was the bringing down of the Berlin Wall. This act of jubilant destruction (and portions of the wall are now as sought after and spurious as medieval Christian relics) marked the end to four decades of Communist rule in eastern Europe and thus of the Cold War. A system of allegiances and enmities, which had shaped the entire post-war period, was effectively cast aside and a huge market made available for the application of free market principles. The integration of the east European nations into a wider European whole is a political issue beyond the conjectures of this chapter (we shall consider this more fully in Chapter 10), instead my concern here is with the new emphasis given to our status as Europeans. In particular, this chapter will look at the notion of what constitutes a European business, having first considered the role of American businesses in reshaping those perceptions. Europe, taken in its entirety, is a huge land mass, rich in natural resources with a well-schooled population who have the potential for affluence. If a united *western* Europe is seen to be a powerful proposition, how much more powerful might be a Europe in which there is no east–west divide. Before we can reach a state of total European unity – if we can even dare to aspire to such a thing – there is an ideological, not to mention a practical, abyss to be traversed, but European history is such that we have substantial precedents for mixing the like with the unlike and for absorbing difference, which augur well. At the end of the twentieth century the outlook for Europe is an optimistic one.

Europe – the gap between the super-powers

Twenty years ago it would have been hard, if not foolhardy, to have written the preceding sentence with such a flourish. Europeans then seemed finally to articulate a malaise that threatened to engulf the continent. High unemployment, slow growth in GNP and sluggish development of the all-important high-tech industries were combining to create *Eurosclerosis*, a term which, briefly, encapsulated the fear of creeping paralysis that obsessed European leaders and commentators alike.

It was this fear which mobilized the likes of Jacques Delors to lobby for the greater union of Europe and, while his vision, energy and ability to take action proved remarkable, it was no less remarkable that it took so long for Europeans to recognize their plight. Perhaps the the closing two decades of the twentieth century have become European decades (in the sense that we in Europe are focused on Europe) precisely because the three that went before palpably were not, despite the manoeuvrings of a narrow elite to construct a European. As western Europeans we owe an enormous debt to America for the post-war reconstruction that brought far greater affluence and security to far greater numbers than pre-war generations might have supposed possible. The relationship between western Europe and America has been 'special' and, to all intents and purposes, west European nations have been satellites of the super-power across the Atlantic. This satellite status extended beyond strategic and defensive terms. The influence of American life entered into the daily life of west Europeans at the most basic level as American-branded goods came to dominate even the food we ate and the gadgets with which we prepared that food, and peoples became united under one banner, that of consumers. If in the west we were subject, emotionally, ethically, financially and strategically to the US then allegiance in the east – an allegiance, perhaps, of necessity or coerced – was to the Soviet Union. As anti-nuclear campaigners (who enjoyed a resurgence of their movement in the early 1980s) reminded us, Europe was little more than the ground on which, ultimately, would be played out the battle between two great super-powers. Europe then during the Cold War period was rather like Janus, looking to east and west but seldom inwards.

Europe in mourning for empire

This tendency to look outwards was perhaps an extension of a nineteenth-century predilection, a throwback to the days when Empires were built, when many European states had subject nations of their own to administer, ready-made markets for products and settlers. The rush for imperial possession is mirrored in the hasty (if reluctant and in many cases very bitter) dispossession as the late 1940s, 1950s and 1960s were marked by the struggles of subject peoples to gain independence. For the colonial powers in western Europe these struggles were uppermost on political agendas. The post-war period saw some fierce battles with the bloodiest battle for independence being fought in Algeria between 1954 and 1962. While this former French colony was to be the scene of the most violent struggles against empire, the struggle was scarcely less bitter in the once British-ruled Rhodesia and Kenya and the Portugese colonies of Angola, Mozambique and Guinea–Bissau. The Rhodesian situation remained unresolved until Zimbabwe was finally born as late as 1980. The loss of power is a disquieting process and the reluctance of the former colonial powers to accept the diminution of a world role can be seen in the zeal shown in 1982 by the British in defence of those few islands (the Falklands) still directly ruled by London. A decade later, the debates around the Maastricht treaty show that there remained a marked reluctance among nations that had once held power to concede that power is theirs no longer (we shall return to this theme in Chapter 9). The relationship enjoyed by the French with its former colonies and the British with the Commonwealth nations testify to the strength of old imperial notions as empire lives on in a muted and more benign form.

Europe is colonized

In the process of losing former empires Europe left itself open to be colonized itself, by American business. Perception has a nagging habit of lagging well behind reality and, even while this process of power loss and economic colonization was underway, Europeans seemed not to notice – witness De Gaulle's comfortable view of the role Europe had still to play and its relation to America:

> *'Europe, the mother of modern civilisation, must establish herself all the way from the Atlantic to the Urals, and live in a state of harmony and cooperation with a view to developing her immense resources, and so play, together with her daughter America, her worthy role in relation to the billion people who so badly need her help.'*

If De Gaulle felt a degree of comfort with the notion of Europe, others were less secure. De Gaulle's contemporary and compatriot, one of the architects of modern Europe, Jean Monnet, showed more circumspection:

> *'Europe has never existed. It is not the addition of national sovereignties in a conclave which creates an entity. One must genuinely create Europe.'*

To American businessmen there was not this ambiguity about Europe – rather Americans reduced the complexity of the network of nations with which Europe's leaders were grappling to a mere matter of geography. American businesses had been active in Europe from the end of the nineteenth century onwards but the real boom period was after the Second World War and, ironically, came to a certain extent on the back of that very vehicle which was to secure Europe for the Europeans – the Common Market. The potential of an integrated market in Europe coincided with an expansionist period for many well-established American companies who crossed the Atlantic with the intention, not just of marketing goods on European soil, but of manufacturing them there too. American companies *en masse* bought up European companies and absorbed them into their subsidiary networks; many companies set up European headquarters in Brussels, Geneva or other cosmopolitan cities. English-speaking networks among American bankers, management consultants and advertising agencies (for American service businesses followed their masters to Europe) facilitated American growth and even a form of American currency in Europe appeared in the shape of the Euro Dollar. The attack by these companies was simple and sweeping and if there were some failures there were far more successes as American brands came increasingly to dominate on the supermarket shelves and in the offices of companies and government departments alike.

Attempts were made by some national governments to resist this American invasion. The French government prevented General Motors from opening a new plant in Strasbourg. GM simply went to Belgium instead leaving France with the frustration of having lost potential jobs while still having American competition on the doorstep. Similarly, despite an inclination to support local companies, European governments were obliged to invest in IBM computer systems since no home-grown company (during the 60s at any rate) could compete with the American giant. Europeans, however, benefited from the growth of American business across the continent as they have in general benefited from most forms of American intervention. Consumers had greater choice, governments could point to increased numbers of jobs and young graduates could enter the realm of organized management training – note in particular the training school set up in Geneva by Procter & Gamble with a specific remit to inculcate in European managers American know-how. This Geneva operation for P&G seems somehow symbolic of the way Americans did business in Europe – there was no sense of 'when in Rome do as the Romans do', nor any cognizance of 'the way we do things here'. Instead the American way was to impose directly onto the indigenous worker the proven American formula for success. The attitude to success was just as uncompromising – if it worked, excellent; if it didn't, too bad. Americans were as relaxed about mounting withdrawl as they were about the initial invasion and that confidence was no small matter in the overall success of Americans in Europe.

European responses to American colonization

The influence of American culture, its movies and, in the post-war period, its music did much to secure European consumer interest in the products on offer. American companies present in Europe peddled the American lifestyle dream for which there were many willing takers. There were, of course, dissenting voices. One of these was Jean-Jacques Servan-Schrieber who in 1967 wrote *Le Defi Americain* (The American Challenge) in which he made what was clearly intended to be an alarmist claim:

> *'The third industrial power in the world following the United States and the Soviet Union, could well be in fifteen years not Europe, but American industry in Europe'.*

Responses to the claim that a challenge should be mounted were, at best, muted. If Servan-Schrieber was alarmist then British writer Anthony Sampson writing *The New Europeans* in 1968 presented a rallying cry:

> *'Many of the European companies ... seem to be becoming more, not less, national in their character, and to reveal old rivalries in new shape. The American giants by luring European companies to collaborate with them, not with each other, can be more divisive than unifying. One is forced to wonder how much sense the context of Europe makes when the continent of Europe has such a background of mistrust, when so many of the keys lie outside it, and when industry has anyway become global ...'*

The response of those on the ground, young graduates entering European business, was to take the American model and learn from it. Indeed, many of those now at the helm of European businesses in the late 60s and early 70s were entering the first-rate training environments provided by American businesses in Europe. The enormously beneficial transfer of skills from the US to Europe is underestimated as, more significantly, is the unifying power of American business culture on those Europeans obliged to operate within it. From the American giants we have had imposed on us a common language in which to do business – English. As Europeans we should be grateful that the decision was so efficiently taken from us. A concern for high standards, of manufacture and, critically, of service are also part of Europe's legacy from the US. The high emphasis placed on management education has helped to transform the standing of business into something more akin to a profession, even a vocation, such that young graduates in the 80s and 90s have aspired to careers in service businesses, such as management consulting, which will give them the platform and experience from which to enter corporations at a senior, influential level. More than this, however, the hegemony of American business united Europeans in opposition. This claim may seem a little spurious but the upsurge in M&A activity from the time the Americans came to Europe (not all of it by any means involving an American party) testifies to the desire to fight the American threat through scale. In one notable, if only partially successful, case prior to 1968 the merger activity was cross-border, involving the Belgian Gevaert and the German Agfa. All the same, one cross-border merger as a representative of European endeavour can hardly have caused concern to the American corporate executive seeking success in Europe. Nonetheless, the approach of American business to Europe must have contributed to an understanding that European commercial unity is a possibility. Europeans joining American businesses, attending US business schools and, later, INSEAD or IMD came to mix more closely together, to forge a common understanding of the principles underlying business. While increased familiarity with other nations and cultures on the one hand reinforced the sense of difference, it also reinforced the perennial message to be gleaned from European history: that difference is no barrier to cooperation.

The European company – the constitution of its identity

Trading relationships may be forged between governments but, on the whole, companies rather than governments embark on the expansion into new markets and so, in discussing European economic renaissance, we need to look at the character of European companies as much as at the character of Europe as a whole. This brings us to the vexed question of just what constitutes a European company. Is a European company one that trades in Europe only? Is it one that trades internationally or even globally but is owned and managed in Europe? Is a European company one that is staffed at the highest levels by representatives of a range of European nationalities? Do European companies reflect the national culture and character of the country in which they are headquartered or can such a company not be considered truly European? These are some of the questions that must occupy this chapter.

Ownership

To use the term either American or European we appear to be talking in terms of possession. So, when we refer to an American company we mean one that is possessed by an American owner. It should be true to say, then, that a European company is one that is possessed by a European owner. In this way a company that is French owned, for instance, could also claim to be European as France is a member state of the European community. We would not bother, however, to define such a company as European – given that the key possessive relationship is French we would simply describe it as French. However, ownership is rarely a clear-cut issue, with many shares being held internationally by a range of institutions rather than conveniently within the confines of one nation. Would we be more likely to regard Danone as French or as European? Danone may be headquartered in France but has also acquired companies around Europe (and indeed in Asia and the USA) which employ locals in the manufacture, sales, marketing and distribution of goods. These companies retain the character, to some extent, of their original national ownership structure while being obliged to report to the French parent all financial results. Over time, strategic direction which comes from the French headquarters will subtly alter the character of the original local business but that operation, be it Spanish, Italian or British, will retain cultural elements that are distinct from those of the parent.

To take another example – what of United Distillers? This is a British-owned business – a subsidiary of Guinness plc which one might be tempted to consider quintessentially British. Its headquarters are in London and its key products are fine Scotch whiskies, the very English Gordon's Gin, and other drinks that are associated with the lawns of Oxford and Cambridge colleges, like Pimms. Alternatively, United Distillers' business operates in global markets, the company has leading brands around the world and its portfolio has been constructed to reflect local taste and local perceptions. Business was originally done around the world via a series of distributor relationships but during the late 1980s and the early 1990s some 80% of those distributors were converted into joint ventures or outright purchases in order that the parent in the UK would have more control over the destination of product. Again many of those local businesses retained much of their local colour and character and key representatives of the previous owners often remained on the staff. The regional directors of United Distillers have a range of reports encompassing all nationalities. Significantly United Distillers is run by a non-Brit – the Swede, Finn Johnston – who sits on the Guinness plc main board, alongside the Dutch Human Resources Director, John de Leeuw. (At a non-executive level the Guinness plc board boasts an even more international cast of characters, including the Dutch Floris Maljers, the German Helmut Sihler and the French Bernard Arnault.) However, if one visits the United Distillers divisional headquarters in Hammersmith or, indeed, the Guinness plc headquarters in Portman Square, the reception areas (smart though both are) do not reflect the cosmopolitan character of the businesses – rather they seem redolent of just another (successful) British business.

The appearnace of parochialism which belies actual internatonalization is nowhere more apparent than in the case of Nestlé. Founded in 1865 by Henri Nestlé, the inventor of processed baby food, the company can claim a peculiarly European character as it has done much to revolutionize the eating habits of an entire continent, not least through the 1938 invention of Nescafé which was a clever ruse to solve the coffee glut in Brazil. More than simply influencing the eating habits of a continent the company was also in the very vanguard of management training provision and founded their own management school in Lausanne – IMEDE, now renamed IMD. The sleek Vevey headquarters reinforce the sense of a truly European company since it is staffed by a host of different nationalities. The company owns operations far beyond Europe, including Carnation Foods in the US and, while being headquartered in Switzerland, derives a tiny fraction of its profits from the Swiss home market. There was consternation when Nestlé took over the British sweet manufacturer Rowntree but as with all Nestlé's acquisitions the majority of the acquired staff retained their positions and, to a greater extent, their autonomy. At the time of the Rowntree takeover considerable criticism was levelled at the British government for allowing such a British institution to fall into foreign hands (so much for European fellowship) and derived in part from a recogition that the same could not have been done in reverse for the Swiss are highly protective of their hugely successful organization. At heart Nestlé is a Swiss company, although its management structure in no way suggests that, for the company is regularly run by non-Swiss executives. Ownership however, is emphatically Swiss, as only Swiss nationals can buy voting shares and key positions (such as President) in the company have typically gone to individuals who are intimately connected with Swiss public life. Indeed, the company has historic links with another great Swiss institution of global proportions, the Red Cross. While most observers would have no hesitation in describing Nestlé as European the company itself would probably – as would the average Swiss citizen – opt for a 'made in Switzerland' label.

European or simply international?

Some would claim that this concern with identifying the European character of a business is a red herring, European business figures amongst them, many of whom would consider themselves 'international' businessmen but would have some difficulty identifying themselves as European. This preference for the term 'international' fascinates me for it is as little illuminating as the term being repudiated. If a company is international (for I am wary of talking in terms of the fully global company) then it may well have shareholders in many parts of the world. It might source its products worldwide, have research centres in one or more continents and have a management structure that incorporates people from many parts of the world. Incidentally, this international head-count is not a mere numbers game – to be truly international a company would need to give influential positions to a range of nationalities. But, for all this evidence of internationalism, the company would presumably have headquarters in one site. In that location would sit the Board and from that place would come the primary decisions. Wherever that place might be would, inevitably, confer a degree of identity on the business. Only if the headquarters were, somehow, to be split would a business entirely forsake its original national identity. I struggle to find examples of companies where national identity is subsumed within a stronger international identity, even those where there is clear intercontinental exchange such as SmithKline Beecham, the Anglo-American merger.

Part of my problem here in finding these truly international organizations may be a mere matter of time. The development of businesses is a slow one and depends upon the cycle of managers who steer that development – thus the evolution of a company is tied to the generational change of top management.

Just as Anthony Sampson writing in 1968 could not predict the less national, more international character of those young graduates just embarking on their careers so I cannot fully envisage that those who are embarking on managerial careers in the mid 1990s will eschew any form of local identity in favour of a fully international, globally realized business. The course taken by all those companies considered briefly above – to start in a local market, move internationally often through distributors and then moving to an owned sales and marketing structure, incorporating local skills in order to play to distinct local tastes and retain local good will – is perhaps a course that will lead to the goal of true internationalism.

Ownership or headquarters – the locus of power

It is not my thesis that the terms *European* and *international* are mutually exclusive. Quite the reverse – my concern is to see European businesses operate in a global market place as successfully as American or Japanese counterparts. Clearly being an American company is no handicap to being international and so there is no reason why the same should not hold true for a European organization; but we are in danger of coming to see identity as being all too bound up with ownership again. Certainly if we look at an American company it would appear that identity does simply come down to ownership. Food is traditionally held to be a very locally influenced product, diet is regional and the attempt to construct a global food business is fraught with difficulties. That said, it remains equally true that some US companies have built vast empires in the food sector. Philip Morris is the world's largest food and beverage organization (although of course its cigarette business also adds substantially to sales and profits) and it is moreover a company that mixes a vast array of international businesses with fascinating histories under a single umbrella. No one in business would question, however, whether or not Philip Morris is American. Similarly, Kellogg. The cornflake has dominated the breakfast tables of the dairy-obsessed Anglo-Saxons for nigh on a century and in the last ten or so years the company has launched an assault on the continental European palate, employing European nationals to spearhead the attack. The company remains, however, steadfastly American as any non-American born executive will testify. If you want to progress a career in the company eventually you will have to transfer to headquarters in Battle Creek, Missouri. The same holds good whichever American company you target. Procter & Gamble has a tremendous record of promoting talent irrespective of nationality but that talent, ultimately, must be prepared to be groomed and nurtured from a Cincinnatti base. At H.J. Heinz the current boss, Irishman Tony O'Reilly, holds court from Pittsburgh and that city remains the focus for the organization as a whole. The salient feature here is that simple one of place. The locus of power is, and always will be, the headquarters of the company. From this site the key strategic decisions are taken, the top management and non-executive team meet to direct the business and from here is disseminated the culture of the business.

European mergers – creating the ultimate European company?

Internationalism requires perhaps a certain cast of mind, a tendency to disregard difference. During the greater part of this century that disregard for difference has been a critical factor in the success of American companies. Nothing has been too alien to resist Americanization. In Europe the ability to disregard difference takes a different form. Difference is not a potential problem, but a strength – something on which the far-sighted can capitalize. This issue leads us naturally to a discussion of companies that are indubitably European – those merged entities that represent the interests of more than one national company. These are not new phenomona; Agfa Gavaert, to which we alluded earlier, was by no means the first such endeavour although it was the first in the more recent round of such company constructions. There are before us two fascinating examples of merged interests, both of which, curiously, are Anglo-Dutch: Shell and Unilever.

Royal Dutch and Shell

The interests of the Royal Dutch and Shell Group of companies were merged in direct response to the competitive threat of John D. Rockefeller's Standard Oil Trust (see Chapter 3) as the two European parties recognized the need to compete on a worldwide basis. The merger took place in 1907 but the Shell company history dates back to 1833 when Marcus Samuel opened a small shop in London's East End dealing, incongruously, in oriental sea shells. On his death in 1870 the business passed to his two sons who split the business in two with Marcus Samuel & Co. operating from a London base and Samuel Samuel & Co. from a Japanese base. In the early 1890s Marcus Samuel saw the opportunity for a large market in kerosene in the Far East, buying in bulk to undercut Standard Oil which was then the monopoly supplier. The timing of this move was fortuitous for in 1885 Karl Benz developed the first viable kerosene-driven automobile. The Dutch partner was formed in 1890 under the patronage of King William III of the Netherlands (hence the Royal of the title) to develop an oil field in Sumatra. A turning point in the fortunes of the company was in 1896 when notorious financier Henri Deterding joined Royal Dutch and set about competing with the American Standard Oil and the British Marcus Samuel in the construction of ships, bulk storage and the distribution of oil and oil products. Samuel's business by this time had grown so extensive that in 1987 he had formed a separate company to operate the oil interests which, in homage to the company origins, was called the Shell Transport and Trading company. In 1901 the discovery of oil in Texas gave Marcus Samuel further strength in the market as his company was there poised to handle transport and distribution. Critically, Shell came to be the first company with worldwide sources of production and the ability to supply gasoline, kerosene and fuel oil. Standard Oil responded to this direct threat by attempting to acquire Shell but Samuel refused the offer. He proved more amenable in 1901 to the offer made by Deterding, then Chairman of Royal Dutch who had similarly realized that it would be more sound to work together than for the two companies to compete separately. In 1903 the English and the Dutch companies came together under the banner of the Asiatic Petroleum Company Limited, with the Rothschild bankers as a third party. With Deterding as Managing Director and Samuel as Chairman the company combined resources for all the markets in the Pacific Rim. In 1907 the success of the endeavour led to the full merger of interests to create the Royal Dutch/Shell Group of companies.

The two parents took a 60% (Royal Dutch) and a 40% (Shell) interest in two newly founded operating companies in charge of exploration and production, headquartered in the Hague with transportation and storage run from London. This ratio is maintained today. The two companies have moved ever closer together. Royal Dutch began as an oil producer and gradually moved towards distribution and trading whereas the sequence was reversed for Shell Transport and Trading, which now has an exploration and refining end. The merger gave a vast geographical spread, a strong portfolio of skills with command of the oil production process from exploration to distribution and has given rise to a decentralized management philosophy. Shareholdings are held principally in the UK, the US, Switzerland and the Netherlands and the parent companies have separate boards of directors, each responsible to their shareholders. Today Royal Dutch Shell is unquestionably an international, if not global, company with over 2000 companies worldwide, more than 130,000 staff, over 500,000 shareholders and combined assets of over £50 billion. The business is currently engaged in designing an organizational structure appropriate to the twenty-first century in which more and more responsibility resides at the local level.

The Unilever model

Before offering any commentary on the benefits of an Anglo-Dutch merger let us look at the second example, Unilever. Where the Royal Dutch Shell company is an example of a direct response to American business the Lever brothers' history shows the ability of the Europeans to harness the American way of doing business to the benefit of their own endeavours. Prior to the development by William Lever of his business, soap in Britain was a commodity product of poor and distinctly variable quality. The American lesson that Lever learnt was that a high quality, reliable, repeatable product would command a high and sustainable price. Lever evolved and refined a method by which the soap would not run the risk of going rancid and thus was able to ensure the production of a uniform product. More than this he adopted the highly American attitude towards his product of making it appeal and then stressing that appeal to a specific target audience. Lever chose the name Sunlight for his soap bar (he was later to think of the equally inspired trade name Lux) which amply indicated the quality of his new product. He then promoted it with a full advertising campaign directed at the housewife. On these foundations he built half of what has become one of Europe's biggest businesses.

The Uni of Unilever came from the Dutch Margarine Union which joined forces with Lever in 1930. The Dutch business comprised Van Den Berghs and Jurgens, a substantial central European business, a meat business called Hartogs and other smaller ventures. Initially the two had come together to look at a way of preventing direct competition since both were large users of oils and fats. It was initially proposed that Lever would focus exclusively on soap, the Dutch Margarine Union on margarines and any other businesses could be subsumed into a third company. This proved unsatisfactory since both companies were required to forego large areas of profitable business and so at the last minute talk turned to a merger of interests. What emerged from this merger were, as in the Shell example, two holding companies, Unilever Ltd (now Plc) capitalized in sterling and based in London and Unilever NV capitalized in gilders and based in Rotterdam, each with identically constructed boards of directors and with an agreement to pay dividends of equivalent values in sterling and gilders. Predictably, Unilever NV was to look after Unilever's interests in continental Europe while Unilever Ltd would consider the UK, the commonwealth and the embryonic American market.

The timing of the Unilever merger was unfortunate. The American depression made penetration of that market extremely difficult and the main competitor Procter & Gamble gained a strong foothold in the UK in the Newcastle business of Thomas Hedley shortly after the merger took place. The war was less than a decade away and with the enforced separation of the two head offices the sense of continuity and uniformity that had been being built up was shattered. Alternatively, what took the place of what might have been a strongly centralized business was a decentralized structure dependent on tremendous trust being placed on local managers. There have been times when this decentralized approach has seemed a handicap, most notably under the stress of Procter & Gamble's assault on the European market. P&G came to Europe with the boast that they would beat Unilever on home territory, which Unilever had singularly failed to do in reverse. P&G came first to France, then moved into Belgium, the Netherlands and Germany and came, critically, with a clutch of brands that were consistently marketed to each of these regions without care for potential local differences – Daz, Tide and Dash suddenly took on the former washing powder supremos of Persil, Omo and Surf. The success of P&G appeared to undermine the strong and sensitive local management of Unilever, which had allowed for such anomalies as a white Omo in one country and a blue Omo in another, and a soap called Astra in the Netherlands but a margarine called Astra in France. The response of Unilever was to set up a structure with co-ordinators for the key operating areas of food and detergents so as to maintain its local strength but to overlay that with a more globalizing approach consistent with the new, increasingly international advertising media. The board structure of Unilever evolved gradually to around two dozen directors, members of both Unilever Ltd and Unilever NV. In addition there was a special committee, with the chairmen of the two operating companies plus a third party who may come from either. Recently the two current chairmen, Niall Fitzgerald and Morris Tabaksblat, have replaced this structure with a seven-man board of executives, a separate advisory board of nonexecutives and, a level below these, a management board. The debate over centralization or decentralization is one that has persisted throughout the company's history, but despite this perennial point of debate the company has come to seem something of a model for how European businesses might converge.

These two examples of mergers give a compelling logic to the notion of European combines. Both are major multinationals, competing successfully with American and Japanese companies (note the recent Unilever success in establishing a fragrance business on the basis of the acquisition of US perfume brand Calvin Klein) and both bring tremendous profits to the coffers of Holland and the UK and offer employment across the globe. Moreover, both are highly respected training grounds for top talent, recruiting and training the top decile graduates from around the world. Further, despite the decentralized nature of the businesses and the extraordinary diversity both display in terms of products and peoples there is a clear and consistent sense of culture, of belonging to an organization with an identifiable character. In the case of Royal Dutch Shell in particular, the rationale governing merger in the first instance was the recognition that there exists common ground between European businesses that makes combination against an external threat both logical and desirable – the vision that is at the heart of this book.

Successful mergers/shared cultures?

The union of these Anglo-Dutch companies is a marriage of similarity and dissimilarity. The synergies between the businesses have been seen; each had something the other wanted and each had access to a market that the other was less well positioned to exploit. The match of business interests was that of shared concerns but different constituent parts, allowing for a clever interlocking without head-to-head competition. What of the likenesses? What enabled the British and the Dutch to work together? Here we can trace a common cultural heritage. Both are flank powers, on the fringes of continental Europe. Both are mercantile nations with a legacy of successful trading endeavours leading to the development in both cases of an early bourgeois society. Both countries have held a special status in the development of financial services across Europe. Both countries retain monarchies (and Britain of course has been ruled by a Dutch family) and both are predominantly Protestant. These factors have played their part. Both cultures are also, by the terms of Fukuyama's thesis, 'high trust' cultures. Indeed, Holland profoundly supports Fukuyma's case against any claim that the ability to generate large corporations is tied to the size of the national economy. Holland is the most industrially concentrated nation in the world, one of Europe's smaller economies and host to some of its largest companies.

Peter Davis, now Chief Executive of that institution some would consider thoroughly British, The Prudential, was one of the primary architects of a third, and more recent, Anglo-Dutch merger between Reed International and Elsevier NV. He would probably not entertain the notion that there are cultural similarities between the two nations that facilitate the merger. His persuasive position is that only one thing can motivate the union of two companies from different countries and that is the commercial logic of the thing. For Davis it was entirely coincidental that he happens to be of Anglo-Dutch parentage (his mother was Dutch) for he has no command of the language and has been brought up entirely within the British educational system. He is prepared to concede that a certain predisposition toward the Dutch may have helped in the process of negotiation but the negotiation came about, not because of any innate interest in developing a European business simply for the sake of being European or any preference for that business being Anglo-Dutch, but because the requirements of Reed International were such that a link-up with Elsevier made the soundest commercial sense. For Davis the merger was the next logical step in the revitalization of the Reed publishing empire and each business found in the other complementary assets, a complementary portfolio of brands and of market strengths, each needing access to the other's market in continental Europe and the US in order to be pre-eminent in their sector.

The merger of Reed Elsevier has resulted in three businesses – a British, a Dutch and an American one – and it is the presence of the latter interest, which is greater than either the British or Dutch, that has helped eradicate the potential bid for supremacy by one merging nation against the other. The process of merging has been calculated to produce in the quickest possible time a sense of shared direction and vision, a feeling of commonality. The merger was accompanied by a painstaking identification of common values that could be articulated and represented in existing professional practices. A commitment was made to move people around the business with particular traffic between Holland and the UK and mechanisms have been put in place to ensure that there is a balance of national representation at all managerial levels. The company has learned from previous mergers that, for instance, rather than befuddle executives with the need for all papers to be duplicated in English and Dutch there has been a straightforward decision that English be the operating language of the company. Peter Davis was, when questioned, prepared to learn Dutch but it was his Dutch counterpart, Pierre Vinken, who pointed out the irrelevance of so doing: 'Why learn a language that is spoken by only 8 million people worldwide?'. Logic, then, has been at the heart of this merger, influencing both sides. Ultimately, despite this logic, the new environment did not prove one in which Davis could continue his career since he and the rest of the Board reached an impasse when assessing the way forward and, as can happen to the visionaries in these complex mergers, he was obliged to leave the new venture to find its way forward without him. A personal disappointment perhaps, but not one that should be taken to undermine the essential soundness of the endeavour.

The less likely mergers

The merger of Reed-Elsevier is one of several major European mergers which have come out of this last European focused decade. We have focused on the mergers so far of European companies where, however irrelevant this may seem to the protagonists, there are clear cultural links and areas of commonality. What, now, of those nations where there is more difference than similarity? Take, for instance, Britain and France. True there have been historically strong links between the French and the Scots but that was because they were united by a common enemy in England. For much of modern history Britain and France have had an uneasy relationship with political alliance being a feature only of the twentieth century and then, as we will see in Chapter 10, not always comfortably. Philosophical traditions (which have far-reaching influence on educational systems and hence on the way a nation approaches problems, on which we will focus in Chapter 9) have been widely different and the small physical distance between the two nations has been completely eclipsed by the sharp emotional divide between them. Since the war, however, the British and French governments have collaborated notably to produce Concorde and, more recently, to build the Channel Tunnel. The completion of the Channel Tunnel and the commencement of passenger services is almost as much a milestone for Europe as the bringing down of the Berlin wall, finally bringing closer together the long standing but distanced elements of a single continent.

These Anglo-French endeavours in the public arena are matched by similar mergers of interest in business. We have already noted United Distillers in our attempt to understand what is meant by a European company but elided a piece of information which makes the company's European status less open to question. With its portfolio of luxury branded goods (United Distillers deals exclusively in premium brands) the company had some common ground with the French luxury goods sector and, in particular, with Louis Vuitton Moet Hennessey, which in addition to its clothing, scent and apparel businesses also had a range of champagnes which sat well alongside the United Distillers spirits range. LVMH had access to Continental Europe, United Distillers – in a pattern we have seen already – to the Commonwealth and the US and the coincidence of interests was clear – the two businesses, in principal, fitted neatly together like the pieces in a jigsaw. The relationship between the two companies stopped well short of full merger and instead each took a 25% cross-shareholding in the other, although the balance has shifted since then and the terms have been renegotiated.

There are other Anglo-French mergers to give the lie to the notion of perennial incompatibility, GEC Alsthom and Arjo Wiggins Appleton (the latter combining, in Appleton, an American business too) are obvious examples. The first, in which top jobs appear to be predominantly in the hands of the French, appears to have had fewer troubles than the Arjo example where the Chief Executive position has passed through both British and French hands in a short space of time, but both have achieved precious economies of scale, access to new markets and products and greater buying power through alliance. We could now embark on an extensive list of mergers between companies from countries apparently unlike – Capp Gemini Sogeti, an Anglo-French–German merger in the consultancy sector, Eurocopter, a French–German merger of helicopter interests, Ferruzzi/Beagan Say, the Italian–French sugar group and the groundbreaking Swedish–Swiss merger of Asea and Brown Boveri to form ABB, currently seen as the model for mergers. Without dwelling in more depth on these we can deduce little beyond the clear fact that the will is there amongst the nations of Europe to combine interests in order to compete better in the global marketplace. We might also be able to deduce from the phenomonally successful Swedish–Swiss merger that there is more flexibility and less reluctance to suppress national characteristics in countries that are less ethnocentric (i.e. less aware of national status, not from the ranks of the superpowers but more culturally and politically neutral) but such a conclusion would be premature.

Can an unmerged business still be European?

Can we conclude then that these merged businesses represent the future for Europe and, further, that when we refer to a European company we mean, exclusively, those companies that are owned by one or more European nation? It is my view that, emphatically, this is not the case. Such companies are, unquestionably, European as they are, unquestionably, international but it is not the mere fact of shared ownership that makes them so.

The term *European* operates independently of ownership, so what else contributes to its meaning? To consider the question from another angle let us look at businesses which do not have shared ownership structures but which merit being considered European. Schroders plc, as a merchant bank is, not surprisingly, highly international. Essentially a London house (although with early roots in Germany) the business is geographically spread across the US, continental Europe and Asia and the board comprises directors from a number of different countries including the US, the UK, Germany, Canada, Belgium and France. The management style of the organization is profoundly decentralized and with its Chairman Win Bischoff it has at the helm someone with a degree of cultural neutrality (German born, South African raised whose first big career break came in Asia).

Petrofina in contrast is a Belgian business with a Belgian in the role of Chief Executive, Francois Cornelis, yet it is a company with very strong European origins. For much of its history Belgian and Romanian interests were merged in Concordia to exploit Romania's oil fields. The company has also for a period been 50% French owned. The pre-war company was effectively dismantled during the Second World War and after the war the Belgian business became involved with Anglo-Saxon businesses rather than European ones, entering into contracts with the British and Canadians. From oils the company moved into chemicals and under its petro-chemical banner was the first to create plastics, this time in association with the Dutch Philips Petroleum. Subsequently the Italian Montedison has replaced the Dutch company as a major partner. Petrofina is now a $20 billion business employing some 17,000 people worldwide with a petrol brand, Fina, which is a highly familiar one across Europe. Belgian owned and run, its history closely allied to that of the European continent as a whole, Petrofina has every right to claim European status.

Polygram is 80% Dutch owned, a subsidiary of Philips but, headquartered in London with a French Chief Executive (Alain Levy) and a portfolio of international and world-class acts and interests in the movie as well as the music business. It is hard to see the business as anything other than international. The business, however, must retain a strong local element with new talent being spotted and nurtured at the local level. This implicit emphasis on local tastes has given the business a strongly decentralized structure. Under Levy's guidance the local has been contrasted with the global as he has put together a range of labels which ensure that a local act can be promoted globally. In particular, Levy has aquired Island Records in the US and forged a distribution agreement with Motown, thereby giving access to the vibrant and growing black music market. He has also masterminded the taking of a 3% stake in Andrew Lloyd-Webber's Really Useful Group. Regional headquarters have been established in the US and in Hong Kong to support the strong decentralized operating philosophy which is, in turn, underpinned by fairly centralized financial controls.

Redland plc (British) operates in the housing sector and domestic architecture has resisted any efforts to be other than local. To have achieved a pre-eminent position the company has been obliged to establish some 185 tile plants in 23 countries and two-thirds of the company's profits come from outside the UK. United Biscuits would be easy to dismiss as a stodgy British business but run by an Anglo-Italian, Eric Nicoli, it is moving rapidly into Europe. In 1989 just 8% of sales came from continental Europe; by 1991 that figure had increased to 26% and by 1994 stood at over 30%. In addition to the established British brands McVities Digestives, KP Nuts and Hula Hoops the company has the European brands Verkade, Fazer, Gyori Keksz, Oxford, Ortiz and Croky as well as American brands Keebler, Chips Deluxe and Town House.

Operating style

At the end of this litany of internationally motivated companies it might be tempting to ask the question 'so what?'. The variety of companies we have drawn together here, in true European fashion, appear to hold in common only the fact that they are entirely different from one another and any more compelling conclusion would seem, at first glance, elusive. However, there is one word which recurs persistently in any discussion of so-called European businesses and that is *decentralized*. My thesis is that identity has nothing to do with ownership or penetration of particular markets, nor even with the composition of the management; rather, identity has everything to do with *style*. It is the operating style and character of a company which confers identity. We have seen how an American company can be staffed with Europeans, even be run by a European (as is the case with Heinz) and yet be profoundly and unquestionably American. The American style is the hugely successful but essentially reductive one of treating all places as like and seeking after sameness. So it is that the same products are marketed in the same way by people who look and act the same. American style is imposed as in the swift and efficient colonization of Europe by American businesses and the dogged refusal to be daunted by regional difference. This impositional, leavening style has paid tremendous dividends and European companies have learnt much from it, not least in terms of the need for standard products and consistent offerings. The European way of doing business is diametrically opposed to this American style.

European operating style: think global, act local

Companies that are European, irrespective of their ownership structure, will acquire businesses with staff and goodwill intact. This is not to claim that there will not be the inevitable rationalization involving loss of jobs and some sacrifice of people who have held power inappropriate to a new entity, but the urge to impose conformity is measured carefully against the need to maintain local expertise. Europeans have learnt the lessons of history – what worked for the Romans will work for modern day Europeans too. The European mind, attuned to the complexity of any international situation and without any single co-ordinating European feature that can bind together the culturally unlike, prefers to remain sensitive to local skills and predilections, to respect and make use of those skills and predilections, rather than to alienate or reject locals and so damage the fortunes of the business.

Still the response may be 'so what?'. America has been hugely successful without pandering to local whim; is not the European caution inefficient? There are a number of potential responses to this. Not least would be that in celebrating difference one enables the decision-making process. Accommodating a range of different views and opinions may be costly in terms of time but ultimately one may arrive at a better truth. Similarly, the tendency to encourage excellence in a range of forms, to foster diversity and heterogeneity, can lead European companies to have a more truly meritocratic approach to people management, which again will lead to better decision making. Still, this does not address the issue fully.

If the Europeans have learned the Roman lesson 'think global, act local' on which Roman greatness was forged, they have also not neglected one of the factors that contributed to the downfall of the Roman empire – the absence of innovation, which we considered in Chapter 2. There is little natural or historical precedent for believing that homogeneity is consistent with innovation. Repetition of genes weakens the breed and the lessons of inbreeding are all too evident in the history of European monarchies – homogeneity being called into question at the most fundamental, genetic level. The universal laws against incest testify to the imperative towards heterogeneity which sustains mankind. Culture is sustained by heterogeneity. Some of the greatest works of high culture are influenced by difference – Gaughin drew his inspiration from the South Seas, some of the finest novels in the English language of the twentieth century were written by a Pole (Joseph Conrad), Spain's fine architecture is highly influenced by an African aesthetic, the courts of the Tudors were painted by a Dutchman (Holbein), those of the Stuarts by the Flemish Van Dyck and, of course, Hollywood, the ultimate American symbol, gained its lifeblood from its European émigré population. As we have seen, some of the loss in German innovation may derive from the loss of the Jewish population. Innovation, indeed, depends upon interchange and interbreeding and the recognition of difference and that some methods may be better than others. The edge the European company has over others is precisely this openness to otherness, a recognition that different may indeed be better. As we have seen, in Chapter 1, the American 'rights'-based culture that has developed over the last 30 years is antithetical to any such notion and reinforces the rule of homogeneity, thereby denying access to new ideas and influences.

Of course, the European company will pay a certain price for its deference to difference. A European corporation may not be as quick to move as one from the US or Japan, having a more diffuse decison-making process, but a rapid response to a wrong resolution is the risk run by highly homogeneous cultures where difference is denied at the expense of better debate. The European company will also need to develop better methods by which it can take advantage of the differences within it. How can a business achieve a focused strategy that is coherent across a number of diverse markets while remaining flexible to local needs? The answer must lie with the professionalism of the organization's board. This professionalism, in turn, resides in a cast of mind. The prerequisite skill the board member of a European organization must bring to that board is quite simply sympathy with his or her international fellows, rather than any partisan adherence to the local. This will go against the grain with some directors whose very presence on the board may be due to excellence only at a local level. Nonetheless, at the level of the board international interests must rate as highly as national. Further, there must be consensus that the board is the custodian of strategy but that operational expertise necessarily resides locally. As one European Chief Executive has put it: 'I may be on the board of a French company that controls the capital and the strategy of operations across Europe, but that board does not, cannot and must not control the hearts of the people in those operations'.

The notion of a European company is a novel one. So much so that it has required a chapter to try and understand what is conveyed by the term 'European'. Ownership structures, which on the face of it would appear the most obvious means of definition, prove unhelpful. Similarly, while the location of the headquarters of a company confers national identity that factor alone does not denote that a company is European – it might remain, after all, entirely focused on its home market and entirely staffed by locals. A European company is one that, certainly, has its headquarters in a European location but also has a particular operating philosophy that draws on the historical and cultural legacy of two millenia. It is a company that learns from others, as in recent decades Europeans have learnt from American companies how to achieve improved product offerings, advertising strategies and management disciplines and, from Japanese organizations, how to ensure the highest standards of efficiency and quality in production. Increasingly, Europeans in a single company are learning from each other. Boards are becoming much more international. Recent research undertaken by Heidrick & Struggles shows that the British boardroom is decreasingly parochial. On the basis of information on 130 of the top 150 UK plcs by market capitalization we find that 54% of companies have at least one non-British board member. A higher proportion of these non-British board members are engaged in an outside rather than an executive capacity but a creditable 38% are full-time executive members of their respective companies with managerial responsibility for large portions of turnover. So much for British insularity. Nor is non-British influence confined to those for whom English is a first language – there are more French directors than Australians or New Zealanders, for instance (a reflection of the fact that distance is a greater hurdle than language difference). Britain, with its considerable concern for governance issues may be in the vanguard of this increasing internationalism of the board but the trend is one that can be seen around Europe. The German Adidas is run by Frenchman Robert Louis-Dreyfus while the Danish business Egmont is run by a Norwegian (and the apparent similarity of two Scandinavian countries conceals substantial cultural differences between the two nations). The European company, then, is culturally open. Still in its infancy, its identity may crystallize as innovative forms of governance are found and shared, but on the strength of abundant European precedents, that identity is unlikely ever to be fully fixed. Ironically, it is almost the very absence of a consistent, dyed-in-the-wool European style which denotes the quintessentially European company. It is one that thinks, empathizes and is increasingly poised to innovate and dominate.

7

Confronting Culture

> '... international life will be seen increasingly as a competition not between rival ideologies – since most economically successful states will be organized along similar lines – but between different cultures.'
> Francis Fukuyama, *The End of History and the Last Man.*

What precedent does Europe have for forging a coherent culture and thus what chance does it have for evolving a new business culture – how, through whom and using which skills? These questions provided some of the departure points for this book and will form the substance of this chapter. We have looked in some detail at the precedents that exist for European unity and shared value systems but must now turn our attention to some of the impulses which lie behind cultural identification and which can be harnessed by those charged with the forging of a new culture. We shall also consider some of the measures by which culture and particularly corporate culture can be assessed. We will then consider the custodianship of culture. How are companies changed? Inevitably this takes us to a consideration of some notions of leadership and, in particular, of what is required of leaders at a time of change. Is there a particular prototype for a European leader who will be equipped to undertake the extraordinary task of developing a new way of doing business in Europe? Through an examination of some people who are – or have been – engaged in the task in companies that are undoubtedly European we will try and arrive at a sense of what is required to lead a European company into the twenty-first century and thus to spearhead Europe's economic charge.

Why culture matters

Culture, as a concept, recognizes that we all have the need to belong, that we all belong to a range of different cross-cultural entities (via race, gender, age, social class, etc.) and studies of culture articulate and make knowable this comforting, if complex, set of confines. Culture has the extraordinary ability, on the one hand, to make something infinitely complicated pleasingly simple while confirming the highly complex nature of the human condition. Thus studies of culture can make the individual seem an ever more potent mix of impulses while bringing that individual closer to a host of people otherwise thought to be unlike. Culture collectivizes the individual on the one hand while individualizing the collective on the other.

Identifying with the local rather than the global

The human sphere of operation tends to be a narrow one. We are loyal to small and identifiable entities, to our families, our schools, our church, the organizations for which we work and, critically, to the nations within which we reside. Can the notion of continentalism ever take on the might of nationalism? Can we embrace something that inevitably eludes our intimate knowledge. For all we can engage in international travel, can learn languages and, increasingly, are involved in broadly homogeneous consumer activities, no individual can ever claim full knowledge or understanding of so broad a locale, a locale so obstinately defying the local. At the moment it seems unlikely that internationalism as an antidote to nationalism will fire us and, even while our leaders talk of combination and a commingling of fortunes, many of us bristle at the thought of subsuming our national identity within some featureless composite. Indeed, during the 1980s and early 1990s, that period which I have characterized as peculiarly European, there was a resurgence of interest in national identity as if in defiant counter to the obsession with internationalism. Curiously, those who sought to celebrate individual nations did so by invoking the very words with which I have been celebrating Europe – difference and diversity.

Ethnocentrism

It is curious that much of the resurgence in interest in national identification has come from France, Germany and Britain. The last work of one of France's foremost historians of the post-war period, Ferdinand Braudel, a historian whose work roamed famously across the entire territory of Europe, was the unfinished *The Identity of France* where in celebrating his own nation he claimed for it:

> 'the dazzling triumph of the plural, of the heterogeneous, of the never-quite the same'.

In claiming such diversity for France, Braudel operates within the tradition of all writers on national identity. Whatever the nation under scrutiny the epithets applied are invariably the same. Writing in 1742, philosopher David Hume made the same claim for the English who represented, to this Scottish Anglophile, the most varied of Europe's people, in whom could be seen:

> 'the least of a national character, unless this very singularity may pass for such'.

For Nietzsche it was the German character that eluded definition, although one could not attribute to Nietzsche a zealous quest to pursue German nationalism, quite the contrary, for he regarded German nationalism as 'a scabies of the heart and blood poisoning'. Indeed, Nietzsche was an early pro-European who stated in *Beyond Good and Evil* (1896) that Europe wanted, even then, to become one and was prevented from doing so by 'the lunacy of nationality'.

Braudel's last work was published in 1986, in the same year as German historians and intellectuals were absorbed in a debate which had as its starting point the meaning of the Final Solution but focused on the future of German identity. Known as the Historian's Debate this issue touched a very sensitive German nerve and led to a rash of publications on the subject, coming from the most learned on all sides of the political equation. In much the same way there was widespread debate on the subject of national identity among the French in 1989 as a response to the encroachment of Le Pen's party on national politics. In the same year the fruits of a British attempt to quantify national identity were published in a three-part study entitled *Patriotism – the*

Making and Unmaking of British National Identity, where are to be heard echoes of David Hume's view of a variegated British identity.

It is tempting to consider that some of the celebration of individual nations has been a response to a paradoxical xenophobic mistrust of difference and diversity. The influx of people to the nation states of Europe from old imperial possessions or less advantaged areas of the world has led to an alarming rise in political sympathy being extended to the far right. In France, where commitment to a European ideal has been better expressed than anywhere else among the nation states of the European community, there has also been seen the rise of Le Pen and the Front National. In Britain the National Front has enjoyed less electoral success but exerts a menacing power on some areas, particularly those with a high proportion of immigrants, and in Germany there is an abiding fear of the rise of neo-Nazi parties. On a more benign level the growth of the heritage industry, an almost nationalized concern in Britain with the National Trust and English Heritage between them taking the responsibility for the custodianship of most of the island's national monuments, represents a sentimental striving after some past paradise lost. Nostalgia, then, is just another manifestation of nationalism.

So what can we conclude from this revived interest in nationhood and, more particularly, from its revival in France, Germany and the UK? Perhaps in the first place we can conclude that it is in the coherence of our notions of identity that we find the conviction to act within the community. Having a clear-cut role seems somehow essential to our capacity to express ourselves, without which we are at large in the anarchy of ambiguity. Fatherhood, motherhood, masculinity, femininity, worker, boss, conservative, socialist – these are just a handful of the constructs of identity which give meaning and shape to our conduct and our image of ourselves; to each there is an understood rubric of behaviour, a ready-made formula of responses which circumscribe, delimit and protect us. The nation is just another of these constructs. The potency of nationhood in France, Germany and Britain may be attributed to, in the case of Britain and France, longevity and in that of Germany, the reverse. In all three cases *great power* status has left its mark on the population where the arrogance of assumed superiority based on an equally fictitious sense of selfsufficiency is only very reluctantly set aside. France and England are the two oldest nation states within Europe in the sense that they have enjoyed the longest political unity, whereas German unity is the most youthful. German nationality, however, is based on geographical rather than political unity, on the ancient status of the Germanic peoples as the people of the middle, anchored geographically at the centre or heart of Europe.

During the last 15 years we have, in Europe, raised anchors and set sail on the uncharted waters of international co-operation. To those ethnocentric nations Britain, France and Germany there is some alarm in the prospect, however much it is the French and the Germans who are at the forefront of attempts to create a full union. It is all the more predictable, this being the case, that the backlash would come from them. It is also not surprising that this backlash takes the form of a celebration of *national* difference and diversity. It is as if those making these claims on behalf of their own nations are asking why there should be any need for international identity when there exists on a national basis sufficient diversity already. Ambiguity is used as a defence against ambiguity. Or perhaps, in direct opposition to this notion, the fear is not of ambiguity but its reverse, a reductive clarity. If we seek after sameness on an international level, throwing in our lot with our neighbours in some artificial construct of European identity, do we not reduce our individuality, our separateness, those factors that inform our very characters? Is this not another sign of the levelling of European society that has been underway since the birth of the mass market and the mass-produced uniform consumer product?

The importance of language in cultural fixity

We have seen already how in Britain notions of national identity can co-exist with profound regional differences and yet despite this obvious paradox Britain, France and Germany have, to a large extent, been insulated from either the ambiguity (or the blinding full beam, whichever way one prefers to perceive it) of internationalism. France famously protects its culture and a part of this protection takes the form of language proscription – the virtual outlawing of Franglais, le weekend, etc. – and, of course, language is at the very heart of all issues about nationalism and internationalism. Countries that are most inclined to be ethnocentric are those that have a strong linguistic culture, one that dominates not simply within national borders but beyond them. For all, within the British Isles, there remain the Gaelic languages and, in parts of Wales, schoolchildren are still taught the Welsh language, the language of

England has come to a pre-eminent position in the Western world, not least because – through accidents of history – it has come to be the national language of America. As English became the practical language of India (and remained so after independence on the basis of pure pragmatism) so the French language is still spoken in former outposts of empire. While French may not be as widely spoken now as English among the peoples of the world, it remains a language that has lent itself to any number of nations, including England. French was for centuries regarded as the courtly language; it was the legacy left to the English by the Normans but, as far distant as the Russian court in the nineteenth century it was the language that was judged appropriate for noble discourse; the vernacular was vulgar. Many of the languages of Europe are Germanic in structure. The German language, like the French, is widely spoken across the continent and European schoolchildren generally have ready access in schools to any of these languages.

Many of the nations of Europe do not have this linguistic uniformity. Switzerland is an obvious example of a nation where the languages spoken vary from canton to canton; Belgium a second example of a state with more than one national language. Other nations may have one unifying language but, as in the case of Holland, the utility of that language beyond national frontiers may be greatly reduced so that the acquisition of other languages becomes a necessity. It is not surprising that we do not hear the same fears that national identity will inevitably decline with the onset of marked internationalism from the likes of Luxembourg, Austria, Denmark – nations where there has long needed to be a compromising of certain national characteristics in order for the nation to support itself. It is interesting to note that some very significant European companies have their origins in countries where there is a high degree of inherent internationalism evidenced by language alone – Sandoz and Nestlé are two obvious examples of very successful Swiss businesses, whereas Holland in addition to its interests in Unilever and Shell is also the home of Philips. It would seem that the absence of ethnocentrism can be a positive factor in building an international business. I am in danger, here, of making ethnocentrism appear a pejorative term – it may be as easily transplanted by the phrase 'culturally integrated'. So we can see that in France, Germany and Britain we have more homogeneous cultures, closer in fact to the American model, than is the case in Switzerland, Belgium or Luxembourg.

Corporate culture with a national perspective

The intersection of different groupings is part of what contributes to an overall culture. National and corporate cultures, inevitably, are very closely related. In recent years a considerable body of work has been produced on the subject first of national culture and then by extension corporate culture of which some of the most interesting work has been done by Geert Hofstede who neatly defines culture as 'software of the mind'. Based on a study of IBM executives across 50 countries world-wide, Hofstede arrived at a method of measuring cultural traits which he condensed into five main dimensions. In his 1991 work *Cultures and Organizations*, he identifies these as:

(1) *Individualism versus collectivism* – a measure of the extent to which peoples within a particular culture are defined by the groups and organizations to which they belong.
(2) *Power distance* – an indicator of attitudes to hierarchy and inequality in a given social structure, of attitudes in a work context of workers to bosses and bosses to workers.
(3) *Uncertainty avoidance* – a guide to the tolerance or otherwise of a particular set of peoples to ambiguity leading to the pursuit or rejection of specific statutory structures.
(4) *Masculinity versus femininity* – relying upon notions of the masculine as bold, showy, goal directed and the feminine as giving greater credence to relationships and quality of life issues, this measure sets out a certain social polarity to be found among differing cultures.
(5) *Short-term orientation versus long-term orientation* – this dimension (drawn not from the IBM study but a later piece of work conducted in collaboration with Michael Bond of the Chinese University of Hong Kong) relates to attitudes to time and is particularly illuminating when Western cultures are set against those of other parts of the world.

Hofstede's work is comprehensive and derives from a carefully stratified demographic sample. The results are illuminating. Wealthy north European nations emerge as the more individualistic cultures whereas Spain and Portugal come out as much more collectivist in their thinking. Employees in Scandinavia, Germany and the UK appear to have a more fluid notion of authority than do their counterparts in France, Belgium, Italy and Spain where there is more evidence of respect for authority. The Danish, Swedish, British and Irish, on the strength of Hofstede's findings, feel less threatened or uncomfortable with ambiguity than do the Belgians, French, Germans, Austrians, Swiss and Finns. German-speaking countries can be characterized as more masculine than the relatively more feminine Scandinavian countries, whereas there are marked differences across the Mediterranean regions.

While the results are illuminating they contain some surprises. For instance Britain, a state we have characterized as ethnocentric and one that appears repeatedly resistant to internationalism at least in the form of full European unity, measures on Hofstede's scale as tolerant to ambiguity, less likely to avoid uncertainty from which we might reasonably expect less reluctance to join forces with other states. On the other hand the French appear much more intent on erasing ambiguity on the basis of Hofstede's findings than some observers would expect. In the course of my meetings with leaders of European businesses I asked one CEO with considerable experience in dealing with Anglo-French meetings what differences he typically encountered and what criticisms either side would lodge with him of the other. The British, he replied, found the French obtuse, prone to changing their minds, given to doing business in their own way and their own time. The French view of the British was a neat reversal of this – the British were too simple, over-crude, prone to jumping to conclusions and (almost their greatest crime) obsessed with speed. Put another way, the French would take their time coming to a clear way of proceeding, carefully considering the options and in the process leaving the way clear for considerable ambiguity, whereas the British wanted greater immediacy, more clarity and thus by implication, less ambiguity. This anecdote, then, would appear to conflict with Hofstede's findings, unless we represent the French as being tolerant of short-term ambiguity if by being so they can ultimately achieve long-term clarity.

A different set of categories

In the study of culture it would seem that there can be as many contradictions as there are conclusions and it is all too easy to dismiss such schema as Hofstede's as arbitrary (although subsequent tests undertaken by other researchers into differently constituted groups amply bear out Hofstede's original findings). Why is it that the five categories above come to have such primacy? Might there not be other categories? Indeed, other people have worked on the subject and have established different parameters of measurement. One such is Edward Hall whose work *Beyond Culture* (1976) cites two main parameters. The first is high context versus low context, the second polychronic versus monochronic. The second of these relates to attitudes to time and so appears to anticipate Hofstede's fifth parameter. The first relates to informal networks. Cultures with a high context tendency are those where individuals maintain a high level of information networks amongst friends, family, colleagues and clients – cultures where relationships are critical and more important than formal rules. Low context cultures, in contrast, are those where there is a much lower dependence on this free-flow of informal information and where therefore more rational and formal rules have greater importance. Working to these parameters cultures that one might term 'Latin' emerge as high context, the 'Germanics' (which category includes those from Nordic nations) are low context adherents. Hall's categories, to my mind, are less satisfying than Hofstede's, primarily because they are less subtle and depend too much upon established national stereotypes and groupings; given that the categories 'Latin' and 'Germanic' have long been in circulation, why attempt to give them a new gloss?

One set of classifications has the unfortunate knack of contradicting another. Hall's high context and low context classifications echo those we have encountered earlier in Fukuyama's high trust/low trust distinction. Under that system Italy, the most Latin of the Latin countries, emerges as low trust, in apparent conflict with the Hall findings. Similarly, Hofstede identifies north European nations as individualist rather than collectivist. Britain boasts the strongest list of large-scale multinationals outside the US and Japan; according to the Fukuyama thesis this denotes a strong tendency to association. As we have seen earlier, Germany and the UK represent two potentially opposing systems of capitalism, the Rhine model and the neo-American model. Sweden – another north European nation – has the most egalitarian social system of any in Europe, which would belie the charge of overt individualism. Alternatively, in America, a rights-based society, a concern with egalitarianism raises the profile of the individual over and above any collective moral absolutes. In short, no classification of culture can offer us any certainty. It is, however, interesting to note that it is not so much the measures that diverge, as the application and interpretation of them.

Criticism aside, such work on national and organizational culture is illuminating not just for the findings thrown up but in terms of the underlying achievement, which is to look at established groupings (nations) from a different angle. Hofstede's delineations of characteristics that are common to more than one culture, characteristics that link as if by isobars nations that we would traditionally think unlike, gives a new meaning to the sequence of international alliances we are in the process of constructing (we shall return to this notion of cultural isobars in Chapter 9). Indeed, Hofstede maps anew the emotional/mental contours of the continent, revealing new similarities and dissimilarities and allowing us new interpretations of existing data. We shall return to this subject in Chapter 8.

The differences between national and organizational culture

So what differentiates national from organizational culture? Here again it is useful to turn to the work of Geert Hofstede who has probed some of the assumptions that lie behind the accepted understanding of organizational dynamics and has isolated a clear difference between the two types of cultural affinity. Hofstede defines culture in terms of four key elements: symbols, heroes, rituals and values. Of these, symbols are the most superficial manifestation of culture, values the most profound. The first three elements Hofstede combines under the generic of practices of culture. Within a particular national culture there is likely to be a high level of shared practices (similar dress codes, sporting heroes, leisure activities) whereas values may diverge strongly. Cultural forces intersect and so the values a child acquires in early years may be the product of divergent cultural affiliations (such as gender, religion, race, social class) which may give two people from one country the appearance of strong similarity and yet that similarity may reside entirely on the surface and not penetrate to the core values which underlie motivation. The traditional way of looking at organizational cultures has been to see shared value systems and differing practices. Values, however, are inculcated at a very young age, long before an individual considers work. Views and values concerning types of occupation, which are fixed later than other values, nevertheless predate first employment since first employment is generally achieved through an educational route which must be decided upon at an early period. People with similar values may well find their way into an organization if there is an impressive and coherent hiring function (or perhaps only those people who share the prevailing value system will choose to remain for any length of time in a given organization), but an organization will not impose a consistent value system on all those who join it. Hofstede breaks with the received view of organizational culture (as purveyed by Peters and Waterman) when he says 'shared perception of daily practices should be considered to be the core of an organization's culture'. He attributes this departure from hitherto commonly held views to a different point of entry. Most earlier studies of culture (from within the US management literature canon) have been constructed around the views and statements of the organization's founder or leader and have not registered the impact of those views and values on the work-force. Hofstede found (after an exhaustive study of all levels within a range of organizations in both Denmark and the Netherlands) the following:

> *'The values of founders and key leaders undoubtedly shape organizational cultures, but the way these cultures affect ordinary members is through shared practices. Founders'–leaders' values become members' practices.'*

Values are tremendously resistant to change. Practices are much more fickle; entrenched in systems, they can be changed by a change in the system itself. Nonetheless, practices that are engaged in by a collective as large as an organization change only under the influence of an extremely strong rationale, and one that is well communicated. It is not the lot of the seasoned manager to take on and alter substantively the *modus operandi* of an entire organization; only an inspired and inspirational leader can take on such a task.

Some reflections on leadership

The inspired and inspirational leader is a charismatic leader. Most of the time groups cannot tolerate too much charisma and merely require sound management (although this is a sophisticated skill in itself). Charisma is an intangible concept that precludes an analysis of its constituent parts. We accord the term 'charismatic' to a number of individuals who appear to have little in common, people as diverse as Mahatma Gandhi and Greta Garbo – we will even extend the word's usage to cover those who have never lived outside fiction but have achieved an almost 'cult' status – Sherlock Holmes or Scarlett O'Hara. In short, we invoke the word at times when we see a concatenation of qualities combined in one being that otherwise defy description. The term charisma and the phrase 'star-quality' beloved of TV talent shows have become interchangeable. And yet, from the work of Max Weber we can find a more illuminating gloss which shows charisma to have almost revolutionary potential.

The term charisma is used by Weber to refer to the *novel impact of a belief-system on social life*. The word, which derives from the notion of the 'gift of grace', has its origin in major cultural shifts such as the development away from polytheism to monotheism or Judaism to Christianity but is equally applicable to less seismic cultural changes. In the strictest sense Jesus Christ would qualify as a charismatic leader, but so too would (to cite one of Weber's own examples) Bismarck. Put in simplest terms a charismatic leader is one who, by virtue of his or her new ideas, can bring about a significant cultural change. Charisma depends, in Weber's words, on the 'heroism or exemplary character of an individual person'.

Charisma, and the changes wrought by the unique properties of a given individual, can be routinized and the routinization of charisma, its *bureaucratization*, is a further concern of Weber's. Through various examples he shows how ideas are transmitted to a body of followers and thence to an entire community or society, enshrined within certain rituals and practices until they begin to stagnate or become, in themselves, traditions. For Weber, alarmed by the increasing mechanization of social life (which he depicted as an iron cage) this routinization represented a tragedy but at the same time there is a certain security in the cycle in that novelty can be integrated into everyday life until ultimately it becomes routine, habit. So from the Weberian thesis we can see that where change in culture is to be effected there needs to be a strong and exemplary figure at the helm.

Towards a definition of a European business leader

The leader of a European company finds himself (and predominantly at the moment such leaders are still male) at a cultural cross-roads. Increasingly, as we have seen in Chapter 6, European companies are operating across national boundaries and employing a mix of locals and expatriates at their various locations. Many of these locations have been acquired by a new parent and so the organizational culture of that entity may be in a state of suspension between old and new. Where this is so – and we have seen that it is a fairly typical route for a European company to expand through acquisition – then national cultures are thrown into relief. With the disintegration of corporate culture (for a new owner automatically imposes some new systems and structures, however generally nonimpositional in style) the collective must take refuge in an alternative construct to maintain unity. A leader then, who is the embodiment (if we follow Hofstede), or perhaps the voice, of the company's culture, must be a figure who will engage the sympathies or excite the respect of a broad cross-section. The leader's task is always to manage difference and diversity and from those things to produce uniformity in terms of product and excellence in terms of service. What then can characterize such an individual? Is there a template for a European leader?

Cultural neutrality

In the first instance we should ask the question: of what should these people be exemplars? The answer would appear to be that they should be exemplars of cultural neutrality. It is a truism that people at a remove from a situation can exercise more dispassionate judgement, being in no way personally implicated by circumstances in which they are placed. So it is that many of the great figures of late nineteenth–early twentieth century English letters who offer a commentary on the English are not themselves English. We have already identified Joseph Conrad but note also Henry James and T.S. Eliot, both English domiciled Americans. The Irish tradition of W.B. Yeats, James Joyce and Samuel Beckett has also developed from a sense of distance, alienation, marginalization. The outsider has several advantages: the gift of perspective; the allure of the other, of exotica; and a certain drive which may well derive from the unconscious need to belong – this drive is often what fuels success. Critically, in the context of a European company, the outsider can identify with the notion of difference.

A survey of some European companies and their leaders shows that there is an interestingly high incidence of outsiders taking the helm and managing change. The European business leader can be seen to eschew slavish allegiance to any one national identity. If we look at a handful of the leaders of European businesses we see a similar pattern emerging. In Chapter 6 we drew upon the example of Polygram, which is Dutch owned, London based and run by a Frenchman with an American management education. Eric Nicoli, the Chief Executive of United Biscuits is the son of Italian parents although raised and educated in the UK. His father had been a prisoner of war in wartime East Anglia and stayed on after the end of hostilities, so in his family background Nicoli was very much accustomed to being an outsider. Curiously, though, Alain Levy's family background also includes profound wartime alienation. Born in 1946, Levy is the only child of a Jewish lawyer who, living some 40 miles from the German border, spent the wartime years in hiding. Levy's mother spent the period covering for her then lover and her brother in the Resistance. Although Levy was not born until 1946 the experience left its mark in a profound sense of the burden of their duty and high moral principles. Levy, then, experienced alienation within the family, brought about by the extraordinary history that is mid-century Europe. Other examples of cultural neutrality abound. Win Bischoff, whom we have encountered as the Chairman of Schroders plc, bears his cultural neutrality in his name, which would be hard to place as pertaining to any one nationality. Frenchman Robert Louis-Dreyfus, Chief Executive of Adidas and a former Chief Executive of Saatchi and Saatchi, has achieved his phenomenal career success in cultures other than that to which he was born. As in the case of Alain Levy, he took the unorthodox step, for a Frenchman, of completing his education in the US. However late, education is a formative period in anyone's life and the relevance of experiencing a period in education outside the country of one's birth is clear – it affords insight into other ways of being, other viewpoints and values. When the education involves an international group its value is additionally enhanced.

For Eric Nicoli, Win Bischoff, Alain Levy and Robert Louis-Dreyfus exposure to more than one national culture has clearly been of benefit and has engendered or enhanced a degree of flexibility, giving the appearance of neutrality. Each of these individuals comes, by birth, from one of the countries that we have previously styled ethnocentric, or strongly culturally integrated – Germany, Britain, Germany again and France (respectively). Others among European leaders have cultural neutrality by dint of the nation from which they hail – those nations that have been obliged somewhat to merge their identities in order that their citizens may prosper. The leader of Petrofina,

8

The Cultural Iceberg: a Guide to Cultural Differences both Above and Below the Surface

'... Men of sense condemn these undistinguishing judgements; though, at the same time, they allow that each nation has a peculiar set of manners, and that some particular qualities are more frequently to be met with among one people than their neighbours.'

David Hume.

National and regional stereotypes abound. Nations are routinely caricatured on the basis of minor behavioural differences in modes of dress, forms of address, gestural idiosyncrasies, eating habits and leisure pursuits. These surface differences are the stuff of comedy but, below the surface, there are many differences in value systems which are critical to relationship building between nations and which, if inadequately understood, can significantly undermine those relationships. This chapter, then, will take a light-hearted look at the surface differences – the tip of the cultural iceberg – combined with a consideration of the submarine differences wherein lie the greater threats to mutual trust and co-operation between Europeans. It builds upon the points developed in Chapter 7 and owes much to the work of two Dutch theorists of culture, Fons Trompenaar and, more particularly, Geert Hofstede, whose work we have encountered in the last chapter and which we will consider again here.

Hofstede's approach to culture is, as we have seen, a holistic one. He considers the outward signs (symbols, heroes, rituals) but also the multiple layers from which cultures are constructed (national, regional, ethnic, linguistic, gender, generational, social, educational, occupational, seniority, status). This holistic approach serves to indicate the extraordinary complexity of the subject. It is not my intention to apply his definitions in painstaking detail to the various national cultures that come together to create something European. Rather, I cite Hofstede by way of raising awareness of the complexity. In terms of management we are uniquely placed in Europe as we move towards the next century and ever closer integration. As we have seen in Chapters 3, 4 and 5, economic greatness has to date been achieved by individual nation states. Some have achieved almost imperial business hegemony, but largely through the imposition of a well honed culture and business ethic upon the subject economy. No business culture has yet developed which brings together people from different nations and asks them to manage peoples of different nations again. Our genetic inheritance proves that as individuals we derive from many other individuals and are thus mongrels, but we are nevertheless innately tribal in our responses to the world, closely affiliated to small definable entities, the nation, the family, the company. In asking people to operate multiculturally we are, effectively, asking them to operate counter-intuitively, to operate against their entire training. We need, then, to consider training them to understand the issues they will inevitably confront in others and in themselves. Part of the rationale behind this volume is a pedagogic concern that culture, no less than marketing and finance, should be on the curriculum of the leading European business schools, especially since Europe's future will depend upon the ability of Europeans to find a way of mediating between cultures that are in conflict.

It is worth noting that this is dangerous territory. It is impossible to stand outside, to be immune from the influence of culture; thus any judgement made of other cultures occurs from within a set of preconceptions and prejudices on the part of the person making that judgement, which can distort the conclusions reached. In these egalitarian times judgement is also something that can cause discomfort. It is not my intention to suggest that any one cultural trait is superior to another – although it may well be the case that one cultural trait gives rise to an ability to achieve the highest standards of production while another impedes innovation. My intention is merely to raise awareness of some facets of European cultures that might illuminate relations between the member states of the Union and those other nations that make up the European land mass.

The study of culture is also dangerous territory because, beyond awareness, it is hard to see what the short-term achievements of such study can be.

Culture is very time dependent – cultures take many years to form and cannot be changed on the instant. We have seen, in Chapter 4, the examples of the German and Japanese economic miracles, but have seen equally that the apparently miraculous turnaround of fortunes on the part of both states owed more than a little to a strong cultural heritage and earlier patterns of industrialization. It should come as no surprise that a good deal of the literature on culture is coming from business rather than academe. It is in business and, more specifically, in the context of the corporation that the study of culture can be put to practical use. It is a mistake, however, to assume that the culture of an organization can be changed overnight by the simple expedient, say, of bringing in a new chief executive and changing the top team. Such a strategy can achieve much – the restoration of ailing financial fortunes, cost and head count reduction for instance – but not a fundamental and irreversible change of culture. Companies may not carry the same emblematic weight as a nation and the status of an employee is not that of a citizen, but that does not alter the fact that companies do develop strong cultures, which prove resistant to change. The custodians of that culture are often those who operate at middle management level, those who are not prepared to make the life style sacrifices to progress to the highest levels of management and who have made a commitment to an organization where they feel some comfort and empathy with the core values. It is this population of people who may outlive the tenure of the change agent chief executive who can bring to bear the greatest influence on culture. They, after all, are often the ones who are recruiting into the organization and do so to a culturally derived, unarticulated template. To achieve a true, lasting change in culture a chief executive should look to commit not a mere five years to a company but perhaps as much as three times that. After four or five years it is still perfectly possible (and all too common) for the die-hards from the old culture to fight a rearguard action and restore the former value set. But for the ambitious chief executive who covets a chairmanship, 15 years may seem an extremely long time to devote to a task with so few guarantees of success. So culture is a troubling concept; it strikes at the heart of individuals, it carries with it the implication of value judgements and it is profoundly resilient, hard to change and of massive influence over our lives. Most troubling of all, culture is insidious: we know it is there but we cannot necessarily recognize its principal features and its primary effects.

The importance of the nonverbal

Style of dress, tone of voice and body language have tremendous impact on the good will or effectiveness of any exercise in communication. An act of communication is an event, a package in which the content is but a part. Admittedly the content forms an important part, but its impact can be enhanced or reduced by the accompanying presentation. In service businesses, where the concern on the part of the service provider is to pre-empt the preconceptions and prejudices of the service user, considerable attention is paid to the nonverbal forms of communication and the overall impression one individual can create. Understanding the impact of the nonverbal can be an important element in taking control of the impression one is making on others. In the context of international business, where language deficiencies may put heightened emphasis on the nonverbal, knowledge of how to manage the perceptions of others and, equally, recognize when one's perceptions are being managed can be enormously beneficial.

Dress code

Caricatures of dress are still live around Europe: the English bowler hat, the German *lederhosen*, the Italian sunglasses, dark greased-back hair and Gucci shoes, the French Breton shirt and beret – situation comedies thrive on such shorthand representations of a nation, no matter how little relevance they now have – and they have scant relevance in a world of branded clothing, where casual and formal clothing alike is heavily branded and internationally available. It is not possible in an international boardroom to identify the different nationalities present by dint of specific items of clothing. However, attitudes to dress will offer some clues. The British and the Americans have a more formal approach to work-wear and the navy blue suit, white shirt and conformist IBM look is one that has been borrowed by many Anglo-Saxon style businesses. A continental European is much less likely to adhere to a strict code and will dress elegantly but more casually, indeed with more apparent individualism of style. Different business sectors are regularly depicted as developing different styles of dress – the British stereotypes of the spinning bow tie in the advertising agency, the open toed sandals of the technical wizard and loud braces in the City of London are not without some basis in truth and demonstrate the extent to which dress confers a sense of belonging. Work (and indeed education) is often associated with the donning of a uniform. That uniform in general serves a practical purpose, providing protection perhaps or providing a means of identification. There is also a sense in which by putting on a uniform we leave behind our private selves and enter upon a public stage. The evidence that we often develop uniforms spontaneously testifies to the emotional importance of uniformity, shared identity and belonging. So it is that attention paid to style of dress can soften or emphasize impact very significantly.

For women in business the matter of a dress code can be particularly fraught. The impression a woman creates in our Western culture remains inextricably linked with appearance and female clothing is infinitely more varied than the standard male uniform of trousers, shirt and jacket. Skirt or trousers, length of skirt, height of heels – all carry particular connotations. Trousers can give the confidence of making a woman feel and appear no different from her male colleagues/clients or opponents but, equally, might appear a defensive/aggressive act. A short skirt can be powerful and defiant or provocative and inappropriate. The wearing of perfume, an apparently innocuous act, can also have some impact on the impression created – the more so since the sense of smell is one of the most evocative, not least because we cannot recreate a scent once we are removed from it. Does a floral perfume denote yielding femininity? Alternatively does a lemon and astringent perfume suggest an acerbic character? Apparently trivial, superficial considerations these surface elements of the overall package have an impact far beyond that which is generally understood.

Voice

The voice can reveal much about the person. Clearly, in most countries it can betray regional or social origins, although only an exceptional linguist could identify these nuances in a second language. More than this, however, the voice can be an extremely flexible tool in presentations. The tone of voice adopted, the volume and the modulation can deliver a message as effectively as the words contained in that message. In an international context it is important to be aware of the influence of the voice over and above the words and to measure the style of others – some cultures will find a particular tone of voice hectoring which to others might appear simply direct and pragmatic.

Alternatively, a softly spoken voice might convey authority to one culture, weakness or vacillation to another.

Body language

The body speaks as loudly as the voice, but is less easily within the conscious control of the individual. The highly intuitive or perceptive person can often sense the mood or true meaning of their companion by an almost instinctive registering of the nonverbal communication made through a combination of gesture, posture and movement. A study of the subject can pay dividends, especially where the verbal and the nonverbal do not appear to be synchronized, where there is in fact dissonance. In such instances the source of conflict can be reached more quickly than without the additional information derived via a deciphering of the nonverbal clues.

The most obvious example of body language is that of the handshake, the vice-like grip versus the dead fish, the thrust-down palm or the two-handed shake much beloved of politicians. First impressions are often heavily influenced by the initial interpretation of the hand. The distance between people when they speak or shake hands can indicate levels of comfort or liking and the ability to recognize the amount of space an individual requires (and so to avoid invading that space) can be an important element in putting that person at their ease. The position of the hands (clasped, at ease by the person's side, or behind the back), the sitting position (cross-legged and cross-armed), the direction of a person's gaze (straight in the eye or beyond to a spot in the distance or to the side) are all instant indicators of levels of relaxation, discomfiture, confidence, trust or openness. Changes in position are useful signs of changes in mood. The body language of one person may interact with that of their companion, often reflecting it, sometimes deferring to it and occasionally at sharp variance with it. If one individual is relaxed but their companion is cross-armed with clenched hands then there is clear dissonance and a breakdown of communication. Allan Pease's 1993 publication *Body Language* provides a very useful guide on how body language can be read and interpreted.

The nonverbal is as culturally conditioned as the verbal – the Japanese, for instance, would expect a far higher degree of formality which would be reflected in voice, dress and body language than would Europeans and decoding the nonverbal is, at best, an art rather than a science. Nevertheless it is a subject that repays study, particularly in an international context, where sensitive communications are critical amongst people who do not start from the position of strongly shared values. In short, an understanding both of the impact and import of the nonverbal can be a very useful skill in the armoury of the business leader who operates internationally.

National traits – a survey of European 'types'

In quantum mechanics, interference in an experiment by an observer can determine the outcome of that experiment. Similarly, in another discipline, literary theory makes much of the role of the reader in the ultimate meaning of a text, undermining the notion of authorial intention. In an analogous way, as noted above, no observer of other cultures comes to the subject without considerable baggage derived from their own cultural conditioning. The following survey of European types may reveal as much about the author as about the cultures of Europe but, drawing on Richard Hill's excellent summary of European culture *Euro-Managers and Martians*, it attempts to bring together commonly held views that have stood the test of some 20 years' experience of businessmen and women across Europe. The survey is not exhaustive. I focus on the larger economies and, exclusively, on members of the EU.

Germany

In the 1970s the author spent time studying theoretical physics at the University of Bonn. Coming from the liberal British university system of the 1960s and early 70s, I was amazed to be required to stand up when the lecturer came in, sit down on his command, copy out reams of notes which could have been photocopied and distributed before the lecture and, most particularly, I was astounded by the embargo on asking questions. It was simply not done. At the end of the session, the lecturer would leave and the students would stand up. Two things struck me: first, the age of the students and the length of their study – half a life-time or so it seemed; second, the deference for authority was something that I had not encountered in so pronounced a form. I was made forcibly aware of my difference from these people, the cultural gulf between a

British and a German student and, by extension, British and German cultures.

Germany is a nation that valorizes expertise, in sharp contrast to Britain where we have long applauded the enthusiastic amateur. Considerable respect is conferred on those who can demonstrate expertise, through hard study rewarded by sound qualifications. The area in which Germany excels is that of manufacture, as we have seen in Chapter 4. The nation has grown economically great through its manifest ability to educate its population in the research and production skills required to produce some of the highest-quality goods in the world. It is impossible to assess whether the Germans excel in manufacturing because of particular cultural traits or whether the long-standing excellence in manufacturing has influenced the development of a certain cultural predisposition towards the proven, the logical, the sequential – the palpable. Not for Germans the grey areas of ambiguity, the spaces within which the French spirit soars. On the contrary, Germans need a high level of detail, of proof, before they will commit to a particular project or agree to a particular view. This native caution is reflected in the predilection for long-term planning and for long-standing relationships with key business partners, as seen in the style of Rhine capitalism the country practises (see Chapter 4), the heavy involvement of the banks in the running of companies and the long-term planning that the Germans have favoured.

Language can give some clues to the culture of a nation – although to what extent language shapes or is shaped by culture must be a subject for separate study. The German language has a relatively harsh, guttural sound (in contrast to the softer, expansive romance languages – and even the delineation *romance* implies some cultural influences). Its grammar is difficult and its vocabulary extremely precise. It is a language that is governed by rules and the learning of those rules can be extremely difficult for someone for whom a less rule-based language is their mother tongue. The German psyche appears to respond well to rules, evident in the respect for authority and the liking for the proven, the palpable. The language has a word with no adequate translation into English: *ordnung*. Apparently close to the word 'order', that gloss offers only a partial translation. It does not convey the same sense of discipline, both personal and professional, of timeliness, tidiness and proper form contained within the German word. It is of considerable importance to the German psyche that things be in their proper order. Lack of structure and sloppiness greatly offend the sense of *ordnung*.

It is this sense of *ordnung* which influences the consensus style of management practised by the Germans (some concern to avoid the autocracy of the past may also play a part in this). Almost fanatically rigorous and thorough, a German organization will operate a long consultative process before taking a major decision. In contrast to a French or British company, where the decision of those at the head of the business is often the only requirement, the German preference for lengthy consultation gives rise to long lead times. However, the pay-off comes once a decision is implemented. I am reminded of a story of a consultant who was trying to sell a similar project to a German and a British telecommunications company. It took seven–eight months to get all the different groups that mattered in the German company to align on the project and to ensure that everyone involved in it from the bottom of the organization to the top understood the implications of the project. From start to finish, the sales process took 11 months. The British took only two months to buy the project. However, when the consultant came to launch the project he found that there was no consensus among the various management levels of the business as to what the key parameters of the project were or should be. In some areas there was considerable resistance to the work. A year later, nothing of merit had come out of the project. In Germany, once the decision had been ratified work proceeded smoothly and substantive findings came out of the project within six months. Not surprisingly, the consultant now does more work in Germany than he does in the UK. The concern for consultation in Germany might appear to contradict the reverence for authority that exists side by side with it. On the contrary, the two are complementary. Germans respect know-how and if know-how resides at a low managerial level then it is as worthy of respect as that at the senior levels. Respect works, as in Japan, on the principle of reciprocity.

The harsh sound of the language and the direct style of communication between Germans often leads people to assume that Germans lack warmth. This mistaken impression is compounded by the formality of the language, the necessity to use *Sie* and to avoid the use of first names until a strong relationship is established. This is merely a further manifestation of *ordnung*, of a preference for the slowly but fully developed over the spontaneous.

What influence do these cultural traits bring to bear in business? Clearly, as we have seen in Chapter 4, short-term innovation can suffer and in an international context the requirement to move at a slow German pace can prove a frustration to the nationals of France, Italy or Britain. The need to know, the antipathy to the over-subtle or ill-defined can further arrest creativity. The overwhelmingly formal style, a reluctance to trust too quickly, might impede the development of service businesses, which could be problematic for an economy where the mainstay manufacturing industries will face growing competitive threats from the newly industrializing nations of Asia. Change, for Germans, is unsettling because of the inherent ambiguity so the option to move into new sectors where rapid change is required is not one that is realistically open to them.

Germans and French share a commitment to the notion of Europe but are otherwise extremely unlike. A case study that was carried out by Heidrick & Struggles in 1992 on the differences between German and French management, in which were surveyed the managing directors of the top 200 companies in both countries, found a number of factors to contrast:

- German managers and leaders were much more likely to be groomed by their current firm than those in France. More than 70% of bosses in Germany began their careers at the level of middle management or lower in the firm and now lead, compared with 30% in France.
- Some 36% of French managing directors were parachuted into their posts from outside the firm while only 16% of German managing directors got their job this way.
- The number of managing directors poached from state jobs was six times higher in France than in Germany.
- Germany stresses training in industry as the route to the top job whereas high flyers in France graduated from elite schools.
- Other major differences showed that the French knew much more about the workings of the government, of the state and the political interplay between government and state than their German equivalents. There are closer parallels with this type of training between the UK and Germany than there is with France.
- Half of the top French managers came from three Grands Ecoles – the Polytechnique, the ENA and HEC – and the German equivalents came from many different schools and backgrounds and had more parallels with the US.

Within these substantial differences, however, there remain strong cultural links, which we shall consider further in Chapter 10. It would be wrong, of course, to assume that the strong German culture implies a wholly homogenous country. Just as its industry is represented by large companies and a huge rump of small to medium-sized businesses, so is its culture more variegated than the above analysis would appear to suggest. Germany is a large country. Its status as the largest European nation at the very heart of the land mass confers a certain identity on the totality of Germany, but it is a country with a strong regional tradition where the separate states, the *Lander*, are very strong. Regional differences between Germans can be pronounced. The Bavarians, for example, are a conservative, farming people, known for their pride and regarded as excessively rural by their more sophisticated (urban) countrymen. The northern states, in contrast, home to Hamburg and Berlin, are much more liberal and relaxed. Their citizens are livelier than the Bavarians, more carefree and share more cultural characteristics with the citizens of Paris or London than with those of Munich. Nevertheless, despite these regional strengths, a common language, a common recent history and, indeed, a strong sense of collective guilt combine to reinforce the strength and unity of Germany's culture.

France

If the German is the most direct and predictable of European cultures the same cannot be said of the French. At the heart of French society is a core contradiction, which manifests itself in contradictory impulses in its people. A strong historical and intellectual commitment to equality and social conscience co-exists with what some would characterize as rampant individuality, which can promote selfishness at the expense of the collective. The notion of schism and dichotomy underpins the French Cartesian philosophic tradition, which posits a split between the mind on the one hand and the body and the material world on the other. It is, however, the turbulence of history to which we must turn to trace the roots of the primary contradiction. The revolution, which fuelled the Romantic movement and appeared to unite peoples under the banner of freedom, in fact gave birth to a certain 'rights movement' which, as we can see in the example of twentieth-century America, leads logically to the individual rather than the collective. Romanticism, of course, is based on the individual sensibility. France's history of autocratic government and a strongly centralized state has added to the actual emphasis on the individual in opposition to the theoretical concern for more abstract ideals such as *liberté*, *egalité, fraternité*. As noted in Chapter 1, Francis Fukuyama's thesis that France is a low-trust nation holds water. Few intermediary associations have existed between the person and the state; thus the person and the state have become the most important institutions influencing French culture. The notion of the French nation, for instance, exerts an extraordinary pull on its citizens. It is harder to uproot French citizens and move them to another country than the citizens of any other state, for there is a firmly held belief that French is best. The passion for France is represented in the passion for its language and the organized endeavours to maintain its purity from the inroads of English/American. Just as it is hard to move people out of France, it is equally difficult to move the non-French into France. Integration is slow and those who have not partaken of the extraordinary French education system find it difficult to gain the respect of their peers in business who will, almost exclusively, be products of one of the elite educational establishments.

I will consider the French education system in more detail in Chapter 9. For the purposes of this chapter, suffice it to say that the system embodies the contradiction between individualism and egalitarianism. In principle the system should develop one of the most meritocratic societies in Europe. Theoretically open to all, French students are educated to an extremely high level from which the very best are selected to run the state and the key industries of state. In practice, the education system has become the preserve of a small elite. Its rigour, furthermore, demands extraordinary dedication on the part of young students and a clear commitment to self-improvement or self-stylization, which is increasingly culturally conditioned within the middle classes to the exclusion of the working classes whom, theoretically at any rate, the system should serve. While it is easy to criticize the form of the system it is difficult to criticize its content. More than any other European education system, the French teach their students to debate, to build rationally from one point to another, to test the logic of a hypothesis and to find the flaws in that hypothesis.

This training is evident in the French approach to business. A French board will be very comfortable with, indeed excel at, the delineation and redefinition of strategy. The French mind is positively at ease with ambiguity and will leave meaning to be found in nuance as much as in the directly spoken word. The development of new ideas, the solution of problems – these are major strengths for the French and the absence of a clear strategy, a well-honed rationale for any action will cause considerable discomfort. Indeed, in managing the French, it is never enough to direct. The logic behind the direction *must* be watertight. Once a French team has tested that logic and found it to be robust then it will work towards implementation as a united team. Implementation, however, is not the first love of the French; instead they prefer initiation. Intellectually innovative, it comes as no surprise that France has spawned some of the best mathematical brains: Lagrange, Leguerre, Laplace (Lagrange was Italian born but adopted French nationality). Today mathematicians and engineers are accorded particular respect within French culture. This level of innovation is highly abstracted. The type of innovation which leads to entrepreneurial endeavour is much less common in France, because it is much more grounded in the concrete.

There is a strong divide in France between the public and the private, reflecting the twin but distinct influences of the family and the state on the populace. The French do not mix business with pleasure but maintain distinct personae to suit either context. This leads to a certain distance but also a clear focus. The French businessman, aware that he is the product of an exceptionally gruelling education, can seem arrogant. The French chief executive can seem closer in spirit to a British entrepreneur for there is a strong (but diminishing) sense that the *president directeur general* (PDG) is the owner of the company. Certainly, in the past, key decisions have been taken by the PDG and the board has been required to rubber stamp those decisions. The board has been happy to acquiesce in this situation because of a shared sense that the PDG is proven to have the exceptional qualities required to lead. This is changing as the need for transparency in governance gains greater recognition around Europe.

In summary, then, a Frenchman on the board of an international company will ensure that the strategic direction of that company is the right one, will insist that the logic behind the strategy is robust and will ensure that it is modified in accordance with changing conditions. He or she will also initiate, come up with new ideas and will probe the ideas put forward by others. His interest will wane a little at the point of implementation. In style the French director will be comfortable with uncertainty and not afraid to increase the uncertainty in pursuit of a better, clearer answer. Subtle and attuned to nuance, he or she will be impatient of the overly direct and reductive style of Anglo-Saxons and this can give rise to conflict and mistrust. Above all, the French director will bring imagination and a set of sophisticated judgements to the board.

United Kingdom

Lord Hailsham summed up the British character thus:

> *'The British are notable for their sentimentality which they mistake for a virtue hence their ability to deceive themselves, which others mistake as hypocrisy.'*

In this damning, if affectionate, indictment there is considerable truth. The British, who regard themselves as scrupulous and fair are often regarded by others as double-dealing and hypocritical. This can be traced to a common cultural obsession. While France is obsessed with the notion of the nation, the British worship the past. The heritage industry is booming and the British identity is bound up with former imperial glory. This confers a natural arrogance on the average Briton, a sense that the British way is the best way, that British institutions are the best in the world. Part of Britain's heritage was a strong aristocratic tradition and elements of that tradition linger, in the British predilection for clubs and in the highly mannered way in which the British interact and from which comes the charge of hypocrisy. The British are no lovers of conflict and nor are they direct. Disagreement may be couched in the form of agreement, rhetoric may be used to conceal rupture and apparent sincerity may prove, on closer inspection, quite hollow.

The British have an abhorrence of trying too hard and a love of the enthusiastic amateur, again a feature of the fiendish class system, the underbelly of the aristocratic tradition, which dictates that the overt creation of wealth is somehow distasteful. Similarly, overt ambition is vulgar. Business, which exists for the sole purpose of making money and feeds on personal ambition, does not enjoy quite the status of some of the professions. Interestingly, no member of the British royal family has opted to enter business although many have spent their working lives in the armed forces. For outsiders coming to Britain the machinations of the class system can seem too complex to be grasped. All elements of life and person are subject to class judgements which, however, liberal the individual, are made almost instinctively by every Briton who can place an accent or an attitude within the social spectrum on the instant. The impossibility of so classifying non-Brits can be disorientating and make the islander feel uncomfortable. In a European context Britain's island status cannot be overlooked. Britain is a reluctant European, more at ease with its former colonies and happier to extend its relationship with the continent across the

Atlantic than the one across the Channel. In part the comfort of a shared language must inform this preference but the continuity with the past is not unimportant. United with mainland Europe only in the last decade of the twentieth century (via the Channel Tunnel), Britain's emotional links still reside in the commonwealth and America, in the sites of former hegemony.

The obsession with the past does not mean that the British are incapable of change and flexibility. On the contrary, the British are good mixers, gregarious, at ease in groups with a relaxed, bantering style which can balance the formality of the German or the distance of the French styles. Wit, humour and spontaneity are all admired in British culture and give rise to outstanding presentational skills. It is no accident that British television and advertising is internationally admired – it builds on this expansive, witty public tradition. Profoundly anti-intellectual, the British have a courageous have-a-go mentality which enables them to try out the new without the prevarication of some of their European partners. Not surprisingly, then, the British have produced a number of entrepreneurs – rarely people from within the ranks of the middle and upper classes, but the anarchic, determined, have-a-go self-made man. The British are pragmatists, the products of an empirical philosophical tradition, more interested in solving a problem than ensuring the problem is fully understood in all its dimensions. This can have its uses in a business context where time to meditate upon a problem is rarely available. Alternatively, a tendency to act first and think later can undermine the success of some enterprises.

The British mentality in business is something of a trading mentality. The immediacy of a transaction plays to British pragmatism and presentational ability without the need for high levels of technical expertise. The British have failed in providing a strong technological education or indeed any form of commercial education. The London Business School, for instance, was not founded until the 1960s whereas the Harvard Business School was founded in 1907. The Industrial Revolution may have come about in Britain (the influence of the courageous have-a-go mind set) but it took the Germans and the Americans to extend it technologically. The British are more comfortable with the inception and development of a new idea than its longer-term planning and extension.

A British director on an international board will strive to make things happen. He will not be daunted by the need to change direction and will have the humour and the interpersonal skill-set to persuade and carry others with him. The British sense of hierarchy has meant that there is little focus on communication down an organization, little regard for gaining consensus (as we have seen above in contrast with the German *modus operandi*), which can undermine the longer term success of a venture. An ironic cast of mind can make the Brit hard to manage, as the British approach authority with a natural scepticism and a strong tendency to judge. A disinclination for adequate planning could make the incautious Brit a liability rather than an asset, but the British director will be strongest where there is a critical need for a swift solution to a problem.

Italy

In Italy the family is the small unit at the centre of social cohesion. Other than the institution of the Roman Catholic church, the family is the only social construct of any moment. Italians are enormously individualistic (and the family is a tribal, clannish unit with a distinct identity and personality) and working together in large enterprises is alien to them. In Fukuyama's terms of reference, Italy is an archetypal low-trust society in which individuals are dependent on their own resources and highly suspicious of others. The prevalent stereotype of the Italian is the gangland Mafioso and, while the stock image is undoubtedly comic, the prototype of the Italian family out of its milieu is not without some interest. The Francis Ford Coppola trilogy of *Godfather* films depicts a migrant Italian family in New York who are at the centre of organized crime. Here the Corleone family has a distinct identity and is the single most important institution in the lives of its members ('Never take sides against the family') but is not immune to mistrust even within its own ranks. As the family extends, Michael the new don culls even his own brother in an attempt to protect himself and his immediate circle. Yet the family's tremendous success is a tribute to inventiveness and flexibility, fearlessness and a disregard for conformity. The films provide a not uninteresting and not irrelevant insight into some elements of Italian culture, which are thrown into relief once Italians are removed from the locale of Italy. I would not wish to imply that the stereotype of the Mafioso is a paradigm for the average Italian, but the cultural elements that gave rise to the organized crime rings in Sicily, Italy and in the US are live ones, which in a different context can be very positive.

In general, Italians function much less well out of their home environment and are ill at ease in the commercial world of the multinational. The business model best suited to Italian culture is the small unit, the family business that manufactures high quality, design-led products. Italy is the home of the Renaissance and if the beauty of the environment has any bearing on the citizens domiciled there then that is sufficient explanation for the strength of the Italian aesthetic. Italy excels in the arena of *haute couture* and fashion and, on the technical side, in the precision business of machine tool manufacture. All such businesses actively benefit from small production units. Indeed, assembly line production is entirely alien to the Italian way of being. Craftsmanship or artisan work in which there is space for individual expertise is all-important. When there is unity of purpose and clarity of direction Italians can be enormously effective, combining flair with determination. Italian football teams are a testimony to this, with many players being highly sought after in foreign leagues.

There is not the clear dividing line between family and business in Italy that we have seen in France. French networks stem from the Grand Ecole system, Italian networks from the family. There is far higher incidence of nepotism in Italy than elsewhere in Europe. One of the negative aspects of Italian culture is that corruption could be said to be endemic, as exemplified by successive political regimes. In striking contrast to Germany, Italy is not a rule-based nation. There is, if anything, a generalized predilection for rule-avoidance – a symptom of a highly individualistic society. Rules exist for others to obey and Italians have turned the bending or circumventing of rules into an art form (they are the most astute of tax avoiders in Europe, followed closely by that other low-trust nation, the French). Commercially, however, this disdain for rules can be highly effective. Italian inventiveness is seldom constrained by rules and Italian entrepreneurialism is given considerable edge by the absence of formal and widely upheld business structures. Business hierarchies exist, but within them the individual relationships forged will determine decision-making procedures far more than any position in that hierarchy.

The face of Italian business is changing. The state sector is in the process of privatization and the large family-run businesses are opening up (Pirelli and Olivetti). At their very best, like the de Beneditti empire, Benetton, the Italians are able to export their entrepreneurial activity. However, unlike Germany, France, the UK and Holland, it is a country with relatively few global companies and has, in recent years, succumbed to dominance by companies from other countries such as Unilever, BSN, Jacob Suchard, Nestlé, Electrolux and Pharmacia, all of which have made strong inroads into Italian business.

Italy needs to strengthen its core businesses in other ways if she is to have the economic horsepower to be self-sustaining.

Italian culture manifests itself in a certain opportunism, a keen entrepreneurial sense and an ability to thrive on ambiguity and risk. As a consequence Italians can be wildly creative, although this creativity may not be fully supported by deductive logic, tactical and implementation skills. Italians are imaginative, innovative and can be the instigators of much – they are the implementers of little. If the Italians are the instigator of something, it takes the Germans, Americans or Dutch to implement it. Money-making skills are highly prized. Timekeeping is not key but personal business relationships, warmth and creativity are valued enormously. In an international context Italians can prove hard to manage, reluctant to be managed and charismatic, but potentially autocratic, managers. Italians have the ability to develop small enterprises very successfully, but making the transition to larger-scale businesses is problematic, necessitating a counter-cultural imposition of and adherence to rules and regimens. Italy, like Germany, was only united in the nineteenth century and as such has sustained substantial regional differences. The north/south divide in Italy is stronger than that in the UK and the central regions, the *Terza Italia* (the third Italy, distinguishing them from the traditionally distinct north and south), are different again. The above cultural traits are evident in varying degrees, with northern Italians resembling the Germans and Swiss and Southern Italians conforming more closely to the standard stereotypes.

Spain

There are clear parallels between Spain and various of the nations of Europe, and the ability to liken the country to several other nations all unlike each other suggests the complexity of Spanish culture. Like Britain, Spain has through history been cut off from Europe. As Britain is an island Spain is one-half of the Iberian peninsula – cut off from the mainland of Continental Europe by the Pyrenees. Very much a maritime culture, Spain – again like those other maritime cultures the British and the Dutch – sailed overseas to build an empire. Spain, then, for some centuries looked across the Atlantic to the Americas. Its empire was won very quickly and dissipated as rapidly for much the same reasons as the British empire (although predating the British experience by a couple of centuries). Poor investment and the tendency of the mercantile classes to seek after status and social position rather than to reinvest led to the decline of the Spanish empire. Physically distinct from much of Europe, Spain has also been politically and economically isolated, re-entering the mainstream of European life as recently as 1975 with the death of Franco (joining the EU in 1986). Like Germany and Italy the country is heavily regionalized and, like Brussels and Switzerland, divided internally by a series of different languages and dialects. Also, like Italy it is a culture where the family and the state have had little between (other than the Roman Catholic church) and it is as a consequence a culture that, by Fukuyama's measure, would be defined as low trust. It has, however, seen an extraordinary transformation in a very few years, moving in the post-war period from being a third-world economy to one of the largest in the world. In this it mirrors the German economic miracle, although the miracle has been achieved by economic liberalization on the French model. The country has also, miraculously, moved from totalitarianism to democracy in two decades – providing a template for eastern Europe. In terms of a business culture Spain does not have one that is uniquely its own. Historically Spain is a largely agricultural economy. Business is being encouraged by the state and the unique institution the *Opus Dei* (an investment arm of the Church), but most business activity consists of large multinationals operating in Spain. There are few indigenous large companies of world-beating order, although as an ambitious education programme starts to bear fruit we can look to changes across the country.

What are the cultural implications or inferences to be drawn from the above? In the first place, Spain – like Britain – is a mannered society where civility and courtesy count for much. This can have the effect of confusing communications as a Spaniard struggles to disagree too openly. The influence of the *Opus Dei*, which seeks to extend Christian values in everyday life through lobbying employers and employees, testifies to a strong moral sense on the part of the Spanish and an equally strong fear of its erosion. The combination of courtly manners and a high moral tone can give the Spanish the appearance of inflexibility and rigidity. However, to have experienced such change at such an accelerated pace strongly contradicts this impression; and here we must cite the diversity of Spanish life, the huge regional variations that make Spain something of a microcosm of Europe as a whole. Spaniards have the ability to change quickly because in their internal national dealings they are perennially confronted by difference and diversity. The manners and morality provide a shell, an outer structure within which there is considerable room for manoeuvre and, like Italy with its family-based society, it is a culture of some individualism in which that degree of latitude is fully exploited. Spain is not a rule-based nation but it is one in which there is abundant bureaucracy, which the Spanish circumvent in much the same way as the Italians avoid structures and rules. To date, however, Spain has not demonstrated the same level of entrepreneurial verve as Italy. Instead, like the French the Spanish venerate the cerebral and, like the British, favour professional service above commerce. Spain's economic future probably rests with those Spaniards who are currently employed in multinationals and are imbibing the cultural principles that enable the development of big businesses. For the moment the country is a patchwork of small and medium-sized enterprises with state-encouraged manufacturing industry but little in the way of promising multinational companies.

Holland

Dutch culture demonstrates an extraordinary dualism between the moral and the material. Various strains of religious thought have long been influential (although the society has become increasingly secular since the 1960s) and, equally, Holland has a long tradition of mercantile success. Indeed, so successful was the Dutch trading empire in the seventeenth century that in his chronicle of Dutch society at the peak of its mercantile success Simon Schama speaks of 'the embarrassment of riches', the phrase in itself conjuring the polarity of morality versus materialism. The tension between these two poles creates, on the one hand, a people who are given to conform, to rally around a particular set of beliefs and values and, on the other, a set of highly assertive individualists who can barter and negotiate with the best in the world. As we have seen, Max Weber has drawn a strong link between Protestantism and the spirit of capitalism, which the Dutch model would appear to support. Similarly, Holland provides another exemplar of Fukuyama's theory that those nations with a tradition of intermediary associations (between the family and the state) are better able to develop multinational organizations than those without that marzipan layer. Holland has a staggering array of multinationals for a country of its size, reflecting the numerous organizations that form the *pillars* of Dutch society.

So how does Dutch culture, or this dualism, manifest itself? One of the most notable features of the Dutch (as with the Germans) is the direct style of upbringing culminating in the award of a Shell International Petroleum Scholarship to Cambridge University. After university he joined a British-owned conglomerate, Rio Tinto Zinc, where he remained for four years before deciding to accelerate his career development by joining a smaller company called Brandts Ltd, a timber merchants. In 1975 he joined the company that was to do much to nurture his innate talent, the pharmaceuticals, horticulture and scientific instruments business, Fisons. Again, Fisons was a British-owned company. He rose to be one of the top dozen or so executives in the business before he was headhunted in 1981 to join Redland plc, of which he became first the Finance Director and then the Chief Executive in 1991. Like many top business people he has studied on a business programme, taking the Harvard Advanced Management Programme in 1987. This, however, was much later in his career than the formal business education undertaken by some of the other European leaders we have encountered and of much briefer duration. The qualities of flexibility which allow Robert to run one company with an impressive European presence and to serve as an outside director on another which is also becoming increasingly European in orientation (United Biscuits) clearly cannot be traced to childhood or educational influences. Rather, it seems to me, there is something to be said about the business function in which Robert has excelled.

Robert Napier had pursued a career in the finance function until he made the move into general management. Finance is an excellent choice of function for those with aspirations to run a business but, curiously, among the leaders considered here most have either a marketing or sales bias, or have a broad commercial background with exposure to more than one function. Many people would throw up their hands with horror if they were to hear me say that there is an element of objectivity to the finance function that is not matched in, say sales or marketing. Numbers, as much as words, can be read and interpreted differently and finance can be as creative as much as marketing can depend upon the numeracy of its exponents. There is, however, a certain dispassionate stance that the head of any finance function is obliged to adopt – the finance director must act as a check and control on all other aspects of the business – which those in marketing or production can disdain. In heavily product-related areas there is and must be a strong identification with the company, a wholehearted endorsement of its image and operating ethos. In finance this must be more reasoned; behind all judgements must lie the consideration whether or not a project is firmly financially founded – a consideration to those in other departments but not the overriding one. I attribute then to the finance function a degree of neutrality within a given business, a certain distance which conveys authority (and there is a strong correlation between distance and authority). More than this, finance is an international language and the skills, as with those of people in the IT or personnel function, are directly transferable from one industry to another. The same cannot be said for research, production or even sales and marketing. This transferability of skills lends further flexibility to a function which is often, wrongly, held to be inward looking and thus insular.

Controlling the devil in the detail

Robert Napier's personal style is challenging and his is a quest for precision. This concern for detail is often associated with the training in finance he has undergone. I have found that it is a particular feature of this group of European leaders. Flexibility must not be mistaken for any degree of fuzziness. On the contrary, each of these people – personally aware of the pitfalls of international communication – is careful to understand and to be understood, to erase unnecessary ambiguity. Crispin Davies would also underline the importance of repetition, of clarifying one's position. His thesis is that consistency is a large measure of what enables a leader to sustain a position of strong leadership. A consistent message (provided, of course, it is well founded) gives those who follow something explicit to support and, in the service of consistency, the regular repetition of a message is more than welcome. An introverted character, François Cornelis shows the same concern for clarity as does Alain Levy and both will call for repetition in the service of clarity – each works hard as a listener, calling upon the highest levels of precision in those with whom they interact.

In my capacity as a headhunter I interview a wide and diverse range of people. In general I am obliged to be the listener but I take great care to assess the capability for listening of each and every interviewee I encounter, for the absence of this skill can undercut the presence of many others. Listening skills in business are equivalent to reading skills in other walks of life (like the civil service, perhaps). This is because business, partly as a result of its increasingly international dimensions, partly because of the speed of response required, is the relative poverty of his family. He worked through his school and university holidays and has always been driven by a desire to avoid future financial need. In Crispin Davies' case determination was almost programmed into him at a young age. One of four brothers, all of whom have been exceptionally successful in their chosen careers, he attributes that success to a considerable degree of coaxing and encouragement in particular from his mother.

Emotional independence

No amount of determination, even where it is coupled with a fierce intellect, can compensate for a lack of independence. The most striking feature about the European leaders I have met is a certain quality of independence and it is this which enables them to look quizzically and questioningly upon every situation that they encounter. As a leader it is inappropriate to depend too closely upon any one person for support and advice for impartiality is a prerequisite of leadership. A person who needs to be liked is not a person who can take on the mantle of leadership for either their desire for approbation or, much worse, their impartiality will be compromised by the demands of decisions that will not always be universally popular or beneficial. For some, independence is derived from overcoming early adversity, learning that one has only oneself on whom to depend. For others it is a function of familial relationships. Robert Napier, for instance, is an only child who is necessarily more accustomed to going it alone. It is interesting to consider the extent to which financial independence can inform a general sense of independence. Robert Louis-Dreyfus is the scion of a wealthy and influential French family. His achievements are entirely the product of his own abilities and actions and, as we have seen, he has never been afraid to seek the most risk-laden opportunities. Perhaps there is, however, some element of security that derives from such a background, which enables him to take these risks? The ability to stand alone depends, however, on a very high degree of self-belief. Self-belief is not arrogance (although occasionally it may take that form), rather it is the unflinching faith in one's own feelings, thoughts and conclusions. I have often thought the quality that most characterized leaders is a certain courage, the courage to believe completely in themselves. Crispin Davis corrected me. In his view, what leadership takes is conviction. Probably leadership is, in essence, about having the courage of one's convictions, a pot pourri of the two views.

Vision

It is conviction and belief that enable individuals to bring about change. It is with the bringing about of change that we come to the achievements that bring leaders to notice. Each of the business leaders considered here has wrought change. Some have built businesses. Win Bischoff built the Asian business for Schroders. Robert Louis-Dreyfus built IMS, a world-wide market research and information business, which under his leadership grew from a $230 million operation to one with sales of around $1.6 billion. Not content with building one business he went on to rebuild one (Saatchi and Saatchi) and is now in the process of rebuilding a second (Adidas). Louis-Dreyfus then is living proof that a successful formula can be repeated. Alain Levy built the French business for CBS before going on to build a substantial US presence for Polygram. Others of our leaders have taken their businesses into new geographical areas: Robert Napier at Redland, Eric Nicoli at United Biscuits, Timo Peltola at Huhtamaki and François Cornelis at Petrofina. Crispin Davies at United Distillers combined the imposition of a much more crisp, marketing-oriented culture with the acquisition of numerous new businesses and their integration into the company. Ultimately he and the Guinness board could not reach final agreement and so he left and has now gone to Aegis, where he has imposed focus and clarity on a business that has undergone several crises of identity in recent years. For others among European business leaders there has been a marked turnaround in a company's fortunes that has brought them to particular notice. Peter Davis has a blend of achievements, having built a new business for British retailer Sainsbury (the Savacentre joint venture with another retailer British Home Stores) and then turned around the ailing Reed Publishing business to the point that it could be merged with the Elsevier business to create a highly competitive whole. Kjell Nilsson, moving from Electrolux to Trelleborg, made his impact on the organization he was later to head up through the turnaround of a newly acquired business, Boliden, in which Trelleborg held 44% of the equity. It was losing so much money at the point at which Kjell took on the problem that it posed a severe financial threat to Trelleborg. Within 12 months Kjell had reduced costs, cut overheads, handled union problems in the process and ensured that a much healthier company could survive. In all these endeavours the leaders have combined a clear vision based on shrewd analysis with articulate and compelling delivery.

Charisma

All have charisma, but in the very nature of charisma, its exact quality defies definition. Some like Robert Napier and Timo Peltola are more introverted but have the authority of highly lucid minds and discriminating judgement to lend them considerable stature. Others are larger than life. Alain Levy, not a tall man, is, however, an impressive presence. This is a mixture of his intense gaze, considered response, leonine head and outsize cigars. With Eric Nicoli it is barely suppressed energy which informs those who meet him of his drive, while Crispin Davies has an energy of speech, a level of emphasis which demonstrates his own self-belief and conviction. Robert Louis-Dreyfus and Peter Davis are very different men but share an urbane manner and very distinct charm, which make them both highly attractive companions. Kjell Nilsson is the most obviously larger than life. He has the power to take over a room, a power that is present even when he is silent. He is not a naturally silent man.

On the subject of leadership qualities it is all too possible to state much and say little, but a picture emerges of those people who can undertake the challenge of leading businesses that we have defined as European, businesses that depend upon diversity and difference. The peculiar challenge in a European business is to be able to recognize these strengths, to allow local difference and diversity to coexist within a consolidated organizational whole which can achieve consistency of standards. In our group of European leaders who, themselves, appear to enshrine the difference and diversity of which so much has been said, we can see that none are partisan. None identify too strongly with any national interest group but move flexibly and freely across the international stage. Indeed, each of these individuals takes their definition not from without but from within. They share a seemingly inexhaustible vein of self-belief that manifests itself in clear vision which is stated with conviction. Win Bischoff confided in me that before a major client meeting he can still feel butterflies, that element of first-night stage fright, while Alain Levy, who defends the earnings of his clients who get up on stage each night, does so with a passion because he is, albeit unconsciously, sharing in the agony of performance. Leadership is about performance, about standing at a distance from most others, presenting an acceptable persona, not diverting from that persona, and ensuring that there is integrity in that persona. Leaders set examples and all of the European leaders we have encountered above are conscious that they are models through which will be ciphered the future culture of the companies they now lead. The European leader then must appear to come from nowhere and everywhere and to be someone who can speak to everyone. In being all things to all people, however, we cannot get too close to them. Few have shared much about their lives beyond the board room and when I read of Percy Barnevik's refusal even to acknowledge the ages of his children I am not surprised. Part of what enables these people to be such public property must be the protection of a part of themselves, their private life, from public scrutiny. However much we can come to understand the leader in the persona of leader, we must always stop short of a more intimate knowledge of the person beneath the persona.

What precedent does Europe have for forging a coherent culture and thus what chance does it have for evolving a new business culture – how, through whom and using which skills? These are the questions I have sought to address in this chapter. Europeans have an enduring interest in culture, be that national or organizational. Colonizers or colonized, they are familiar with the harsh lights of a cultural laboratory. In the maelstrom of change which has been the twentieth century, the need for some fixed point of cultural identification has been profound; and, as we have recorded and shall consider further in Chapter 10, there are ample examples of cultural similarities that bridge the apparent chasms between peoples unlike across Europe. The internationalization of European businesses is being driven not by governments but by businesses themselves – witness the mergers that we charted in Chapter 6. The will to combine and to diversify is undoubtedly present and, whatever the challenges faced in the EU, there is clearly a will for some political combination. The will to change, experience of change, fearlessness but respect for difference – these are all critical factors in Europe's ability to forge a new culture. That individuals with a high degree of cultural neutrality are being given the opportunity to develop these cultures should give further encouragement. There is no single methodology for changing culture, but the single biggest attribute is a recognition and respect for difference and an ability to distil different elements into a coherent and distinct whole. While the culture of Europe's companies is in the hands of custodians who understand the dynamism of difference, their chances of becoming increasingly competitive are high.

and Assistant to the Chief Executive of the entire operation, further opportunity to understand the mechanics of leadership. At an earlier juncture in his career Alain Levy had a similar opportunity to witness the pressures and pleasures of running a major company. Leaving business school, he approached CBS and was offered the job of assistant to the International President. He held this job for four years and it was of enormous significance, allowing him to anticipate many of the issues that now govern his time – the need for a sense of direction, clear priorities and an understanding of those factors that can make someone a success or a flop in the entertainment world. Clearly, the latter is not an entirely learned skill – some of it is intuitive – but part of what can be derived from proximity to strong leaders is a sense for the style of leadership. Much as this assistant to the president role enabled Cornelis to take a great leap forward so did it for Levy who moved next to be the Vice President, Marketing, for the whole of Europe.

Turning potential into performance

So far we have looked at a number of factors which seem to be shared among our European business leaders and deduced that in combination these contribute to the elusive leadership quality that we are pursuing. Some of these factors are, however, entirely down to chance, the facts of one's birth, the circumstances of another's education, and while we have seen some skills that are important we have said little about achievements. Implicit in the notion of leadership quality are two fundamental questions. What does one have to *be* in order to be a leader and what does one have to *do* in order to be a leader. To some extent being and doing are intertwined. One truth about each of these leaders is that they are all extremely bright and most have achieved significantly in their educations. The quality of intellect informs every aspect of their demeanour, the ability to stand back and assess a situation and to articulate both problems and solutions. Many extremely bright people, however, do not flourish in a corporate environment; rather they shrink under the multiplicity of choices that face them, are rendered impotent by their very ability to assess the merits of each independently. It is more than mere intellect, then, that marks a leader. Determination is an obvious factor integral to the emotional make-up of any leader. For Timo Peltola, the Finnish Chief Executive of one of Finland's top companies Huhtamaki Oy, part of his determination was an oral culture. More and more we depend upon the spoken word, through the telephone through which we can now run international meetings or more sophisticated technology such as video conferencing facilities. From the words people say and the manner in which they say them we can learn infinitely more than when that person expresses the same sentiments in writing. The written word is formal and it is also robbed of inflection, of nuance, of all the subtlety and signs that abound within the spoken sentence. Ironically, in an international arena nuance and subtlety become potential traps so the listener must be on guard to capture every ounce of meaning. This calls for a degree of restraint, which would appear to quarrel with the inflated egos it is customary to associate with leadership. Listening requires the suppression of assumptions and, if really valuable information is required, it also demands the manipulation of that most sinister weapon, silence. Many people are afraid of silence and will talk to fill its vacuum. As any reader of detective fiction will know, the private detective or the cop will always fall back on silence when he or she needs to uncover the truth. So it is with the leader who must constantly examine and re-examine the current best truths to ensure that the company of which he is leader is on the best possible course.

Exposure to excellence

Access to leaders is an important factor in the subsequent success of young people. The role of mentors in the lives of this group of business leaders cannot be underestimated. François Cornelis has spent his entire career with Petrofina. That he is a 'lifer' does not imply that Cornelis' experience has been narrow, merely that it has been within the context of one organizational culture. Although not educated in the US, an early and critical part of François' business training came from the States when he was transferred to Dallas and given the role of Vice President and assistant to the President and Chief Executive of the American subsidiary of Petrofina. Experience of the American way of doing things was invaluable to François (as it has been to all of our European leaders who have lived and worked in the US or, at a remove, with an American company in Europe). As important was the experience of shadowing the Chief Executive, of experiencing at first hand the concerns that shape a leader's life. Returning to Brussels François became General Manager

Chief Executive François Cornelis, is a Belgian national and his command of both French and English and the small-power status (thus nonthreatening) of Belgium allows him to sit comfortably in an international setting. Kjell Nilsson, President and Chief Executive of Trelleborg, a Swede born in Malmo who, interestingly, spent a period of his childhood in West Africa, comes from a country where the native language is not much spoken beyond Scandinavia and, like most Swedes in business, Kjell has been obliged from a young age to cultivate a persona that does not immediately brand him as Swedish. It is possible to come from a country with a strong, easily recognizable culture and yet to acquire neutrality by dint of working within another equally strong, easily recognizable national culture. In his two most recent roles Robert Louis-Dreyfus has worked first for a British-owned company (Saatchi and Saatchi) and second with a German-owned company (his current organization Adidas). In both cases Louis-Dreyfus has been hired to bring about change, to make a difference and his own difference in national terms (although he is a truly urbane international businessman) has been an important beacon of impending change. As a clear outsider he has been able to make changes that do not implicate those on whom the changes are being thrust. In a sense, his very difference encourages the assumption that he would do things differently and takes away some of the sting of being judged and found wanting by someone who visibly carries the same values and judgements.

These individuals with a pre-existing capacity to merge identities with other nationalities lend themselves very naturally to international experience and each of them was early singled out to operate beyond the home shores of their chosen company. Kjell Nilsson, when first joining Electrolux, was put onto the sales side where he focused on the Middle East. For a ten-year period he made regular trips from Sweden to the Middle East covering the territory from Beirut through to Tehran. This proved invaluable experience for Kjell, giving him first-hand experience of a culture that is very markedly different in all aspects to the north European environment within which he lived.

Early international success can often lead to very rapid promotion – it is as if there is general recognition of the inherent difficulty in doing business with people whose values may be derived from quite alien belief systems. If I were to isolate one role which was to lead to Win Bischoff's future success it would be that of Managing Director of Schroders Asia Ltd, a position to which he was promoted in his very early thirties. This was a Hong Kong-based company and those with whom Win dealt as clients and customers came from other south-east Asian countries with very different practices and beliefs to west Europeans. Undaunted, however, Win was to build this company in some 11 years to become the major player in Hong Kong and the Pacific Rim in general. At a similar (if slightly younger age) Crispin Davis – Chief Executive of Anglo-French media buying house Aegis and former Chief Executive of United Distillers – made his mark in the Procter & Gamble organization when he was selected to head up the German operation, one which faced the additional competitor of Hoechst (a German company much less dominant in the detergent markets elsewhere in Europe). Robert Louis-Dreyfus' experience of international success was to take him in a different direction. After obtaining his MBA he returned to Europe and joined the family business where he became Managing Director for Diversification. This was not a role that inspired him for long and he seized the opportunity to manage the company's Brazilian subsidiary, an important but autonomous subsidiary the management of which played to Louis-Dreyfus' strengths. It was the risks and gamble of working in such an operation which proved the enticement and, as his subsequent career has demonstrated, it is risk which enables him to achieve his personal best. Both of his two most recent appointments have involved applying leadership to businesses which have previously been founder-led but which have lost their direction. Following a founder is never easy and is best accomplished by a seasoned manager, assuming the circumstances allow for such an eventuality. When they do not, when there is a clear need for a different style of leadership, but leadership nonetheless, the challenge is peculiarly heightened for the individual who accepts it.

The neutrality of function

In meeting these leaders of European businesses it has been, on the whole, relatively simple to spot the characteristics that have made them successful. The above cultural characteristics (or the very absence of them) are among the most marked signs of success. One figure, however, amongst this hall of fame puzzled me more. Robert Napier is the highly able Chief Executive of Redland plc, a business which, in the light of its merger with Braas to be Europe's largest roof tiler, is indisputably European in its orientation although it operates from a UK head office. An only child, Robert had a traditional British an education system that is truly comprehensive. The openness of its systems of government is also held up as a potential model for the EU. The representation of women in public life is also far in advance of countries like the UK and France, with 38% of legislative seats being held by women in 1990 compared with a miserable 6.8% in Britain and an even more pitiful 5% in France. With a legacy of empire, followed by war-induced deprivation and poverty, Sweden's stance to the outside world during the twentieth century has been characterized by neutrality, a position adopted in 1914. For a country with a population of a mere 10 million, Sweden has an extraordinary number of world-scale corporations, which account for over 40% of the stock market. Fiercely international in outlook, these corporations do the bulk of their business abroad. In conflict with the egalitarian and open social structure of Sweden, its businesses are organized along highly conservative lines, with numerous state monopolies and cartels. Does the mix of the liberal (Sweden is seen by some to be permissive in its liberality) and the conservative find expression in the cultural characteristics of its people? Certainly Swedes are notoriously cautious. The structure of the economy reflects the absence of a strong entrepreneurial drive, although the focus of education reforms has been on increasing skill levels in high tech areas. While unnecessary risk is anathema to Swedes, ambiguity does not generate high levels of discomfort. On the contrary, Swedes are among the most flexible of Europe's business people, able to interact easily with other nations. Part of this is down to the linguistic skills Swedes are obliged to develop but part must also be due to the same drives that enable the nation to stand independent from world affairs, confident in the strength and validity of its own position and able to mix with ease with its neighbours. Neutrality has not always won friends for Sweden and a clear cultural stereotype is of a nation of chilly people, at a remove from the mainstream of Europe, standing aloof and determinedly keeping their options open. In the context of the late twentieth century the stereotype no longer seems as pejorative as once it might. Part of the strength a Swede can bring to the board room is a capacity for distance, an ability to see all sides clearly and the confidence to take and uphold a position that he or she deems to be fair. The fierce commitment to egalitarian principles (and Sweden can demonstrate actual democratization of many of its institutions) gives rise to an equally fierce commitment to fairness and open-handedness. The flip-side of this admirable trait can be a tendency to compromise, in the interests of fair representation and avoidance of conflict.

Denmark

Denmark has long been one of Europe's most generous providers of welfare. Indeed, an OECD survey in 1996 found that a sizeable percentage of Danes stood to gain rather than lose from unemployment. The price of this welfare state, then, is a certain diminishing of levels of personal autonomy (the so-called welfare trap). On a practical level the price is a punitive tax regime, which disincentivizes those in senior management positions within the corporate sector. Being a company man or woman is not the means to the substantial financial gains it can be elsewhere in Europe. The Danes have a liberal government and an attitude to life that is equally liberal, with a strong emphasis on the value of leisure and the need for balance. The common character given to Danes around Europe is of a nation of very relaxed, balanced people – a balance which is reflected in an ironic humour. Critics claim that Danes lack the motivation of some of their European partners but, welfare trap aside, Danes value their autonomy and take a sceptical view of being managed. The nation has some strong international businesses – Grundfos, Danfoss and Lego among them – but also has an impressive level of entrepreneurial activity. This is in part a response to the impossibility of attaining financial independence from within a corporation in Denmark but also reflects the independence of the average, affluent Dane. Indeed, independence, manifested in different ways, is a feature of the Nordic countries. No lovers of being classified as a single homogeneous bloc, Scandinavians, nevertheless, have greatly interwoven histories and Denmark once controlled Norway and Iceland. It has, then, some of the confidence of a one-time colonizer. Geographically, Denmark occupies a position on the flanks of both the mainland of continental Europe and the other Scandinavian territories, and the independence of the Danes (note the similarity of their response to Maastricht to that of the UK) owes something to this geographically induced ambivalence to interdependence.

Finland

A final brief word on a nation that, as a new and enthusiastic member of the EU, appears to be demonstrating some cultural characteristics that are quintessentially European, in the sense that I defined 'European' in Chapter 7. In the last couple of years Finland has made an art form out of uniting the apparently unlike. In political terms the country is run by a five party 'rainbow' coalition put together in 1995 apparently effortlessly. In business a series of mergers has taken place in an effort to modernize and streamline the economy. The country's two biggest banks with a long history of rivalry combined to form Merita Bank, the largest in the Nordic region. Forestry group Kymmene merged with Repola, forming Europe's largest pulp and paper company, and Enzo-Gutzeit took over Veitsiluoto creating Europe's fourth largest pulp and paper business. The Finns, then, are nothing if not flexible, as they are obliged to be, given the low international penetration of their language. Geographically and hence geopolitically vulnerable, it is easy to read a certain insecurity into the national psyche and the education system supports such a thesis, inculcating in students the need for absolute conviction, certainty and proof before action or a decision is taken. This apparent inflexibility or caution is belied by the keen intuition and sense of regard for the interests and concerns of others that Finns can demonstrate. Again, this may be the watchful response of a vulnerable people or the flexible skills of a nation obliged to be external in outlook. Either way the combined emphasis on fact and feelings makes for a skilled and chameleon nation, given to a higher than average emotionalism but capable, as recent history testifies, of overcoming considerable obstacles in the interests of pragmatism.

Combining cultures

What is the value of such a cursory delineation of national stereotypes? If Europe were not increasingly integrated there would probably be little value in such an apparently facile exercise. However, Europeans are being called upon to interact with one another to an increasing degree. Having even the most simple appreciation of some of the deep-seated differences between nations can be of immense benefit in the quality of interaction achieved. A French chief executive of my acquaintance illustrates this point with an anecdote relating to his initiation into the art of international, cross-border management. As a newly appointed chief executive he was appointed chairman on some international subsidiary boards. In one company a specific problem called for an unscheduled, emergency meeting of the board. The chairman made a couple of phone calls to his new German and Spanish colleagues. To each he put the same request, that they attend the meeting, in the same terms. The response he received was directly contrary both to that which he had intended and to the other. The German thought the meeting was optional, since the tone my associate used had not been sufficiently directive, while the Spaniard was offended by what he saw as the hectoring tone in which he had been addressed. My associate's error? Simply an inadequate understanding of the differences between cultures – shared equally by the German and Spaniard who did not decipher the cultural coding implicit in the Frenchman's mode of address.

Analysing national cultures

The thrust of this chapter, then, has been to heighten awareness of some of the differences between cultures. This has been done quite scientifically by Geert Hofstede, to whose work we referred in Chapter 7. He measures culture against five dimensions, the fifth (short- versus long-term orientation) being added at a later date than the first four. To recap, the first four measures are: individualism versus collectivism, power distance (the extent to which a culture respects authority), uncertainty avoidance (meaning tolerance to ambiguity) and masculinity versus femininity (reflecting the toughness versus the tenderness of a culture, the extent to which a society values ambition, and assertiveness set against one which places value on co-operation and caring). Hofstede's research shows the extent to which national cultures incline towards these poles. I reproduce Hofstede's indices below, highlighting those for the European nations considered above. On these scales Denmark scores 74 on the individualism index so inclines heavily towards individualism, with 18 on the power distance index showing a culture that does not set store by authority and hierarchy. The score of 23 on the uncertainty avoidance index indicates a relatively high level of comfort with ambiguity and risk taking, while a score of 16 on the masculine/feminine scale suggests a culture that is less concerned with aggressive achievement than with a more general social well-being. These scores are consistent with the brief outline of Danish culture above as one concerned with the welfare of its citizens, entrepreneurial and so, by implication, not daunted by risk, motivated by factors beyond work and wealth generation and sceptical of authority.

The French education system

It is the French system of education which perhaps offers the best paradigm of conformity to the system of thought that has dominated since the eighteenth century.

Indeed, the political culture of France was spread from the 1880s onwards by means of a centralized education system. Designed to be liberal, lay and egalitarian, it was not meant to be totalitarian but was intended to be uniform. It was based on the frame of mind of the writers of the eighteenth century French enlightenment, on the proponents of rationalism. Despite considerable reform and modernization the system, fundamentally, remains one that is based on intellectualism, on what John Ardagh in his revised *France Today* terms 'inspired academic pedagogy', concerned to train a mind rather than a whole personality. A common criticism of the system is that it does not attempt to instil any sense of leadership in pupils, having no prefect system such as remains common in the UK. It is seen, at its worst, to stifle individualism and creativity. The thrust of the system is on deductive reasoning, rhetoric and style. The syllabus of the lycées is geared towards providing pupils with the apparatus to solve problems step by step and conforms very closely to the Romantic model above. Until 1965 the student studying for baccalaureat (*le bac*) might have to take as many as nine hours' philosophy a week plus five hours of science even if he were taking a predominantly arts option. Today le bac has eight main options, of which the literature and philosophy option used to be the most prestigious, although the maths, science and economics option is now seen to be the choice of the future elite. Academic study squeezes out all but a fairly perfunctory experience of music, art, sport – central to education in an Anglo-Saxon environment. Performance in le bac determines not entry to the grandes écoles, but at least the chance to pursue further study in order to qualify for entry to the elitest of elite systems to which a mere 1 in 20 of students in higher education can aspire.

The Ecole Polytechnique (X), the Ecole Normale Superieure (ENS), the Ecole des Hautes Etudes Commerciales and ENA the newer national school of administration between them produce all but a small proportion of France's governing elite both in business and in government. Although ENA was set up with a view to democratizing entry to the grandes écoles, it remains the province of the elite who can afford to prepare their, admittedly highly able, offspring for entry via expensive schools and crammers. So, while in principle the grandes écoles system is a meritocracy, access to that meritocracy is effectively limited. Five of the last six Presidents of France are graduates of ENA. Between them ENA, Ecole des Hautes Etudes Commerciales and the Ecole Polytechnique provided some 60% of French CEOs, only 4% of whom had been promoted from within the enterprises they ran.

The British education system

The British education system conforms neatly to the Lessem–Neubauer model in being concerned with the experience of the individual, taking a person rather than an intellect and offering a more generalized training. The emphasis of course work is, especially with the advent of a national curriculum, self-expression through project work, with a significant proportion of study taking place outside the classroom. The educational school trip has long been a feature of British education. Music, drama and sport also play an important part in the curriculum and lend those who excel considerable prestige within the school culture. While offering an apparently broader range of study than French schools, British school children are required to specialize considerably earlier, taking at Advanced Level (in England and Wales) only a handful of subjects rather than the broad canvas of the bac or the Abitur. University entrance requirements are based on an average of 3 A level passes. So, from an early age a school child makes choices about subjects of study which reflect individual choice, interest and ability. The obvious shortcoming of such a system is that it can allow huge pockets of ignorance, even when considering that all children must study mathematics, English and a foreign language until they are 16. The Scottish system, it should be noted, gives greater credence to the need for breadth and an 18-year-old would study, at Higher level, more subjects than an English or Welsh contemporary.

The subjects taught are less significant in the British education system than the structure within which they are taught – which has long reflected the British social class system. The 1944 changes to education reinforced class divisions by separating education into secondary modern, technical and grammar schools. The occupational pattern of pupils attending each category was, broadly, brown collar from secondary modern, blue collar from technical, professional and white collar from grammar schools. Professional status would usually require further education, at a university. Until very recently further education was divided between academic universities and vocational polytechnics – although the distinction has now been removed. Adjacent to the state education system was the private system consisting of independent grammar schools and the 260 public schools, which are expensive and socially significant. Attempts to democratize state education in the 1960s led to the introduction of comprehensive schools, along the lines of the mixed-ability high school in the US. Alongside these, however, the private sector has continued to attract a fee-paying middle class and the recent Conservative administration has changed the system in such a way as to give comprehensive schools the option of becoming increasingly selective.

The British education system, then, is rather schizophrenic, geared around choice, and produces mixed results. On the one hand Britain in 1980 had a significantly higher proportion of the children of manual workers in university education than any other nation in Europe – a staggering 30%, the second highest being the German 18%. On the other hand, power in Britain is still in the hands of the privately educated (although in the wider sense than merely the public schools). The Economist's survey of Britain's 100 top people found that 67 of 100 went to private school in 1972, 66 of 100 went to private school in 1992. Of course, the top 100 people were educated some 20+ years prior to the years of the study, but the trend is not encouraging. An Oxbridge education remains a significant asset in occupational terms – but there is evidence that the older universities at least are an increasingly accessible meritocracy. In 1981 Anthony Sampson found that Oxbridge were admitting more students from the state sector than from the private sector.

Education, elites and entrepreneurs

The common factor emerging from the above study is a focus on elites. However hard the governments of France, Germany and the UK have attempted to democratize education and however successful those efforts have been, it is still predominantly the middle classes who benefit from the systems. This is the case in Sweden as well, which has one of the most egalitarian of education systems. Modelled on the US system, Swedish education is free and open to all up to university level. All students are educated in one common system akin to the comprehensive ideal that has not been achieved in the UK. However, it is still the middle classes who dominate tertiary education and the key positions in business and government. Why should this be? The explanation would seem to reside in the home and the levels of cultural development that exist in and between the various class strata. It would seem that despite a high degree of social levelling that has been experienced across Europe since 1945 there remain clear distinctions between the social groups which are manifest in attitudes to culture as enshrined in education. John Ardagh, in his study *Germany and the Germans*, suggests that the importance of parental supervision of a child's homework places a relatively uneducated parent at a substantial emotional disadvantage and disinclines that parent to push a child into an educational establishment that might expose the parental educational deficit. Similarly, in Sweden, the lifestyle gap between the manual and the managerial classes is thought to restrict the chances of the children from the first sector in competition with those from the second as far as educational advancement is concerned. In summary, then, Europe offers its children an education system which is, by and large, meritocratic but due to the insidious effect of class access to that meritocracy remains restricted.

What are the implications of the above as far as Europe's chances for future business hegemony are concerned? In the first place the existence of a knowable community of highly educated Europeans must be an asset. Despite evidence of change in the various education systems we have studied there remain constants, particular styles – pragmatic, intellectual, technical – which dominate. While the weighting of individual education systems might, in the long term, have an adverse effect on an individual nation state (as has been the case in Japan where the focus on learning by rote has led to a stifling of creativity and innovation), group the products of a range of European education systems around the board room table of a multinational company and the probability is that the differences will be complementary and the output, in terms of a decision, superior.

There is a case to be made, however, that current educational practices in Europe favour an economy that is based upon large-scale, well-established companies rather than smaller entrepreneurial vehicles. European education systems currently ensure that power is exercised by a small, privileged, slow-changing elite. Such an elite is innately conservative and concerned to perpetuate its status. The careers that the elite will select will be those that confer the appropriate status and satisfy the conservative requirement for stability and a certain guarantee of progression and reward.

is derived from the Germanic philosophical tradition and so prevails in parts of Germany, Austria and Switzerland. The fourth dimension they dub humanism, being related to Italian art and culture but having branches in Greece, Spain and Ireland.

Do these models have any use – can they teach us something of how we, as Europeans, should interact? Lessem and Neubauer have established certain consequences in a business environment following from each model which can be tabulated as follows:

Model	Type of manager	Best case	Worst case
Pragmatic	Experiential	Free-spirited individualism (entrepreneurialism/creativity)	Rampant materialism (disregard for effect)
Rationalist	Professional	Meritocracy	Bureaucracy
Wholist	Developmental (considering the case from the bottom up)	Wholistic (covering the angles)	Totalitarian (inflexible, too rigidly adhering to the principles)
Humanist	Convivial (consensus, gaining agreement, discursive)	Communal (inclusive)	Nepotism, corruption

NB The interpretations in parentheses are the author's own inference rather than the direct views of Lessem and Neubauer.

There is a danger in any such tabulation of ascribing values and the use to which this understanding can be put is not immediately obvious. As in any attempt to apply broad categories to peoples such as the psychological profiling of Myers–Briggs such definitions are a guide, offering some indication of the types of assumption we might encounter in those who conform to a particular type. For a consultant staffing an international case study team, or a chairman at an acquisitive organization looking to put together an international advisory board then these types of loose definitions can be helpful. In dealing with board colleagues, overseas customers and clients these summary guides can be helpful. My own interest in pursuing this exercise at this point is simply to demonstrate that there is some agreement on the broad cultural

Drawing some cultural isobars

The three sources at the head of this chapter led to a hasty delineation of an English, French and German model of thought. The English are pragmatic, rooted in the facts, the hard evidence, the French rational, building stone on stone and the Germans essential, getting to the heart of the matter, establishing first principles. Nothing is ever quite so simple. The Empiricist tradition is as much Scottish as it is English, while rationalism is perhaps more accurately a continental than a purely French tradition, with Descartes being followed by the Dutchman Spinoza and the German Leibniz. Nevertheless these categories have been echoed regularly in studies of European cultural types.

An Andersen Consulting study, *Doing Business in Europe* cites three dialectical models. The first of these is the Teutonic model, which is a reasoning and negotiating approach seen to prevail in the Germanic, Nordic and Central European regions and derives from a legalistic methodology, beginning with the conclusion (the big idea, perhaps), proceeding to the supporting points (the underlying principles) and returning to the conclusion (reinforcement of that big idea). The second is the Romantic model, being largely French, Mediterranean and South Eastern European, which is in contrast highly formalistic and structured, beginning with a theoretical introduction, moving logically through two or three sub-points, each clearly supported, and all together leading to an inescapable conclusion. The final model is the Anglo-Saxon model, which is largely inferential, beginning with the concrete and observable and proceeding to a logically inferred conclusion. The Anglo-Saxon model is probably on a cultural isobar with the US (rather as in the neo-American versus the Rhine model seen in Chapter 4), but also with the Dutch and to some extent the Scandinavians. It is no accident, of course, that some of these models follow linguistic patterns, the very structures of language having bearing on, or being an expression of, styles of thought. Similarly, religious patterns are evident in these groupings, which themselves mimic the spread of languages.

Fred Neubauer and Ronnie Lessem see similar categories, somewhat differently aligned and with an interesting fourth to set against the three which formed the starting point. Pragmatism, they agree, is rooted in an empiricist tradition, the tradition that highlighted the rights of the individual, and dominates in the British, Scandinavian and Dutch ways of doing business. Rationalism is fundamentally Gallic but has been exported to parts of Germany, Scandinavia, northern Italy and French-speaking parts of Switzerland. Wholism

It is not entirely irrelevant to consider the background against which education systems developed. Mass education in Europe is a feature of the final quarter of the nineteenth century. Education served at its most elevated levels to provide a cadre of governors, of individual countries and empires. The German, British and French civil services have traditionally (as has the Japanese) recruited top performers from their respective education systems to participate in the governance of the nation state. Education systems have therefore reflected the interests of statehood and government (in a liberal arts bias) and have been successful in manufacturing a product to suit the initial specification – a bureaucrat. The French system best exemplifies this, with the cream of grandes écoles graduates going into the various ministries, government departments and nationalized industries. Whereas in the US it is common practice for people from the private sector to move into the federal service for a period, in France the shift is in the other direction and even has a name: pantouflage. There is increasing incidence of top performers selecting business over bureaucracy, not least because of the potentially higher rewards. However, the fact remains that the system is geared towards the provision of safe and conservative careers. In the UK and in Germany there is a similar relationship still between government and academic excellence. The British civil service has identified a potential problem in filling its senior posts from within. A Career Management and Succession Planning Study undertaken by the Cabinet Office notes:

> *'Modern attitudes in society have changed ... There are certainly those for whom the attraction of a career in public service is as strong as it ever was, but there is much more readiness to contemplate job mobility and career changes; indeed, most fast stream entrants now openly acknowledge that they expect to keep their employment options open, and do not feel committed to the Civil Service until 60.'*

This is good news – the best trained do not automatically seek a sustained career in the civil service (although a high proportion still do). The public sector in the UK at least has lost prestige and top graduates increasingly transfer their interests to the private sector. The education system, the conservatism and the guarantee of rewards can incline those graduates towards private sector organizations which have a similar monolithic structure and similar lifestyle/status benefits to the old corridors of power – the large companies.

The British civil service compares itself, in the same document, with Shell, British Petroleum, Marks & Spencer, British Telecom, Unilever, Bass and IBM. In short education systems, originally devised to support large national bureaucracies, still continue to do so, albeit those bureaucracies are now in the private rather than the public domain.

A top-flight graduate from a European university with an interest in pursuing a commercial career is likely to select a large company that will provide a strong training. Very often that big company will not be European at all. A number of would-be future chief executives will embark on a career with American majors such as Procter & Gamble, Mars, Ford or a leading US investment bank or a premier strategy consultancy. In short there is a marked preference for the high-image, secure, conservative institution. This may bode well in a global economy where the multinational corporation is king. Europe will provide a generation of first-rate corporate animals who have the potential to work together in international teams and to out-compete Asian or American counterparts. The prize of a seat on the board of a listed company will often entice well-trained products of American companies back to their native country – indeed, the fear that Americans stand the best chance of securing the top job in an American company will incline Europeans to seek a post in their country of origin. In this way the current education systems, however much they perpetuate unfair social distinctions, may support the European cause, or at least not undermine it – assuming the future lies with the major multinational.

The failure of Europe's high-tech industries – the influence of cultural values

However, European experience offers us a paradigm which suggests that an educated elite that is conservative and too bureaucratic in orientation can suffer in a fast-changing global market place: the failure of Europe's high-tech industries. Olivier Cadot and Pierre Blime, in their paper *Can Industrial Europe be saved?*, offer several reasons as to why Europe has competed so poorly in the scramble to corner the high-tech market. The authors cite the low incidence of link-ups between universities and businesses in the R&D field (a problem covered in Chapter 4 in relation to German decline), government policies in favour of large national combines developed through distracting mergers, poor investment, an environment that has not been conducive to the growth of small- to medium-sized businesses (poor start-up funds and limited managerial education for those with the scientific know-how) and managerial/operational inefficiencies.

Several of these factors are directly related to the educational environment that has developed in Europe – and other deep-seated attitudes allied to those that inform our educational systems. Not surprisingly, the grandes écoles system comes under fire, for taking a disproportionate share of funding resources (to the detriment of the universities in France) and providing a cadre of bureaucrats and businessmen who actively deprecate the university system as somehow inferior. The French attitude perhaps merely writes large what is implicit in other parts of Europe. There exists a hierarchy of occupations – the professions (law, medicine, academia, government service) – which are held in higher esteem than business. Harold Perkin, charting the rise of the Professional Society, notes of the English experience that:

> 'The public schools and ancient universities were not intended to educate business men or their sons and, far from setting out to convert them to the public service ideal, did what they could to keep them out and to embarrass them with contempt for "trade" when they insisted on coming.'

What they were intended to do was to provide public servants, a category that included teachers in universities and public schools. We see a clear distinction between business and academia. Indeed, academia is a focus of aspiration for the self-made businessman and it is an interesting commentary on this that some of Britain's early, great self-made men – Lord Nuffield, Isaac Wolfson (of Great Universal Stores) and Sir David Robinson (pioneer of rental television) – all endowed Oxbridge colleges. The relationship between business and universities, then, certainly in France and in Britain, is an uneasy one in which the status of those within the university system is somehow superior to that of their business counterparts. It is a small step to extend this mentality to other parts of Europe who had imperial interests and a public service ethic which their education systems were set up to serve.

The gulf between management and science works in both directions. A European scientist might have an excellent, commercially viable idea, but will be at a considerable remove from the management education that would enable the development of that idea into a business. It is not merely the absence of the practical skills that would hold back the scientist but a conservative, risk-averse cast of mind that would counsel against departure from the sure prestige of academia to the risk and random reward of entrepreneurial activity.

So the failure of universities and businesses to link up in Europe is rooted in a certain distaste on the part of the so-called professions for business, which in turn is rooted in a European fixation with hierarchy, with ordering and ranking. In 1994 a McKinsey study (cited by Cadot and Blime) attributed the competitive failure of European electronics firms to managerial weakness. In particular, a poor level of delegation in European firms led to low-quality products and escalating costs. Managers manage, workers work. Inflexible organizations that failed to bring manufacturing and R&D together developed products that were difficult to manufacture and hard to redesign and the same inflexibility hindered innovation. That distance from the shop floor maintained by European managers – a disdain for getting one's hands dirty – the antithesis of the Japanese managerial ethos, can be seen as a major contributory factor in Europe's fate in the high-tech race.

The European obsession with (or perhaps merely familiarity and comfort with) the large-scale enterprise – the monolith or bureaucratic machine – is another instance of hierarchy at work. Big is best. So each European nation championed the development of one super-company to pioneer its high-tech development, promoting a series of engineered mergers which created managerial problems of such magnitude that the commercial objective became all but obscured.

Ultimately, Europe has failed in competition with Japan and the US in the high-tech marketplace because of an absence of an entrepreneurial spirit. Our educational systems appear to be perpetuating a rather cautious, no doubt able, but risk-averse manager who is most likely to excel in a big company, hierarchical and prestigious environment. Clearly, European education systems are not without their shortcomings. The values they perpetuate or enshrine are not always conducive to economic superiority – although companies operating across the continent can draw upon an extremely able population with well-honed and complementary skills. In general the standard of European education is high and becoming increasingly multicultural, decreasingly parochial. The lessons have been learned from the experience in the high-tech arena (around Europe, for instance, there is increasing support being given to the development of an entrepreneurial spirit – witness the launch haps the most interesting. Distinct and different traditions, the German, French and English taken together lead to the construction of a strong, well-built and eminently inhabitable edifice. In the eighteenth, nineteenth and twentieth centuries, then, observers have seen a 'national character', a 'national cast of mind', a set of philosophical and cultural traditions which are measurable and which, happily, can integrate and work together – or so these sources would suggest. Can the legacy of Locke, Descartes and Hegel, of Enlightenment and Romantic thought, have any bearing on the future business success of Europe? It is the not altogether fanciful claim of this chapter that they can. Particular cultural traditions have given rise to particular practical institutions, which have in turn led to particular approaches to problem solving which, taken together, can lead to the strongest solution.

In previous chapters we have looked at the difference and diversity which make any constitution of a single European culture seem both impossible and, arguably, unnecessary. This chapter will look, briefly, at some of the cultural isobars which have been drawn linking certain parts of the continent and will then turn to consider the implications of some of those isobars on particularly influential institutions and attitudes. The terrain of this chapter, then, is both the distinctions and the inter-relatedness of the various European cultures, and its aim is to arrive at a rubric of values that are somehow quintessentially European, and to assess whether in a race for economic power they represent assets or liabilities. It is not wholly bizarre to speak in terms of the quintessentially European for the Americans and the Japanese have encountered nothing but success when dealing with the land mass as one homogeneous unit, susceptible to a single, uniform approach, and are mystified by European introversion and reflexivity. In dealing with Europe as a single bloc we run into a set of assumptions, which are broadly the following. Europe is a continent marked by very different peoples who are nevertheless united by having won and lost imperial power. European dreams of past glory are linked with an aristocratic heritage which lingers in the ubiquitous gradations of class, a preference for the professions over commerce and a disdain for money as a measure of success. In short, the sun has set over Europe and in some twilight zone we have become sentimental and nostalgic, concerned with the provision of care rather than with active engagement in competitive commerce which will secure the means for continual provision of care to our communities. In the following pages I shall attempt to probe the veracity of these assumptions.

9

European Culture: Asset or Liability?

'We could say that the philosophical centre of gravity in Europe in the eighteenth century was in England in the first half, in France in the middle, and in Germany towards the end of it.'
Jostein Gaarder, Sophie's World.

'[The Marxist doctrine] is the legitimate successor to the best that men produced in the nineteenth century, as represented by German philosophy, English political economy and French socialism.'
Vladimir Ilyich Lenin, The Three Sources and Three Component Parts of Marxism.

'In the trinity Founding–Building–Inhabiting, the French build and the Germans lay foundations, but the English inhabit.'
Gilles Deleuze and Felix Guattari, What is philosophy?

Three quotes from three very different sources, one popular, one political and one philosophical, suggest on the one hand quite distinct cultural traditions in each of the three strongest European economies but on the other a certain inter-relatedness. In his popular summary of Western philosophy, which has been an international best-seller, Gaarder charts the linear progression from English pragmatism, through French rationalism to the German adherence to the big idea. Lenin's delineation of the best that men produced in the nineteenth century shows the inheritance from those distinct traditions – English political economy deriving from its empirical tradition, French socialism from a rational one, Marxism, the ultimate 'big idea' in Lenin's lexicon, is of course German in origin. It is the construction of a trinity by Gilles Deleuze and Felix Guattari, which for our purposes is per-

Country	Individualism versus collectivism	Power distance	Avoidance of uncertainty	Masculinity versus femininity
Australia	90	36	51	61
Austria	55	11	70	79
Belgium	**75**	**65**	**94**	**54**
Canada	80	39	48	52
Denmark	**74**	**18**	**23**	**16**
Finland	**63**	**33**	**59**	**26**
France	**71**	**68**	**86**	**43**
Germany	**67**	**35**	**65**	**66**
Greece	35	60	112	57
Hong Kong	25	68	29	57
India	48	77	40	56
Ireland	70	28	35	68
Italy	**76**	**50**	**75**	**70**
Japan	46	54	92	95
Korea	18	60	85	39
Netherlands	**80**	**38**	**53**	**14**
Norway	69	31	50	8
Portugal	27	63	104	31
Singapore	20	74	8	48
Spain	**51**	**57**	**86**	**42**
Sweden	**71**	**31**	**29**	**5**
Switzerland	68	34	58	70
Thailand	20	64	64	34
UK	**89**	**35**	**35**	**66**
US	91	40	46	62

Source: Geert Hofstede, *Cultures and Organisations*; McGraw Hill Book Company (UK) Ltd.

Hofstede's indices give immediate insight into the direction in which particular cultures trend. This is, of course, not to suggest that every citizen of the particular culture will respond in precisely this programmed way. Rather, this is the prevailing or dominant but by no means exclusive response. Knowing the areas of comfort or discomfort can enable international communication, in the sense that areas of potential conflict can be identified from the outside and either deflected or at least correctly interpreted. Further, these indices can be a useful tool in understanding team dynamics when that team numbers several individuals from different cultures.

Analysing individuals

Hofstede's research considers national preferences but considerable work has been undertaken looking at individual preferences. In particular, the mother and daughter Myers–Briggs partnership developed a mechanism for identifying individual types in the 1940s, building on the work of Carl Jung and Ernst Kretschmer. Their work identified four pairs of polar opposites which give rise to a possible 16 personality types. In simplest terms these oppositions are:

- *extroversion (E) versus introversion (I)* – denoting those who are energized by contact with others versus those who are enervated by contact with others (the extroverts making up the bulk of the population);
- *intuition (N) versus sensation (S)* – denoting those who are speculative, looking to the future, the type to back a hunch versus those who are rooted in the present, pragmatic and moved more by fact than by fantasy;
- *thinking (T) versus feeling (F)* – denoting those who are moved by objective judgements, by clear principles and a strong rationale versus those who are more comfortable with the subjective, who rate values above laws and the personal rather than the impersonal;
- *judging (J) versus perceiving (P)* – akin to the short-term, long-term horizons of Hofstede's work this opposition reflects those whose preference is for action, decision and moving things forward versus those who keep their options open, allow more room for manoeuvre and can feel some discomfort with the finality of a decision.

The various categories should not be seen to carry judgements. A thinker is not, for instance, somebody incapable of feeling. On the contrary, their emotions may be every bit as deep as those of a feeler but the thinker will internalize more. On the basis of a battery of tests every individual can build up a profile of four key variables – for example, the ENTJ is someone who is extrovert, intuitive, thinking and judging and there is considerable body of work identifying the implications of the 16 different types. The work of Myers–Briggs provides an extremely useful schema for understanding the vastly different motivations of individuals. Over time it is possible to become skilled at identifying the preferred mode of people on quite a fleeting acquaintance and, indeed, by extension to identify the type of culture that may predominate in an organization (which is, after all, a collection of individuals who to a certain extent are selected in a particular image or self-select to a particular image). The subject is a complex one (explored with clarity and depth in Kersey and Bates' *Please Understand Me*) but, when united with an approach such as Hofstede's, can be extremely illuminating for the student of interpersonal dynamics. As tools in the kit bag of the international chief executive, both systems are invaluable.

The survey of European cultural types conducted in this chapter shows up the clear differences that exist between the peoples of neighbouring nations. These differences can lead to catastrophic misunderstandings between those who are unaware of the influence of culture and who cannot therefore adapt or make some allowance (as in the case of the French Chief Executive and his German and Spanish colleagues). On the other hand, the cultural differences point to the opportunity that presents itself to Europeans in the form of increasing integration. The skills and values of Europeans are complementary. A French strategist, a German manufacturing director and a Swedish managing director could make a formidable team on the board of an international company. Their ability to work together constructively depends to some extent on the ability to enter the relationship from a position of mutual respect and flexible expectations. The Frenchman, to be simplistic about it, might need to guard against the charge of being obtuse, while the German might similarly need to watch a tendency towards pedantry if some fundamental frustrations are to be avoided. Learning to read culture is equivalent to learning a language and as valuable, but to read culture one reads at the level of subtext. What is visible on the surface – a disinclination to take a particular decision, a reluctance to toe the line, an insistence on consensus – is likely to be just the tip of the cultural iceberg. In looking below the surface, the deposits of experiences and values made over the generations become apparent and recognition of the cultural processes of history can allow the apparently unfathomable other to be better understood. Working on a daily basis with people from other cultures is not for the insensitive or the inflexible and early exposure to more than one culture, as we have seen in Chapter 7, can make the difference between success and failure. The difficulty of managing an international team can incline some to stay in the safety of the domestic arena, but to do so is to deny the extraordinary potential dividends deriving from the successful management of diversity. Economic success in the future will depend upon the ability of individuals to work together with representatives of other cultures, united by a common commercial ethic. It follows then that economic supremacy will go to those who can best understand and work within the constraints of culture, and the most practised in this area are, without question, modern Europeans.

Belgium

Belgium is a fitting place for the EU to locate its primary institutions. A country divided into two peoples with two national languages (the Flemish and the Walloons), it has been occupied by most of its European neighbours, in turn by the Spanish, Austrian, French, Dutch and, most recently the Germans. The country also plays host to the European headquarters of numerous multinational (often American-owned) corporations. Almost more than any other European nation, then, it has been subject to a plurality of influences. This has not undermined the development of a strong, recognizable national culture. Belgians have, historically, pulled together in the face of adversity and so the culture is based on a strong communitarian principle. Belgians are an urbane, sophisticated people with a strong streak of optimism, borne of their collective ability to weather the vicissitudes of invasion (however benign). A long tradition of being subject to diverse influences has made the Belgian mentality one of opportunism, a willingness to grasp the nettle and act as soon as opportunity presents itself. The flip-side of this opportunism can be seen in a tendency to take shortcuts to economic success, for example through short-term, opportunistic pricing policies. The same accident of history that has made the Belgians optimists has also made them comfortable with compromise. They are not natural leaders. Greatest respect is accorded to engineers and process is more respected than creative, innovative ideas or high-quality products. The Belgian mixed economy perhaps reflects their comfort with the middle ground – a few large-scale, multinational companies (Petrofina and Solvay, for example) and a large number of small to medium-sized enterprises. Many of Belgium's capable, highly educated executives work for the ubiquitous visitors in the non-Belgian multinationals. Belgians are nothing if not adaptable and the economy is responding to the need for greater entrepreneurial verve and is training impressive numbers of its youth in the high-tech sectors that promise to provide substantial profits for the future. Belgians have the same cultural dexterity (although very differently packaged) as their Dutch neighbours and so they are similarly well placed to play, as individuals perhaps rather than as a nation, a prominent part in an integrated Europe.

Sweden

Sweden is among the most affluent countries in the world. It also has one of the most egalitarian social systems in Europe, with a strong welfare state and speech. Not for the Dutch the well-motivated insincerity of the British or the Spanish – the Dutch tell it like it is. This direct style might have its origins in a moral concern for truth at any price. A tradition of thrift has also given rise to a stock image of the Dutch as the mean men of Europe. Natural traders, the Dutch have transformed the skills that built their mercantile empire in the seventeenth century into the modern skills of the salesman and marketer (and notably the Dutch are good at both activities). These skills – the ability to understand the needs of a market and meet them at the best possible price – also suggest the flexibility of the Dutch, or rather the chameleon quality. This latter is derived from Holland's small nation status. The Dutch language is spoken by a mere eight million of the world's population. As a maritime nation on the flank of the continent, the Dutch have long mixed with other cultures and its people are some of the most linguistically gifted in Europe. The Dutch, then, are able to empathize with other cultures while losing none of their own cultural distinctness. This ability to remain culturally distinct but also to integrate with others has enabled the Dutch to form such powerful jointly owned companies as Royal Dutch Shell and Unilever, which we considered in Chapter 6. Again, evidence of Dutch dualism.

As might be expected of a nation of traders and marketers, the Dutch are strong on detail. Indeed, some of the finest artefacts of high Dutch culture are tributes to a long-standing Dutch eye for detail, with the fine interior canvases of Vermeer. A nation with strong democratic principles and some of the most liberal laws in Europe (in contrast to the religious conformity that also characterizes the nation) the Dutch are more comfortable operating within than outside structures. The dependence of the economy on large, efficiently run multinationals suggests a tendency amongst the Dutch to be professional managers rather than entrepreneurs; and certainly the shortcomings of the Dutch culture are in the areas of imagination and innovation. The Dutch are not naturally entrepreneurial. They are, however, excellent managerially, being clear, concerned with consensus and – consistent with the prevailing morality – scrupulously fair. In an international context, Dutch executives are particularly well placed, having the cultural dexterity to move with ease around other countries and the linguistic skills to support that movement. They are also skilled in the dynamics of big company management and, in terms of European integration, it will be the large companies that can and will unite.

isobars that bind us together as Europeans rather than simply residents of particular nation states.

Within and across nation states there are any number of regional affiliations that exert a strong pull on their residents. Not even strongly identified European ministers, figures prominent in the drawing together of Europe, have been immune from regional loyalties. Adenauer, a Rhineland Catholic, could be impatient of so-called Prussian characteristics, whereas De Gaulle did not entirely forsake his Breton allegiances. There are any number of ways in which the map of Europe can be redrawn. An obvious modern dimension, but one which has coloured the lives of three generations, is that of the Communist versus the non-Communist worlds – even when the events of 1989 are many years past the legacy of those brought up under a Communist regime will inform the attitudes and thinking of the children they in turn are charged to rear. There are isobars that connect the smaller nation states, and still more linking those newer entrants to the EU, which are developing economies and dubbed by most commentators as peripheral. Then there are the areas which together comprise a heavy industrial triangle – the Ruhr in Germany, the Nord/Pas de Calais region in France, Belgium, Lorraine, Luxembourg and the Saarland. Doubtless one could write an entire chapter, if not a book, on the cultural isobar that links the landlocked nations together and another for those with a maritime border. Certainly, much is made of the fact that Britain's attitude to the EU is necessarily different from that of her continental partners, by dint of geography. As an island there are simply not the same issues in Britain as in some countries which may border as many as nine different countries. From whichever angle one approaches the land mass there are as many similarities as there are differences, the consequence of this being, culturally speaking, an old continent.

Styles of thought mirrored in education systems

The model with which the chapter began – styles of thought – and which we have seen replicated a couple of times is perhaps the most powerful because it informs that most fundamental of modern institutions, the education system. The style of an education system can determine not just the fortunes of individuals but of entire economies, channelling energies and intellects along predetermined lines, closing off particular forms of conduct, venerating others. The links between the models above and the patterns of education evident in Germany, France and the UK are compelling.

The German education system

The German education system, for instance, allies closely with the Teutonic style of reasoning identified in the Andersen Consulting model above. Certainly, the German ruling class is dominated by those who have been legally trained. Ralf Dahrendorf calculated that in 1962 85% of all civil servants had law degrees and the mandarin culture of Germany is dominated by the law. So a legally biased education system then influences the development of bureaucracy and hence of government which must inform business. The structure of the West German education system also conforms to the Wholist model of Lassem and Neubauer. A common four-year primary system splits at the secondary level into three tracks: the five-year continuation of primary school, the six-year intermediate school, and the nine-year senior grammar school. The first two systems are geared towards provision of a vocational/technical training, the last towards university entrance. Once based on the classics the offering in the third stream (Gymnasium) is a modern curriculum embracing arts, languages, mathematics and science, leading to the school leaving certificate, the Abitur. The system is criticized on the one hand because it reinforces social differences but praised because it yields Europe's most highly trained population. 59% of all German youth are in school until the age of 18, as opposed to 24% in England and 41% in France. 44% are licensed to practise a trade or craft, as opposed to 20% in England, 10% in Italy and 6% in Spain. However, only 15% of university entrants come from working-class backgrounds and the Gymnasium is predominantly middle-class territory. To some extent this reflects a German concern to maintain a balance in the skills of its population and, as we have seen earlier, some of Germany's success has derived from its ability to train a skilled work-force.

of EASDAQ) and the proliferation of management training. Even the old seats of learning are now competing with the established business schools in management disciplines.

We have seen in Chapter 5 that the south-east Asian nations do not necessarily have education systems that are any better geared towards the development of innovative thinkers than those in Europe. Indeed, there is a case to be put that education operates in opposition to innovation, that implicit in the process of education is the imposition of received ideas, the schooling in particular practised modes of thought. It is often the autodidact, after all, who is most capable of original thought. To expect any education system to provide an arena for entrepreneurialism may be misguided. Equally, to encourage entrepreneurialism at the expense of knowledge may be foolish. Neither Europe nor Asia seem to have struck entirely the right balance. Has America?

Comparing the European educational experience with the American

America has achieved tremendous success in the high-tech arena where we have seen Europe fail – does its educational track record shed light on this?

On the contrary, an analysis of the American education system can only cast doubt on the long-term sustainability of the nation's economic supremacy. At first glance such a claim seems absurdly alarmist. Where the American system far outshines that of any country in Europe is in the higher education sector. A massive amount of funding is poured into the world's greatest array of research universities and scientific institutions which carry off a disproportionate number of Nobel prizes and have the prestige to attract the best brains from overseas both in terms of students and staff. However, at the level below the story is entirely different and the gulf between school and higher education is reducing the flow of good students into the research fraternity. America is increasingly recruiting foreign doctoral students and professors. The American school system is profoundly egalitarian and highly decentralized. It would also appear to be failing monstrously. Compared with other children in the world, those in the US acquire substantially less education, between 175 and 180 days per year compared with a European average above 200 and a Japanese norm around 220. By the age of 18 the average Japanese or Korean pupil may have had three or four years more education than their American counterpart. A recent science test put to the children of 17 countries placed American pupils behind Japan, South Korea, all the nations of western Europe and ahead only of Hong Kong and the Philippines. In mathematical proficiency tests Americans again were close to bottom. A mere 15% of school children learn a foreign language, just 2% for a period longer than two years. One in seven American adults cannot locate their own country on a world map, 25 million adults cannot read sufficiently to understand a warning label on a medicine bottle and 22% of American adults cannot correctly address a letter. Close to one-fifth of all high school pupils (rising to half in inner city high schools) drop out annually.

The problems in the education system must inform the widespread social ills of the nation – the dramatic crime rates and escalating poverty. They may also be a direct reflection of the values of a consumer-driven society. America is the home of instant gratification, of fast foods, ephemeral entertainment, a popular culture based on cartoons, game shows, soap operas. A drug culture, a gun culture (instant pleasure, instant death) – a profoundly anti-intellectual culture. This is America at its worst – but with an education system, at best, in deep malaise it is hard to see where the impetus will come for a reversal. The breakdown of the family, the decline in religious values – the checks that used to exist upon rampant individualism are in abeyance. The gap between the haves and the have nots is one of the highest in the world – and growing. Oxfam America channels aid into America itself. Perhaps this is the logical consequence of capitalism – or at least capitalism on the neo-American model? Perhaps also it should not matter to America's future economic hopes, however much it may matter on humanitarian grounds. Perhaps an environment that venerates individualism and does not stifle individual endeavour with formulaic education will breed still more entrepreneurs? Possibly, but a society with large-scale social injustice cannot, surely, be infinitely secure and stable. A society in the process of creating for itself a new aristocracy – a minority of very conspicuous haves – a century after most of the world's aristocracies have been disarmed, makes itself vulnerable. A disaffected, underprivileged underclass can organize itself – or be organized – to rebel and disaffected, underprivileged, undereducated underclasses are not reliable as a source of defence. However, we need not pause to consider the possibility of apocalyptic strife which, in all probability, overstates. America has an immediate reason to feel concern over its poor education standards and that is the rise of the knowledge society.

The rise of the knowledge society – implications for America and Europe

Economic theory forecasts that the race for economic/business supremacy will be won by knowledge-based societies. The influence of access to raw materials has ceased to be the economic differentiator of the past as the major developed economies have reached something like parity in this regard. The explosion of the high-tech sector is just one indication of the scientific and knowledge-driven focus of the future: microelectronics, biotechnology, the new materials science industries, telecommunications, civilian aviation, robotics plus machine tools, computers and software – the future lies with these industries. Certainly it is fair to say that there is a huge future also in service and it is in the service sector that the US has created so many jobs but the growth in white collar and technical jobs, requiring a college level education, is rising. The Hudson Institute survey, Workforce 2000 has predicted that as many as 52% of newly created jobs by the end of the decade will require a level of education that the American system is not currently providing.

Demographics are against America here. While the work-force is expanding, the best educated sector of the work-force constitutes a declining percentage of the whole. White males will constitute just 15% of the new work-force, the remainder comprising women, minorities and immigrants – the very groups that have least exposure to education.

In an age to be dominated by knowledge, Europe undoubtedly has the edge over the US. However much the European system is elitist and insufficiently geared towards entrepreneurialism, each nation can nevertheless demonstrate raising rather than falling standards of education and increasing breadth of opportunity and choice in terms of the curriculum. The favoured styles of teaching in most of Europe are geared towards problem solving and independent thought and so might also be more flexible than the rote-based systems which still dominate in the highly knowledge-driven Asian societies. America might maintain a strong lead in terms of the provision of management education – but first it must produce the calibre of manager to be educated to MBA level. On present showing, Europe is doing rather better.

Attitudes to business

One corollary of the knowledge society is an increasing disdain for the very structures and systems (capitalism) that have brought it into being by the community in possession of that knowledge – intellectuals. Capitalism encouraged a rational critique of feudalism in order to cement its own existence. In the second half of the twentieth century that rational critique has been turned against capitalism itself. Capitalism has broadened the intellectual class – that class being those who wield the power of the spoken or written word and who are distinguished from the labouring classes by the absence of direct responsibility for practical affairs. These intellectuals are onlookers, commentators, outsiders who, typically, criticize the existing order and challenge the ethics on which it is based. The highest numbers are in the higher education system, which has proliferated in the post-war period. Capitalism has given rise to a community of opinion-formers who undercut the moral supports that have held the potential excesses of capitalism in check. In the post-war period (and beforehand) religion has come under fire as archaic, the bourgeois family as patriarchal, private property as immoral and competition, saving and personal effort/self-improvement are scorned as stultifying. In short, the knowledge society brought into being by capitalism (and, indeed, largely sustained by capitalism) is disputing capitalism's very creed. Post-war intellectual thought has focused on the absence of moral certainties implicitly promoting a creed of anything goes, encouraging therefore the rampant individualism and materialism which we have sketched as America at its worst. If we are to give any credence to these views then Europe's future looks bleak indeed, especially in those states where there is a clearly defined intelligentsia such as France. The experience in Germany, as we noted in Chapter 4, finds a younger generation who have embraced a different political ideology (the Greens) and seem less inclined to engage in business – or at least in manufacturing industry. However, while capitalism and the knowledge society may generate a group of critical intellectuals it is impossible to believe that a group at a remove from economic activity will have sustained influence. But does this intellectual revolt against capitalism and hence against business have any bearing on the value system at play in Europe? Does it not feed off a long-held disdain for commerce in certain circles, a disdain that has its cultural roots in anti-Semitism?

Just what are European attitudes to business? We have seen earlier that at the time when the primary European education systems were forming there was a general perception that the professions were superior to commerce. Offered a choice between a role in commerce or in public administration Frederick Lugard wrote:

> 'If I go in for this I have to throw overboard the Indian Civil Service which if I passed it would be an infinitely better thing besides being a thoroughly gentlemanly occupation, and look at it how I may, I can't bring myself to think that an Assistant in a Sugar Factory is such.'

This was written in 1875 and, although it makes the point that administration is superior to commerce, how relevant, nearly a century and a quarter on, can such values truly be? The social milieu in which such a view could be advanced has been altered beyond all recognition – there are no European empires or aristocracies to validate such a choice or the language in which it is couched. At the time the super-wealthy (in Britain) were the aristocracy – in the 1880s 250 territorial magnates in the UK were millionaires, 29 multimillionaires. In 1994 a list of the 500 richest individuals in the UK was dominated by businessmen (some three-quarters of the list were self-made men). We do not have comparable statistics for other European nations but Britain is often seen as the most class-ridden of Europe's nation states, the one whose decline rested on insufficient investment in commerce and overenthusiastic homage to an aristocratic principle, so if the pattern is so altered in Britain it follows that it will be as much or more so on the continent. It is, furthermore, interesting in the light of the comments above concerning education systems and entrepreneurialism that the bulk of that 75% made their fortunes by their own efforts. Cultural attitudes towards business clearly do not inhibit commercial activity.

The levelling of European society

I have referred casually above to a general levelling of European society. In Europe only Britain has income inequality approaching that of the US, although there is less real poverty in Britain than in the US. In most European countries in the last 50 years the income gap between the upper 10% and the lower 10% has actually narrowed. 60–70% of Britons and Germans, and 80%

of Italians and Austrians, are committed to further reduction of income disparities, compared with just 29% of Americans. Since 1945 the structure of employment across Europe (and indeed the US) has shifted substantially away from manufacturing industry towards the service sector, giving rise to the phrase 'post-industrial society' and the term 'service class'. As early as the 1970s over half of all workers in western Europe were already employed in services and the shift from manual labour to service has led to an apparent *embourgeoisement* of society – in other words a drift from the working classes to the middle classes, which can be measured in part by the decline in trade union membership. Service class workers are salaried rather than waged – a traditional status symbol – usually better educated and have greater spending power and a higher number of consumer goods in their homes. Members of the service class act as individuals and have much less class identification. Class divisions remain – to be seen in styles of dress, accent, preferred leisure activities – especially in Britain, France and southern Europe, but terms such as gentleman, notions such as gentility, contempt for trade have little or no meaning. In a society where most people of the appropriate age aspire to work and where unemployment carries a certain stigma, class-based resistance to business is breaking down.

The prestige of the professions

It might be the case, however, that there remains a residual preference for the professions over commerce. On the one hand the professional adviser carries considerable cachet particularly in the UK – the lawyer, the accountant and the consultant all occupy a position of knowledge and power, and part of that power is intellectual power. Indeed, very often that intellectual power is registered by a professional qualification, the standards of which are fiercely controlled by professional associations. The cult of the qualification has more force in Europe, but also in Asia, than in the US. The MBA is increasingly carrying weight but outside the business world does not have the immediate impact. The professional adviser can also have substantial influence but without some of the risks taken by those he advises. In general, if the rewards are not as great as for some chief executives of major corporations, they compare extremely favourably at most other levels. Historically, since the nineteenth century the solicitor, the doctor and, to a lesser extent, the teacher have had a certain cachet and status in small towns – and some of that status lingers, transferring itself to the large practices – in the case of accountants and solicitors – that have taken the place of the original small operations. Typically, professional advisers have organized themselves into partnership structures – built on such values as trust and equality. While the old-style partnership format is not meeting the needs of partners today and is undergoing substantial change in a number of professions, some of those values are still associated with these organizations and their practitioners. As the figures above testify, Europeans have a concern to narrow income differentials between the very rich and the very poor and are much more prepared to support welfare systems via sometimes quite punitive taxation regimes than American or Asian counterparts. This evidence of social concern would reinforce the status of those in the caring professions.

Commerce and culture

While members of the professions populate high culture, featuring as linchpins in nineteenth-century European novels, the businessman has not been so well served. Despite the reality that some of Europe's major corporations began as relatively benevolent, paternalist institutions and retain some of the best elements of those early cultures, business is the terrain of the antihero rather than the hero. Only rarely in Europe do we see business heroes making the front pages, or enshrined within art forms – save where there is something sinister or shady to report. Charles Dickens' portrait of Mr Merdle, the unscrupulous banker in Little Dorrit, whose suicide reveals bankruptcy and financial ruin (not just for Merdle but for those in the slipstream of his activities) eerily prefigures the mysterious circumstances of the death of Robert Maxwell – an event which brought business to the front pages of the tabloids and broadsheets alike in Britain. Ernest Saunders, Bernard Tapie – these men are more likely to be recognized by Europeans than the Chief Executives of the top 50 European businesses. Rupert Murdoch is perhaps the closest we come to a universally known name, but again he is seen as more of an antihero than a hero – a figure who is controlling our thoughts by the insidious medium of television and newspapers.

Contrast the European situation with that in the US. America boasts an unrivalled literature concerned with business, far in excess of anything Europe can muster, and has a gallery of business heroes. A cross-section of the public would know the names of Lee Iacocca of Chrysler, Jack Welch of General Electric, Tony O'Reilly of Heinz. Popular culture, that reliable barometer of public opinion, gives prominence to business in the US. Two successful television exports from the US to Europe have been soap operas (the very concept of the soap being commercial) with their plots revolving around the machinations of two business empires – Dallas and Dynasty. While the Ewings and the Carringtons may not be the most positive images of the US business environment they are certainly compelling ones which, furthermore, testify to the glamour with which business is invested in the US. In Europe these have been watched avidly, but equally have been the focus of amused critical condescension. A business magazine profile of a CEO can read like an interview with a matinee idol, as this random selection from Fortune Magazine testifies. Under the heading 'Is Herb Kelleher America's best CEO?' comes a profile of the CEO of South-west Airlines couched thus:

> *'Herb does not disappoint. A lean man, just a shade over six feet, with a weathered face and thinning white hair, he glides to the microphone, Merit Ultra Lite in hand and begins speaking in a honeyed baritone ...'*

The reader could be forgiven for thinking this a profile of Frank Sinatra. The heroic image is further built up as we learn that this hard-drinking, heavy-smoking CEO – a sort of boardroom cowboy – was once a 'star athlete' at college, names as his hero Winston Churchill and is approaching his 40th wedding anniversary. He embodies the spirit of frontier America – the wholesome, John Wayne spirit, that is – and if the tone appears to come perilously close to caricature, with Kelleher emerging from the column inches like some latter day Roy Rogers, it is likely that that is simply the slant of a cynical European.

European cynicism towards business does not necessarily denote a deep-seated cultural antipathy to business. America's hegemony in the twentieth century has been predicated upon its business and economic success. The presidential remark, much quoted in this text, that the business of the American people is business would not have been uttered by any European head of state. Small wonder, then, that business, which has been the means by which many

Americans have acquired status, is accorded considerable respect. In the US there has long been a direct correlation between money and status. In Europe the relationship between the two is less obvious. If in America capital is primarily a matter of money, in Europe great store is set by cultural capital. Art, literature, music – high culture has left a legacy of heroism that is more closely connected with travails, suffering and poverty than wealth and status. *Buddenbrooks*, *A La Recherche du Temps Perdu*, two of the greatest written works to emerge from twentieth century Europe, show the decline of fortunes and invest that decline with a certain grandeur. Perhaps there is a certain inverted snobbery in celebrating decline. This is not to say that America is without its own high cultural traditions, but the primary cultural legacy from America is Hollywood – itself an industry, bent upon spreading the notion of glamour and providing all those involved in production – the studio bosses, the stars, the writers – with massive fortunes. Cinema has been taken up by the critical intelligentsia and even in its most popular form is fodder for sophisticated critique but, predictably, the intellectualization of cinema, via the arthouse, has been a European phenomenon – the Italian Visconti, the Swedish Ingmar Bergman, the French Jean-Luc Goddard, the German Fassbinder. Are these varying attitudes to money and culture between Europeans and Americans symptomatic of the different class regimes (can America really consider itself a classless society) or simply of divergent histories?

European culture – asset or liability?

It is hard to predict exactly what will be the determinants for economic success in the future. We can only extrapolate from past experience and assume that the major trading blocs need to be clear that they have a skilled work-force motivated to compete, governments capable of providing the appropriate infrastructure to support innovation within a society that has a high level of stability – both social and political. But populations also need to be able to change, to adapt to different external pressures.

During the course of the twentieth century change has become a constant factor for Europeans. The very landscape has been carved up by two world wars on its soil, leading to revisions and counter-revisions of frontiers. Nationhood – and the sense of identity that nationhood confers – has been in flux with various states being annexed or occupied while political ideologies have careered from far right to left, sweeping aside long-established modes of living. Through this Europeans have endured and adapted. Vestiges of old value systems inevitably remain – a fondness for the values implicit in professional service rather than corporate competition – but do not ultimately impede progress. Europeans are also good students. They have learned the lessons of American corporate models, are learning those of Japanese manufacturing processes and, most importantly, are coming together to learn from the lessons of their own past. Europeans understand the variable. The differences between the various nations, although sometimes deep, are in general variations on a common theme. Judged by the yardstick of flexibility, Europeans are more than equipped for future success.

To what extent, however, do the cultural factors considered in this chapter affect Europe's potential economic success or failure in the next century? We have seen that the rich European tradition of thought has allowed for the development of education systems which, against Asian and American models, are nothing if not robust but which, equally, can change. On current showing, the conservatism of the educated European elite would perhaps be better served by an economy where the corporation is king but entrepreneurialism is by no means defunct. As we have seen, the wealthiest are those who have made their money through commerce. Value is placed upon money, but money is not the sole measure. European veneration for social justice, at the expense of some individual wealth, is a factor likely to contribute to long-term stability – especially when compared with the American model. We have used the notion of a race for economic supremacy throughout this volume. One of the most famous races to emerge from the annals of European culture is that between the hare and the tortoise. Europe cannot be characterized as having the swiftness of the hare, as might the US or the newly industrialized nations of South Eastern Asia but, dogged and tough, may well have the resilience of that most ancient-looking of creatures, the tortoise.

10

Europe: the Practical Realities

> '... in the most general sense, Europe is distinct from America because of its greater emphasis on the social requirements of sustainable wealth and it is distinct from Asia because of its insistence on basic freedoms and democratic processes.'
>
> Ralf Dahrendorf.

What is Europe, relative to either Asia or the United States? The notion of the three areas or regions as distinct trading blocs is one that underpins this book and most others that consider the shape of the world in the coming century. But are they comparable entities? Asia, like Europe, is a continent comprising a number of different states, each of which has one dominant economic power. Europe's western states, however, have enjoyed far greater political stability and economic power for far longer than have Asia's newly industrializing nations. Both regions have a Communist legacy to consider and a mixture of ideological, religious and cultural influences to contain. These inevitably make for an uncertain future. The US, on the other hand, is one nation with significant regional differences but broad similarities in government and culture. It shares a common set of laws, a common defence policy, a common economic policy and a common language. Unlike the separate states of Asia or of Europe, it also shares a common set of risks and exposures. Asia and Europe, by dint of being a collection of states and skills, spread some of those risks. Is it better to be the homogeneous state that we see in the US, which has been such a successful formula in business terms and copied to great advantage by Japan and Germany? Or does diversity offer both the opportunity for greater innovation and creativity and the comfort of not having all one's eggs in one basket? Is there something in between? The formation of the European Union would suggest that there is – a spreading of risks, an easing of restrictions but a maintenance of distinction and diversity. An easy target for criticism, the EU for all its flaws is a remarkable, pioneering development which makes it hard to believe that the twentieth century represents the end of Europe. Perhaps in the closing years of the century we are simply seeing the end of Europe as we have known it – if we have ever fully known this unknowable entity. The next century will be no less Europe's than the last – but Europe might look, and indeed behave differently. Lord Dahrendorf's vision of a Europe which has a social and a political conscience and a will to provide the economic power to support those inclinations is perhaps a utopian one, but nonetheless fitting as an aspiration for the next millennium. The fulfilment of that aspiration will rest on our ability to overcome some of the practical impediments to union.

The concern of this chapter is to look at the practical issues that Europe confronts in an age of a global trading bloc, with multinational corporations turning themselves into global companies. Some of these issues will be influenced by and will influence in their turn the cultures of the separate nations that comprise Europe. Indeed, the vexed question of which countries should comprise Europe is rooted in culture. The practical considerations cover geographical, political, economic and social spheres. We cannot hope to do justice to them all but will look at the issue that lies behind the minutiae – what balance to strike between sameness and difference, uniformity and distinction.

The two big issues that this chapter will consider are the effects (and indeed the actuality) of the European Union and those of the fall of Communism and the entry of the former Soviet bloc into the plane of activity of the Western nations. First, we will look at some of the common complaints about Europe's lack of harmonization and consider the prognosis for overcoming them.

First, the minutiae

In modern technological economies there can be no question that a large economic unit is more efficient than the sum of its parts. America as a distinct continental unit has the benefits of unhindered movement of raw materials, labour, capital and finished product to all parts of the country, allowing for high productivity and specialization in favourable localities. In Europe the existence of national frontiers has, historically, imposed a very different set of circumstances. As an illustration, in 1989 goods travelling from the north to the south of Britain covering 750 miles would require a mere 36 hours to complete the journey. Once the channel had been crossed, however, the same distance required an additional 22 hours because of border stops, giving a journey time of 58 hours. Small wonder that the 11,000 businessmen consulted by Paolo Cecchini in his European Commission report into the impediments to the free flow of goods, services, persons and capital within Europe declared in favour of wholesale standardization of European practice. The report published in 1988 found that impediments such as different testing standards from one country to another or different bureaucracies (fiscal regimes, etc.) cost Europe some 5% of its GDP annually. The report also found that the removal of national differences in key areas would result in a one-off gain somewhere between 4.3 and 6.4% of GDP and deliver noninflationary growth of 7% in the medium term and around 5 million new jobs.

The single market

Less than a decade later the situation is considerably altered. Driven by Jacques Delors and Lord Cockfield a single market was designed comprising some 282 legislative measures which would bring member states of the then European Commission into alignment. By December 1992 some 260 of those legislative measures had, remarkably, been achieved. Single market legislation focused on the simplification of bureaucracy governing the transit of goods, on value added tax regimes, tax-free sales and tax-paid goods. The story is a little less encouraging in the context of public health, product safety and consumer protection – this is left to industrial bodies to administer rather than any public authority. Nevertheless, the tale is compelling and supportive of the notion of European Union.

Add to this the types of international co-operation fostered by the spirit of union. A lone Rolls-Royce developed the RB211 engine during the 60s and 70s. Development costs escalated far beyond estimates, the company could not find the money and went bankrupt. On the other hand, when British and French firms combined in the design and manufacture of Concorde, they produced one of the most advanced civil aircraft in the world. Then there is the extraordinary working monument to the notion of a truly continental Europe – the Channel Tunnel, which has altered travel times from the UK to cities in Europe by a substantial factor. The journey to Paris in 1989 would have taken 5½ hours, but now requires 3, to Brussels would have been 5 hours and is now 2¾, to Bonn a 9-hour journey is now cut to 6¾. The project is also giving rise to others such as the north European project which links Paris, London, Brussels, Amsterdam, Cologne and Frankfurt using both the Channel Tunnel and new sections of line designed for high-speed trains. The scheme will also incorporate regional as well as national needs. For example, the development of a London rail by-pass to take goods straight to the north of England and Scotland.

From these few examples it is clear that pooled capital is leading to increased innovation and increased access – that Europe is quite literally coming together.

Lifestyle differences

In my professional life as a head-hunter I find I can certainly move around the continent more freely – with the opening of the European skies in 1997 I shall be able to do so more than ever – and yet there are any number of hurdles that I have to scale if I wish to woo a Belgian businessman to come and join a UK plc or send a Swedish businessman to the French subsidiary of a Swiss-owned business (to choose randomly). There remains a fairly clear resistance to relocation on the part of a number of business people, which appears to me to be largely divorced from latent xenophobia, parochialism or fear of the unknown. Instead, they are practical and bound up with family structures. Increasingly, the community of European business leaders are in their 30s and 40s and merely one-half of a working couple. Can a working spouse guarantee a job commensurate with their skills in a country other than the one where they have gained the bulk of their experience? Possibly, if that spouse is engaged in commerce – but if the spouse is a lawyer, doctor or accountant the different legal, medical and fiscal systems which are practised and the differing qualifications required in order to practise from one state to another will preclude an easy transfer. Then there are the lifestyle issues. What of earnings levels? There is no clear parity of pay, the same compensation for the same job, across Europe. Nor is there even similar recognition of what constitutes a fair package of perquisites. To what extent those perquisites should be weighted towards health provision, life insurance, pension entitlements, bonus payments and living subsidies varies considerably and according to national custom and levels of national welfare. A Belgian couple relocating from Brussels to London would find that the spouse would in all probability earn less in real terms while being obliged to pay considerably more in child care costs. Older children will require international schools if they are to maintain the standards required for maximum achievement within the educational system of their native country. It might be the case that the family will need to split if educational needs are to be met in the country of origin – or the needs of one child might have to be put at risk.

However, some of these problems are red herrings. It is not easy to move people from one town to another in the same country – a move from east to west coast America will not be lightly contemplated. Different states have different laws and while they may not be as dramatically different in the US as in Europe they are nonetheless material. Colleagues in Asia find that moving people from one place to another, from Singapore to Hong Kong, is no less difficult than a move from Paris to London. Cultural affinity, family networks are all at play in the move from one locale to another, even within a very restricted radius.

The international market in senior appointments, although extensive, affects only a very small number of individuals and here the role of the corporation should not be underestimated. A business that regularly requires its top managerial tier to rotate through international assignments will offer support systems to the family and will reflect sacrifices made through hardship allowances or particularly tailored compensation packages. The type of person who contemplates an international career is also, increasingly, someone whose lifestyle decisions are geared around that ambition. Increasingly, international managers are people who have already been exposed in childhood and early life to more than one culture, who may have been educated outside the country of their birth or gained their early career training in another country, or pursued a course of management education overseas. Lifestyle changes will not provide insurmountable barriers to international moves.

Corporate Differences

International managers are more likely, in moving around the continent, to find themselves bewildered by the vast differences between corporate structures that exist around Europe than by the lifestyle differences that confront them. We deal separately (see Chapter 8) with how some corporate differences manifest themselves and what a German and a Swede can expect of one another when they are obliged to sit around a board room table – but here, briefly, we need to look at the style of the board. There is a growing literature about the role of the board, but in essence the board is the vehicle by which a corporation is governed. It has a chairman and a team of directors, some of whom will be executive, others non-executive (or outside). Generally, the board will be the custodian of strategy and ethics for the corporation; but it is difficult to speak in generalities since there is no one norm that dominates in a consideration of board structures and practices. Differences pertain in several areas, neatly glossed by Ada Demb and Freidrich Neubauer in their study of the corporate board.

The unitary board versus the two-tier board

The UK follows the pattern of boards in American corporations, which is to have just one board in which the ratio of non-executives to executives will vary from company to company. An alternative model is that which is mandatory in Germany, the Netherlands and Finland – the two-tier structure, comprising a management board of around five members and a supervisory board. The management board comprises executive members of the organization. The supervisory board brings together experienced executives from outside the organization. The two boards will have a common chair. In some countries, France and Switzerland for instance, there is some choice as to which structure to use – although the unitary form is probably most common.

Clearly, there are operational implications behind the preferred structure. The two-tier structure suggests a clear divide between management/strategic direction and a supervisory/watchdog function. Not surprisingly in view of the cultural model we have seen of Germany as legalistic (see Chapter 9) there are specific regulations governing practice on either board in Germany. It should be noted, however, that the two boards rarely operate in splendid isolation from one another – they will generally meet up, but only on an infrequent basis.

Companies with a unitary board structure will in all probability have regular and separate meetings of just the executives, but the primary vehicle for governance, the body that will ratify decisions, is the full board of executives and non-executives.

It should be noted that, while there is considerable variation from country to country in Europe as to which structure will predominate and what the legal requirements are pertaining to directors, there are also differences state by state in the US. Some dozen states legislate specific responsibilities while the others are much more vague.

Labour participation

In Holland and Germany labour interests are directly represented in the board room, although the two nations have evolved distinct models. The German supervisory board grants equal interest to shareholders and labour, while the Dutch works council system does not involve labour on the board but does insist on labour input to key decisions. In France, a company with more than 50 employees must have labour observers on the board. There is no labour involvement on boards that follow the Anglo-Saxon model.

Committee structures and frequency of meetings

The unitary boards meet more often than the supervisory boards in the two-tier structure, usually some 9–12 meetings per year compared with just quarterly meetings of supervisory boards. However, the management boards in the two-tier structure would meet on a fortnightly basis. Unitary boards make increasing use of committees (very common on Anglo-Saxon boards) which, in essence, parallel the function of the supervisory board. Common committees cover audit, remuneration, strategy and nomination (for senior recruitment).

The person of the chairman/chief executive

There has been considerable debate in the UK surrounding the role and person of the chairman and chief executive. Should one person hold both roles? A growing consensus suggests that there is considerable merit splitting the role and looking at a structure with a full-time chief executive and a part-time, non-executive chairman. This model is becoming more common in continental Europe but has tended to be used more as a mechanism for securing succession in French and Latin countries than as a model of good governance.

The implications of different board structures

The manner in which a board is organized reflects a host of cultural and political influences. The role of the PDG in France, for instance, reflects the centralization of the state. The PDG may act very much as if he is the owner of the business and so there is some disinclination to split the roles of chairman and chief executive and some discomfort with the degree of labour participation that law now demands. A director coming to work in a country where a different structure predominates from that to which he is accustomed will need to understand the rationale that informs that structure and assess the limits upon his own role accordingly. This adds to the difficulty of transferring from one environment to another that will not affect someone moving from one US company to another (even in the case of someone moving from one state with no legislation governing director responsibilities to another with statutory requirements for directors).

The problem, in this light, is one of local adaptation – a feature of European life. But how much of a problem is this? In the days of multinational companies the decisions made by a board are complex and cover issues at a far remove from the domestic base from which that multinational has grown. A particular board structure, be that American, Japanese, British or Italian, will not suit all circumstances and the interplay of local interest and expertise with transnational strategy is complex and irreducible to one structure of governance. The demands placed on international managers are profound and require a high level of personal adaptability, for which European difference is a good preparation.

One of the important things to emerge from the increasing attention being given to national idiosyncrasies in board structures is a concern not simply to level out all differences but to consider best practice. Across the business community in Europe there is growing interest in achieving the highest standards of corporate governance. The work of Adrian Cadbury in the UK has been of enormous influence across the continent and the principles contained in his report are, to varying degrees and at a varying pace, being adopted across Europe (note the Vienot report in France). Once again, the existence of difference can be seen to lead to debate and an overall upgrading of performance.

Some bigger practical problems

As I have tried to suggest above, the myriad differences that exist in the operational styles and practices of Europe's countries and companies can be overemphasized. If we subject any matter to inspection below a microscope and compare it with some other matter that appears similar we will uncover difference – but that difference may have little actual effect on performance.

There are, all the same, some real consequences of different fiscal and legal regimes around Europe. Paolo Cecchini calculated that the burden of different tax and audit regimes around Europe can account for between 10 and 30% of the costs of an organization's finance departments. Similarly, if a European were to undertake a grand tour of Europe's nation states and change money into and out of the local currency at every different national stop, over 50% of the capital would be consumed in the exchange transaction. But here we start to strike at the bigger issues that confront Europe – the extent to which we can or, indeed, should contemplate increasing standardization, which must take us into a consideration of the European Union, what it is, what it stands for and what are its limits.

The European Union

Brief background

The European Union (EU) is a unique European vehicle, the product of twentieth-century historical forces, the vision of several key figures and the support of a group of intellectuals in the elites of the six founding members. It has never been, as have communism or nationalism, a movement with massive public support but has established itself as an essential tool of governance by dint of the success of many of its measures. Entry to the Union is now increasingly coveted by European states who remain on the outside, but the extent of involvement is a political hot potato in some of the existing member states.

Brief history

The impetus to European integration was political, economic and military. The desire to prevent war between European states and to foster friendly relations between France and Germany was a critical factor. The US was keen to engage Europe in the orchestration of its own recovery, so encouraged the economies of scale implicit in union. America had the additional incentive of wanting to restore one of its most important markets. All parties became increasingly concerned to secure the western states of Europe from the threat of communism to the east – the 1948 Communist coup in Czechoslovakia and the withdrawal of some US troops from Germany to fight in Korea made many Europeans uneasy about their Eastern border of Germany. The chronology of integration has been:

1947 The Organization for European Economic Co-operation (OEEC), founded by 17 nations to distribute funds from the US Marshall plan. East European nations excluded (the will of Stalin).

1949 The Council of Europe established. A permanent European assembly to plan European integration. East Europeans not involved. Britain a reluctant, obstructive participant (due to Commonwealth and Atlantic focus).

Formation of NATO

1950 Schuman Plan first proposed by French Commissioner of Planning Jean Monnet and Foreign Minister Robert Schuman. A pooling of European coal and steel resources that would bind France and Germany together.

1951 Treaty of Paris leading to the European Coal and Steel Community involving France, Germany, Italy and the Benelux countries, which comes into being in 1952.

1954 Failure of plans to develop a European defence council and a European political community.
1955 A common economic market and forum to deal with atomic energy proposed.
1957 Treaty of Rome signed in March by the six ECSC members.
1958 The European Economic Community (EEC) and European Atomic Energy Community (Euratom) come into being.
1965 The executive bodies of the ECSC, EEC and Euratom merged to form the European Community.
1973 Enlargement from six to nine members with the addition of the UK (entry previously vetoed by De Gaulle), Ireland and Denmark.
1981 Admission of Greece.
1986 Admission of Spain and Portugal.
1987 Single European Act formalizes political and institutional change to enable the Single Market to be achieved.
1991 Maastricht Treaty agrees plans for Economic and Monetary Union with a single currency to be introduced by 1999 and the three pillars concept incorporating economic union and the development of a common foreign and security policy and co-operating on justice and home affairs. Significant opt-out clauses inserted by Britain and Denmark.
1993 The term European Union comes into force.
1995 Enlargement to 15 with the admission of Austria, Finland and Sweden.

The institutions of the European Union

The European Commission

The executive, permanent civil service of the EU, headquartered in Brussels with a staff of around 13,000 people – a third of whom are engaged in translation and interpretation. The body that prepares and formulates policy proposals and legislation, responsible for administering the Community and for ensuring that decisions are carried out. It has the legal authority to bring legal action against persons, companies or states that have violated EU rules.

The Commission is directed by 20 Commissioners – 2 each from Britain, France, Germany, Italy and Spain and one form the other ten countries – who are nominated by their governments and approved by agreement of the 15 states for a renewable five-year term. The European Parliament approves the Commission as a whole, but not individual nominations. The President is chosen from among the Commissioners who act in the interests of the EU, not in defence of national interest.

The Commission acts in a collegiate fashion with decisions made by majority rather than unanimity. Each Commissioner is assigned a specific policy area or areas and has a cabinet, a small staff of aides.

The Council of Ministers

The main forum for decision making consisting of representatives of each of the 15 states who must approve the proposals of the Commission before they can be implemented. The Council is not a fixed group of people. Its membership changes according to the subject under discussion – finance, transport, agriculture. The Minister in each of the states responsible for this portfolio will take up the seat at the Council. The most regular meetings are those on foreign policy, which take place monthly. The principle of majority voting applies in most but not all areas (tax matters require unanimity). The Council has 87 votes that are weighted; 62 votes are required for a qualified majority so votes can be blocked by a coalition of 26.

The Committee of Permanent Representatives (Coreper) – comprising the representatives of the member states who hold ambassadorial rank – meets weekly and acts as an important conduit between the Commission and the Council of Ministers.

The European Parliament

The developing political assembly of the EU and composed of 626 members directly elected in the 15 states for a 5 year term in accordance with the size of the population of the state.

Country	Numbers of MEPs
Austria	21
Belgium	25
Denmark	16
Germany	99
Greece	25
Spain	64
France	87
Ireland	15
Italy	87
Luxembourg	6
Netherlands	31
Portugal	25
Britain	87
Finland	16
Sweden	22

Members come from over 60 political parties and usually come together in political groups rather than national blocs. Parliament meets one week a month in Strasbourg, its 3600-strong secretariat meets in Luxembourg and its committees meet in Brussels.

Parliament has the power to dismiss the Commission on a two-thirds majority (never exercised), the power to approve or reject the budget and since 1975 has been involved in drawing up the budget with the Commission for approval by the Council of Ministers. The Parliament has no formal powers over the Council but is consulted prior to nomination of the President of the Commission. The Single European Act extended the Parliament's legislative powers. It can accept, reject or amend some proposals, ratify new international agreements and veto some agreements concluded by the Council and the admission of new members to the EU.

The Court of Justice

The Court of Justice sits in Luxembourg, administers EU law and arbitrates in disputes involving the EU treaties. It checks that the budget is being spent appropriately. The court consists of 15 judges – one from each state – plus the President of the Court; appointments run for six years. It works by the rule of unanimity and EU law is accepted by the member states as superior to national law if there is a conflict between the two. By 1995 the Court had made some 3800 judgements.

The Uniqueness of the Union

The brief history of union above and outline of its key structures cannot convey the extraordinary endeavour that it represents. The following is an attempt to do justice to the practical role the Union plays in the future of Europe, deriving from the impassioned and thoughtful recent studies by Ralf Dahrendorf (*Why Europe Matters*) and Paul Hirst and Grahame Thompson (*Globalization in Question*).

Q. What is the European Union?
A. It is the most developed and complexly conceived and constructed of the major trading blocs.
A. It is an entirely new venture for which there is no pre-existing political model for it is neither unitary, federal or confederal. The powers of the European Union derive from the principal treaties and the role of the individual nation states remain critical, giving political legitimacy and accountability to the supra national construct.
A. It is a laboratory, an experiment in government – political, social and economic – which may have far-reaching consequences, offering a new model for something that stands between the global and the national.
Q. What is the significance of the European Union?
A. It has come into being through a concerted desire to eliminate the possibility of internecine war, in recognition of the intolerable strife that has caused such suffering in Europe during the twentieth century. It is thus one of the most sustained efforts at pacifism ever conceived.
A. It is a vehicle to ensure the collective well-being, through organized trade over a large economic unit, of the population of the member states. It is an organization that will ensure the voice of Europe's citizens can be heard in world affairs.
A. It is a testimony to the power of European culture to devise innovative methods for safeguarding its own future and providing a new model for governance as powerful, potentially, in the next century as the nation

state has been in the last. It is a union that complements but does not replace the nation state.

Q. What has the European Union achieved?

A. A methodology for a group of nations with sometimes conflicting interests to come to majority decisions on critical areas of policy.

A. A forum to ensure continual dialogue on a political party rather than a purely national level between the peoples of Europe.

A. Provision of an arbitration facility which can defuse potentially incendiary disagreements such that violence or unilateral action by any member state towards or against another has not occurred.

A. Creation of a single market which has materially affected the lives of the citizens of Europe.

A. Provided a paradigm of international co-operation which is attractive to non-members.

What are the challenges it faces?

The answers above attribute rather lofty aspirations to the Union but the original vision underpinning the Union is, rightly, an ambitious one – to secure lasting harmony amongst the member states.

The preamble to the 1951 Treaty of Paris which created the ECSC includes the following grand claim on behalf of the principal players, that they were

> *'resolved to substitute for age old rivalries the merging of their essential interests; to create, by establishing the economic community, the basis for a broader and deeper community among peoples long divided by bloody conflicts; and to lay the foundations for institutions which will give direction to a destiny henceforward shared ...'*

The governing principle as set out in Article 1 of the Treaty of Rome is put in slightly less grandiose terms but nevertheless conveys a similar message:

> *'The community shall have as its task, by establishing a common market and progressively approximating the economic policies of Member States, to promote throughout the Community a harmonious development of economic activities, a continuous and balanced expansion, an increase in sta-*

bility, an accelerated raising of the standards of living and closer relations between the States belonging to it...'

Any entity of such scope must, inevitably, face challenges of some scale and the EU is, in the closing years of the twentieth century, confronting several critical issues which if not satisfactorily resolved could substantially reduce Europe's chances of securing a strong global position in the next century. These are issues of extent, employment, immigration, enlargement and, contained in the issue of enlargement, inequalities within member states, especially those to the south and east. We shall look at each of these in turn.

The question of extent
In January 1963 De Gaulle, contemplating British entry to the EEC declared:

> 'England in fact is insular, maritime, bound by her trade, her markets, her supplies to countries that are very diverse and often far away ... The nature, the structure, the situation that are peculiar to England are very different from those of the Continental countries. How can England, as she lives, as she produces, as she trades, be incorporated into the Common Market as it was conceived and as it works?'

De Gaulle's stance has been interpreted as one of reluctance to relinquish the primary position of France in the EEC, to hand over a certain amount of power to Britain who, after all, were seeking preferential terms of entry which it would be hard not to extend to others. However, the British attitude to the EU has consistently been one of scepticism and writing over three decades later, Paul Hirst and Grahame Thompson note:

> 'Britain is, quite frankly, a menace to the Union. Britain's institutions of economic and social governance deviate so far from the continental norm that, without major structural reform, the UK is a liability to Europe.'

Both the comments by De Gaulle and the modern commentators may have a high degree of truth. Britain's experience during the Second World War was very different from those of her continental neighbours. Her Commonwealth and US relationships, moreover, were binds every bit as important as (more so than) those in Europe. Britain, for all Churchill's pioneering support of a 'United States of Europe', did not feel the same compulsion to put economic and political affairs between the nations of Europe on an equal footing. Confidence in British institutions also remained high, not for Britain a sense that new supranational institutions were appropriate to guard against any perceived excesses of the nation state. So Britain had few of the motives for union that the other members had and, once admitted, little fundamental sympathy with the mechanisms of the Union. The decision-making system within the European Union is built on consensus. The British political system is adversarial. The entire understanding of political debate and decision making differs in Britain from that which prevails in Europe. Again it is not surprising that commentators and the lay observer in the UK feel little empathy. All the more ironic, then, that Britain's entry to the Union was heralded as a prelude to diminishing the democratic deficit. Indeed, it was widely felt that Britain's long parliamentary traditions would come to the aid of Europe's nascent democractic systems and render them more efficient, accountable and transparent. Britain's record is not good. The lowest turn-out in elections, the most grudging attitude to the extension of the powers of the European parliament and a continuing rivalry between the national and the supranational institutions of government – to date this seems to be an not entirely unfair assessment of the British contribution to the Union.

It would be wrong to overplay the role of British dissent – it would be to borrow some of the hubris that informs the attitude towards sovereignty, the dream of independent glory. Britain alone will not shake the union. The Union began without Britain and can continue, should it need to, without Britain. Equally, it would be mistaken to assume that there is not considerable dissent elsewhere in Europe concerning the various European institutions. However, Britain is perhaps guilty of a form of filibustering – constantly hindering the development of improved institutions by a return to issues that contain implicit contradiction. A case in point is the obsession with sovereignty. As Hirst and Thompson point out, Britain cannot on the one hand embrace the free market principle of the single market, which has necessarily eroded a central plank of national sovereignty, but on the other oppose in general the principle of erosion of national sovereignty. To do so is to run with the hare and hunt with the hounds.

In the assessment of the significance of the Union above we stress that it is an evolving form of government that could have far-reaching consequences for global democracy. There is no template for the architects of Union to follow; it is a tortuous learning process and in any learning process there needs to be debate. I do not mean to deny the validity of the debate as to the extent of the Union. However, one of the critical issues the union faces at the moment is the need to be able to act quickly and decisively and so it needs to have its house in order, its structures clear. A watering down of powers into a bland subsidiarity is no more appropriate than an attempt to construct a macrocosmic supranational state – what is needed is clear, innovative, creative thinking on the extent of the Union's powers. Europe does not have much time and what can seem sometimes to be time-wasting tactics on behalf of Eurosceptics could undermine the position of Europe in global affairs and squander a carefully built legacy.

Union for union's sake

In the same breath that it is possible to criticize Britain for filibustering, it is possible to criticize the Union for stubborn adherence to a facet of union which appears to be more likely to lead to division than increased harmony and which serves as something of a distraction from other pressing concerns. This issue is the fraught one of monetary union. The European Monetary System was established in 1979 with the European Currency Unit (ECU) and the exchange rate intervention mechanism creating a zone of monetary stability throughout the Union. This was only a partial success since Britain did not fully join the system. The Delors Report of 1989 proposed further economic and monetary integration. The rationale behind this was that the gains derived from the single market could be greatly enhanced by the creation of an economic and monetary union (EMU) and, ultimately, a single currency. Exchange rates would remain the same and the there would be no need to change money from one currency to another. The Maastricht Treaty set a timetable for a three-stage transition to EMU and a single currency by 1999. Parity of economic performance and policy was deemed critical to any single monetary policy and so the Treaty stipulated certain 'convergence criteria' which members must meet by 1997 to qualify. The four criteria are:

- a high degree of price stability with a rate of inflation close to that of the three best performing member states;
- the elimination of excessive public sector deficits;
- observance of the normal fluctuation margins provided for in the ERM for at least 2 years with no devaluation against the currency of any other member state; and
- stable long-term interest rates which should not exceed by more than 2% the average interest rates of the three top performing member states assessed by price stability.

Currency turbulence in the early 1990s followed by recession has called into question the ability of many members to meet the convergence criteria. Thus we face a situation of two-tier entry and, as a consequence, variation in status from state to state. There is no hard and fast evidence that monetary union will yield the results hoped for from it. Best estimates suggest that the elimination of money changing costs will yield about 0.33% of GDP. Some regard the race to meet the convergence criteria as having deflationary consequences. In short, monetary union might represent premature, misplaced effort. Given time, however, monetary union might deliver substantial benefits and the need to meet convergence criteria could lead to genuine infrastructural changes, which could create more jobs (notably through public sector reforms). Time, however, is running out.

The issue of monetary union is tied up with the notion of the extent of the union and the timeliness of any extension of unity. As noted at the outset to this chapter Europe has to strike the right balance between sameness and difference, uniformity and distinction, and to this we should add that Europe also has to find the appropriate pace for change. At present the unseemly dash for monetary union seems likely to deliver disunity and as such should be questioned. The context has changed so perhaps the timetable should change too. The fundamental idea, however, remains sound.

The issue of unemployment

Unemployment is part of a wider set of demographic problems that confront Europe (and, in fairness, are of consequence in all the developed economies of the world). In 1992 unemployment across the union was five times the figure of 1973. A crisis was identified but by the end of 1996 nearly an additional 1 million were out of work. Barley 70% of men of working age are in employment compared with 85% in the early 1970s. There has been a rise in the number of women working – from 43% to 49% between 1973 and 1994, but this does not make up for the shortfall in male employment and, predictably, a good third of those women are in part-time work. Compare the situation in Europe with that in the US. For every 100 jobs that there were in America 25 years ago there are now nearly 160, for every 100 jobs that there were in Europe 25 years ago there are now 96. In a number of states unemployment is below 5%, half the European average. Many of Europe's jobs are in the protected state sector rather than in dynamic, growing, open markets. This would appear to support the argument for monetary union and the moves to meet the convergence criteria via a substantial reform of the public sector, but the point about timing remains constant.

The causes of unemployment in Europe are not easy to assess. Some are structural, the product of rigid labour markets. However, a Bank of England Inflation Report in 1996 stated that the decline in employment had less to do with the absence of jobs than a rise in what it termed the 'economically inactive'. In other words, society is structured in such a way as to allow people to drop out. This brings us to the fraught issue of welfare. One of the happy consequences of living in a European state is the level of care exercised towards the population by the state, exemplified by the British welfare state. There is no question but that welfare systems in western Europe have been a major success in providing social services and transfer payments to all those who need them, thus attempting to ensure a decent standard of living for all. But there might be an argument that social welfare has broken the automatic link between personal effort, between work and saving and personal reward, income and consumption. Studies of developing underclasses show that while social welfare does not directly cause rising crime and has not in itself led to the breakdown of the family, the presence of a safety net might establish the conditions that enable social decline. If we were to subscribe to the notion that single parenthood is more likely to lead to juvenile crime, for instance, then there could be some link with the social welfare systems that have enabled single parenthood to exist. The stigma that surrounded illegitimacy 30 years ago has been displaced by a range of welfare rights, which have underpinned and normalized lifestyles that were previously deemed unacceptable. Such an argument would need some careful study and strong statistical support but it would not seem unreasonable to suggest that welfare systems have established a sense of an individual right to income irrespective of behaviour or effort. In this way, modern welfare systems may, unintentionally, have contributed to an erosion of personal responsibility and legitimized the increasing incidence of the 'economically inactive'.

Whatever the causes of unemployment there can be no question that it represents a critical issue for the European Union in coming years. Assuming that we do wish to sustain our welfare systems we need increasing rather than decreasing work-forces to support them. The greying population across Europe with accompanying pension and health-care costs is one of the demographic trends that intersects with the issue of unemployment. Pensions alone account for about 25% of the increase in public expenditure across Europe since 1960. As we have seen, European societies are concerned to minimize the gap between the richest and the poorest and this commitment is one of the few defining features of being European. The harsh practical reality is that Europe needs to find a formula for maintaining high levels of care and personal responsibility in parallel with one another in order to fund the commitment and thereby preserve a population which is affluent, aspirational and therefore inclined to compete and innovate.

Immigration, inequality and enlargement

Twentieth-century European conflict has had nationalism as its focus. Any substantial rise in immigration inevitably gives rise to fears of a resurgence of nationalism in its most sinister, neo-Nazi form. The growth in popularity of right-wing politicians is alarming. Far-right parties gained 22% of the vote in Austria in the last general election and 12% in France. Germany, inevitably the focus for fears of neo-Nazi activity, shows little sign of movement towards a fascist revival but, nonetheless, suffers increasing levels of dissatisfaction on the part of its indigenous population towards the huge number of immigrants. In 1992 Germany took in about 75% of all political refugees seeking asylum in the EU, in the decade from 1985 to 1995 Germany took in five times as many immigrants as France, the next most popular destination for those seeking asylum. In 1989 prior to German reunification West Germany recorded about

100 attacks on foreigners by right-wing extremists. By 1992 the rate had risen to well over 2000. Inevitably the immigrant population become scapegoats for any social and economic problems. As we have seen, social welfare programmes are already stretched by the demands of an ageing population and high levels of unemployment. Widespread immigration, then, constitutes a considerable potential problem to the European Union assuming that migrants will require social support. In reality the Turkish immigrant population to West Germany is an important source of taxation revenue and a consumer market – but reality and perception are not always in harmony. In fairness, as with most of the demographic issues that affect the Union, immigration will also affect the states with which Europe finds itself in competition in Asia and in the US.

Much of the influx of foreigners to the European Union comes from countries that are in the process of applying for membership to the Union – Turks and Poles in particular are sizeable migrant groups into West Germany. If the Union is enlarged to include other poorer nations and given that entry to the Union grants any citizen the right to move freely between member states, might that not serve to increase the problem of immigration while simultaneously placing an additional burden on the coffers of the Union and thence its members (either by the need for additional funds or the deflection of funds from the existing to the new members)? Germany has more Italian and Greek immigrants than it has Polish immigrants, which might be attributable to ease of access through EU membership.

Case studies of previous enlargements

Although the enlargement of the Union currently being contemplated is well beyond the scale of previous enlargements, it has been the case before that the EU has given admission to countries substantially poorer than the core members. Ireland, which joined the EU in 1973, provides one interesting example. Having received total subsidies from the EU in the region of IR£2 billion Ireland enjoys a much improved standard of living and in 1995 saw real GDP growth of an all-time high of 8.6%. Thanks to European assistance Ireland's economy has grown faster than any of its European partners, bringing Irish income per head to 92% of the EU average. In the past quarter-century since joining the EU, Ireland's rural population has been almost entirely rehoused, excellent roads have been built, schools have been transformed, universities hugely expanded and a generous welfare system constructed (supported by high levels of income tax). As a consequence EU subsidy levels can now be reduced.

The story is not one of unalloyed successes, however. Greece joined the EU in 1981 and since 1989, despite receipt of substantial EU funds (2% of GDP from 1989 to 1994), has had severe economic difficulties, with unemployment at around 9% and high inflation at 12%. Greece is further from meeting the convergence criteria than any other EU member. Nevertheless, there are signs of regional growth, spearheaded by EU money. The picture in Spain and Portugal is better. Both countries joined in 1986 and Spain subsequently enjoyed five years of very rapid growth with GDP growth at 4.5%, well above the EU average for the period. In 1992 the economy went into recession but there have been good signs of growth. Inflation currently stands at 5%, but unemployment is a serious problem at 20%. Portugal is an EU success story. On admission GDP stood at 51% of the EU average but now stands at 66%. The economy is growing at a rate of 3.2% per year (compared with 2.3% for the EU as a whole). Unemployment has risen but at 6.8% is relatively low and inflation at 4.5% in 1994 was the lowest it had been for 25 years. For both, the chances of meeting the convergence criteria are relatively low, but the overall economic prognosis is generally fair.

What do these case studies tell us? That although admitting relatively poorer economies to the EU is an expensive strategy it is one that, over time, yields results. As Ireland is now starting to pay its way, so in time will the other nation states. Quite apart from the humanistic imperative to contain poverty (and the numerous by-products of poverty) the admission of more nations to the EU extends the market and so the opportunities.

Set against the encouraging signs from the southern states of the EU the scale of enlargement we are currently contemplating. Formal EU membership applications have come from Turkey, Malta, Cyprus, Poland, Hungary, Slovakia, Romania and the Czech Republic. It is the East European states which pose the greatest potential problem.

First in line for admission to the EU are the central European states, the so-called Visegrad countries (Poland, Hungary, the Czech Republic and Slovakia). Under current EU rules admission of just these countries would increase the EU budget for agricultural support and regional development by as much as 75%. This would place an almost intolerable strain on an already groaning EU budget. Then there is the matter of the Common Agricultural Policy, a thorn in the side of the EU for a number of years, a monster that consumes half the EU's budget and is in urgent need of reform. Central and east European countries are relatively more dependent on agriculture than those in western Europe. Farm workers make up 32% of employment in Romania, 27% in Poland, 17% in Bulgaria, 10% in Slovakia and 8% in Hungary. These figures compare with western figures of 2% in the UK, 4% in Germany and 6% in France. Bringing east European countries into the EU would be very expensive under the present CAP regime. This may simply be another argument for the urgent reform of CAP. Unemployment is a problem in the east European states (15% in Poland – the current average for member states is around 11%) and the catapulting of the populations of eastern states from state support into the maelstrom of free market forces is an additional pressure. On the positive side, however, the central and eastern states represent a large potential market for EU goods with the Visegrad nations having a total population over 60 million. Moreover, east European nations have a well-trained work-force, ready to take on skilled manufacturing. This factor is, for some, as much a negative as a positive, for inevitably there would be fears that the huge low-wage pool represented by the eastern states would prove alluring to investors to the detriment of other parts of the Union.

Quite apart from the additional costs of integrating the east European nations into the EU there are the structural implications. The institutions of the EU were designed around an original group of just 6 members and are already overstretched by the necessity to serve 15. Any further enlargement will require substantial revision of the mechanisms of government.

The problems attendant upon enlargement are massive. However, the rejection of east European states might bring a different, larger set of problems. Simply because the Communist regime has come to an abrupt end in eastern Europe does not mean that any threat from the region has automatically been defused. The dismantling of a Communist ideology and its replacement with a free market ethos happened almost overnight. Mental attitudes, however, change far more slowly and a culture or set of ethical practices that have had 50 years and more to become entrenched cannot be eradicated on an instant. For the moment, east European states look to Europe as a model and aspire for membership of the Union. If left out in the cold by the West, however, how long will that reverence for the Western way of life remain? High unemployment, a resentment of the higher standard of living in the West and its closed markets plus a lack of clear leadership could substantially alter attitudes to the West. Francis Fukuyama, in his fascinating cultural study *Trust*, paints a picture of a deeply individualistic society in the former Soviet state (and by extension others in East Europe):

> '... the Soviet state was very powerful, and there were many atomized individuals and families, but in between there were virtually no social groups whatsoever. The ironic consequence of a doctrine designed to eliminate human selfishness was that people were made more *selfish* ...'

Fukuyama describes this phenomenon as being a society without a middle, that middle being the network of civil associations (church, clubs, business networks) between the family and the state which engender and encourage trust between peoples unrelated. The picture of rampant individualism he depicts is akin to that we have seen in an earlier apocalyptic vision of the US (see Chapter 9). The presence of such a society on Europe's doorstep is not a comforting thought. The need to secure the West against the volatility in the East is expensive whichever method we select. Economic support, however, would appear to be more likely to pay dividends than defence through military means. Both the EU and NATO in accepting any new members are likely to give priority to the most advanced states and so, ironically, neglect the very ones that pose the greatest threat.

The story is not all bad. Portugal's GDP at admission was lower than Slovakia's is today and, as we have seen, Portugal has turned in its strongest economic performance for generations with EU assistance. Long transition periods were granted to Spain and Portugal to bring them to a common standard with other members. Longer may be required for some of the states of western Europe – but there exists a precedent.

South-east Europe presents another major challenge to the EU. Apart from the former Yugoslavia, there is Albania, a poor Muslim country in the throes of considerable civil strife, Macedonia and, most importantly, Turkey – a loyal NATO member and an important ally, already refused entry on economic grounds and because of concerns about Turkey's record on human rights. There are also the microstates Malta (already refused admission once) and Cyprus.

Since the reunification of Germany the Eastern Lander have received some $100 million per year in net transfers from Western Germany. The Eastern Lander now have a state-of-the-art telecommunications infrastructure and are in the process of acquiring a good transport network. They have the most modern production facilities in Europe as well as a superb new housing infrastructure. However, they are now growing more slowly than their Eastern neighbours partly because labour costs in the remainder of the former Eastern bloc are at third-world levels and undercutting those in Eastern Germany. As West Germany has taken seriously its obligation to East so should western Europe take seriously its obligation to the states to the east. Hirst and Thompson put forward the view that the EU should mimic West German action and give long-term infrastructure investment aid and long-run trade credits. The increase in public works would remedy unemployment and trade credits would enable the purchase of capital goods for reconstruction. The effects of trade credits would stimulate Western firms in the depressed capital goods sector, leading to rising employment in the West, increasing domestic demand and the tax base for social measures. It is the claim of Hirst and Thompson that such 'continental Keynsianism' would be the most effective means of replicating the economic boom after 1945. Such a vision, however, remains a utopian one for, as Jacques Delors found, there is considerable resistance amongst member states to expanding the EU central budget and allocating those funds to reconstruction.

As we have seen the EU's decision-making methodology is one of consensus and consensus, inevitably, leads to moderate rather than radical action. In the case of the enlargement issue, the only sensible, realisable course is probably the moderate one. The logical halfway house would seem to be to offer entry to some states making explicit the promise that entry in time would be forthcoming to others. Given that the requirement to maintain peace in Europe and to resolve historic enmities was one of the founding principles behind the European Union it would be a betrayal of the vision if the current members turned their backs on the opportunity to secure – or attempt to secure – something like stability and prosperity on their neighbours to the east and south with which there have been long cultural and trading links. Moreover, it would be sheer folly to ignore this opportunity and, if nothing else, the argument of enlightened self-interest should hold some sway.

Conclusion

Writing in the late 1980s and predicting which of the world powers would be pre-eminent in the twenty-first century, Professor Samuel Huntington (an advocate, incidentally, of culture as the most powerful influence on the human spirit) wrote:

> '... it is possible to conceive of a European ideological appeal comparable to the American one ... A federation of democratic, wealthy, socially diverse, mixed-economy societies would be a powerful force on the world scene. If the next century is not the American century it is more likely to be the European century.'

Despite the, at times, gloomy consideration of practical hurdles confronting Europe the reality of the situation remains that Europe has a great deal going for it. Many of the problems Europe faces are those that confront her main competitors – not least the demographic issues. For all their diversity and apparent conflicts of interest the current states of the European Union are broadly united ideologically in a commitment to maintain the level of social well-being and political stability consistent with strong economic performance. The precedent for support being given to poorer regions and the largesse shown by the Western Lander of Germany to the Eastern Lander are encouraging signs that the European Union is not the focus for cronyism that its harsher critics would claim. It would appear that Europe is committed to some form of self-extension which can only lead to extended opportunities for growth and success. The Union itself, for all its flaws, is perhaps the most encouraging symbol for Europe – a testimony to European innovation and co-operation. Moreover, it is a living, evolving organism and the scrutiny to which it is subject can only ensure its health and well-being. As a collection of states committed to the development of common ethics and principles of conduct the Union is a fitting expression of European identity – something between the national and the global, between the polar opposite and the mirror image. In an age where globalization has become a by-word and the fate of the nation state is at least in question Europe is, once again, a path-finder.

11

Conclusion

'Having experienced the horrendous irrationality latent in the nationalist form of recognition, Europe's populations have gradually come to accept universal and equal recognition as an alternative.'
Francis Fukuyama, *The End of History and the Last Man*.

'What is proper to a culture is to not be identical to itself. Not to not have an identity, but not be able to identify itself, to be able to say "me" or "we"…'
Jacques Derrida, *The Other Heading*.

The primary concern of this book has been with business and with which power will seize business supremacy in the coming decades. The assumption underpinning the book is that we are at something of an impasse at present, with no one clear power in the ascendancy. This creates an opportunity for the most enterprising or visionary to move into pole position. I might have called the book *The Trade Wars*, given its focus on business and trade. That I did not do so reflects the fact that far more than mere trade is at issue as we move into the next millennium. In the previous chapters we have surveyed, in some detail, the economies of the United States, Japan, the emerging Asian economies and, of course, Europe, and what becomes apparent is that there is not a great deal to choose between the trade practices of these various players. Industrial capitalism, which gave rise to the corporation-dominated business arena, has provided the model for each economy and the cycle of development has, broadly, been parallel. The most successful economies are those which have managed to develop large, multinational corporations but which have balanced these with a range of smaller, more innovative companies from which can come new technologies, new developments. The ability of economies to support those smaller companies through the transition to larger companies, while not neglecting the imperative to continue to encourage entrepreneurial endeavour, has also been a marked factor in success. These last elements are bound up with the notion of culture, with the development of values and attitudes consistent with success. No successful business economy has been built without a strong, shared cultural imperative – the pioneering zeal of early America, the determination of the devastated Japanese and German peoples to recover their pride and prosperity – these have been the principal factors giving these economies their initial impetus. No successful business economy will be sustained without due cognizance being given to the force and influence of culture. So it is that this book is called *The Culture Wars*, since it is with the weapon of culture that the battle for business supremacy will be fought and won.

Culture is no more fixed than the histories and circumstances which contribute to it. The cultural advantages enjoyed by one group of peoples may be reversed with changing trends, values and opinions. Culture can only be predictable over a very limited time horizon, as can future events. We have seen already how South Korea and Ghana experienced similarly low levels of GNP 30 years ago and that while Ghana remains one of the world's most impoverished nations, South Korea is in the elite of developing nations. The factors that have given rise to the vast discrepancy between the two nations can be readily explained with the benefits of hindsight, but how easily might they have been predicted? Eric Lomax, a survivor of a Japanese prisoner of war camp and author of a book charting his dramatic shift in attitude to his former captors notes:

> *'It was astonishing to be walking around this handsome town: a few years before I could not have imagined meeting a Japanese person voluntarily and now I was strolling in streets full of them, a tourist in my seventies, an honoured guest of two good people. Everyone we met was extremely courteous, and it was wonderful to me to see these crowds of smiling, well-dressed young people who are heirs to an economic superpower that leads the world in electronics, when I remembered my patient explanations of how a radio transmitter works in that wooden room in Siam in 1943.'*
>
> Eric Lomax, The Railway Man.

The human capacity for change on both an individual and a collective level in a very short space of time can be quite breathtaking, and defiant of any attempt to predict or second-guess. People may change, events may give rise to very different responses to situations and people encountered previously, but some cultural traits are very deep rooted and while the shoots above ground level may respond to prevailing conditions those roots will remain secure. The cultural factors that gave rise to Lomax's enduring hatred of his Japanese torturers were the very same that enabled him to understand the torment of his torturers and to forgive. So, we can be more confident in our prediction of cultural influences than we can of the outputs of those influences, since the outputs are subject to many and various influences. We can, then, have some confidence about the cultural factors that will influence the conduct and the fortunes of American, Japanese and European businesses but must, inevitably, have less confidence about the conditions within which those cultures will be put to the test. Are there any certainties that we can cling to?

The economic conditions

In the first instance we can be fairly sure that the primary players on the world business stage, at least in the early decades of the twenty-first century, will be those we have considered in this book: America, Japan, and Europe. In the early 1990s 80% of world trade was conducted between the main economies of the OECD, 70% of that being between the leading five economies. While south-east Asian nations may take an increasing share of international trade, they currently constitute a very small part of the world economy. The strength, longevity and stability of America, Japan and Europe ensure that, whoever else may enter the running, they will be strong contenders in a race for economic supremacy.

Much of that economic supremacy will depend upon the robustness of the multinational corporations that each economy can develop and sustain. Our survey of the emergence of business cultures in the leading economies demonstrates the extent to which the economy is based on successful corporations of size and scale. The multinational corporation is almost as old as organized trade itself, if one were to stretch the facts and claim as an embryonic multinational the Hanseatic League of the fourteenth century. Certainly the Dutch and British East India Companies, the Muscovy Company, the Royal Africa Company and the Hudson Bay Company, with their seventeenth- and eighteenth-century origins are testimony to the enduring importance of efficient, large-scale vehicles by which business can be organized and expedited. As we have seen, many of the organizations that feature amongst the top valued global corporations in the late 1990s are as old as the economies that gave rise to them – Unilever, Royal Dutch Shell, Ford, General Motors, Mitsubishi. This is not to suggest that an economy can be sustained simply by the large-scale organization. On the contrary, the nature of the marketplace is such that many services supplied to large companies must come from small organizations. Machine tool manufacture, for example, where sophisticated engineering, quality monitoring and customer service are paramount, is one area where small is definitely beautiful and it is notable that Italy, home to so much small-scale rather than large-scale business, is strong in precision tool manufacture. In some sectors large, monolithic structures cannot compete with streamlined, sleek, small-scale organizational structures as we have seen in our case study of Europe's failure in the high-tech arena. This pattern was repeated in the US where IBM was undercut by the smaller company DEC, which in turn suffered at the hands of the later, smaller still, Sun Microsystems. In the same way, the Japanese have had to go out and buy small businesses in an attempt to maintain their competitive position in the high-tech marketplace. However, the notion that small companies will take over from large is as unfounded as the supposition that large-scale multinational corporations will take the place of governments in the management of human affairs. The monstrous global corporation is a myth. Most corporations, being run by and for groups of humans (the board, the work-force, the shareholders), will retain a national focus and allegiance, however international in scope their operations may become. A large multinational corporation which is a slow-moving monolith governed by the force of tradition is not one that will enjoy enduring success. Recent decades have seen the triumph of expertise over amateurism. Specialist skills are increasingly bought in to a company or contracted out and the need for a large corporation to be flexible, capable of loose, arms-length management, is more acute than it has ever been. The trend towards lean head offices, shrinking bureaucracies and abbreviated lines of command is evidence of the multinational making sure it has sufficient manoeuvrability to secure success in an environment that is governed increasingly by networks. These networks are networks of associated companies (those who supply or whom the company in turn supplies) and international networks, companies within the company itself.

There can be little doubt that the trend will continue towards increasing internationalization. Technology has given the impetus to a network of global communications, systems of global banking and information exchange, which have brought the nations and the markets of the world into ever closer contact. As some markets have matured, the world's multinationals have looked to new locations to provide increasing profits and to give a chance to secure market share ahead of competitors. Internationalization is a phenomenon which will be taken best advantage of by large-scale companies but also by those which are culturally predisposed to manage international difference with sensitivity. The nation state is no more dead than the global corporation is its devourer. Nationalism likewise is alive and well. If anything, internationalism serves to heighten nationalism, to make people increasingly aware of the national identity they possess in distinction from those of the international population with whom there is increasing contact. In an international age, therefore, acute sensitivity to national sensibility is a prerequisite for success in dealing with others.

The paradox of global/local is one that we have invoked a number of times in the course of these chapters. Before leaving it once and for all it is useful to stress once again the inter-relatedness of the two notions. Bruno Latour, French sociologist, in his consideration of the condition of being modern *We have never been modern* gives substance to the idea:

> *'Is a railroad local or global? Neither. It is local at all points, since you always find sleepers and railroad workers, and you have stations and automatic ticket machines scattered along the way. Yet it its global, since it takes you from Madrid to Berlin or from Brest to Vladivostok. However, it is not universal enough to be able to take you just anywhere. It is impossible to reach the little Auvergnat village of Malpy by train, or the little Staffordshire village of Market Drayton. There are continuous paths that lead from the local to the global, from the circumstantial to the universal, from the contingent to the necessary, only so long as the branch lines are paid for.'*

The continuous paths which Latour identifies are networks. It is his contention that: 'the two extremes, local and global, are much less interesting than the intermediary arrangements that we are calling networks'. Whether or not this is the case, as far as the thesis of this book is concerned, it is the management of these intermediary arrangements – these networks – which represents the most challenging aspect of the present and future environment in which business will be conducted. So the several certainties to which we can cling are:

- Business will continue to be dominated by the established triad of economic powers, America, Japan and Europe.
- South-east Asian nations (and others) will mount an assault on existing powers but will find it hard to erode the long-established hegemony.
- The economy will feature a mix of multinational corporations with small, flexible businesses, where national focus and global reach will be twin, paradoxical influences.
- Multinational corporations will exist within networks, at the national and the international level, and network management will be critical to future success.

Assessing the triad in the light of the prevailing operating environment

The simplest measure by which to assess the probable future performance of the triad of leading economic superpowers is that of the multinational corporation. Here America is quite clearly in the ascendant. In earlier chapters we have referred to the global top 1000 companies by market capitalization produced by *Business Week*. The 1996 results show the overwhelming strength of American companies, with 422 entries accounting for some 46% of the total value of the 1000. In contrast Japan accounts for just 23% both by value and by number of entries of the global 1000. Germany, France, Britain and Italy – Europe's four largest economies – together account for 17% of the total value of the list (but 19% of entries). This figure rises to 25% in value (28% by number of entries) when the composite figure for all European companies represented on the list (the list excludes Portugal and Greece, which feature on the separate listing for emerging companies) is calculated. The results are clear: America has more companies of greater value than either Japan or Europe. Of course, the value of the global companies is measured in dollars and American companies have gained from an extraordinary bull market; nonetheless the figures are compelling evidence of American corporate strength. The figures produced just eight years previously told a rather different story. In 1988, Japanese companies accounted for 48% of the list's total value. Whether this indicates the depth of Japanese recession or the height of corporate performance (and corporate flexibility) on the part of American companies, or the extent to which the methods of measurement influence the outcome, is unclear. For our purposes, however, it is clear that the global pecking order in terms of multinationals is America, Japan and, trailing slightly, Europe. The rest of the world accounts for a mere 6% of the total value of the list, reinforcing the initial point made that new contenders for business supremacy will find an already crowded marketplace. The extraordinary disparity between the 1988 and the 1996 figures may simply confirm that business leadership is very much up for grabs, or will at least rotate between the triad.

The measure of culture

Above we have considered the issue of muscle. It is the firm belief of this author that it is the mind set rather than the muscle tone of the key economic players we are looking at that will determine future success – that competitive edge will be conferred in the next century by culture. How do the members of the triad measure up on this scale and in the prevailing economic conditions that we have sketched above (those conditions being ones where networks are a primary feature requiring flexibility, especially on an international basis)?

A point made earlier in this text is that while America and Japan are single nations Europe is not. Europe is, in fact, a network. We have wrestled with the notion of Europe and what it is to be European and found that the concept ultimately defies tight definition. Europe is a loose federation of alliances and it is easier to think in terms of the spirit of Europe than the body. Is Europe just those members of the EU? Is it those countries that have always been defined geographically as European? The geographical and the political distinctions blur and while membership of the EU is, in this author's view, an important element of being European, the Swiss, who are not members, are no less European and, indeed, make an important contribution to business activity in Europe. The point is less what Europe is than what it is not. It is not the cultural monolith that we see in either Japan or America. As we have seen in an earlier chapter, some of Europe's constituent parts display high levels of what we have termed ethnocentrism – a tendency towards a monolithic cultural type. Certainly this has been the case with the largest economies and the nations which have held superpower status in the past. Germany, France and the UK have less fluid cultures than the smaller nations, Sweden, Holland or Denmark. Nonetheless, taken as a whole there is no one European culture. We have also seen that European companies have a higher tendency to deal with companies from other European countries than do Japanese or American organizations to deal with foreign companies. Europe is a network of companies in countries which network with one another. By being so identified with the notion of networking perhaps we can infer that Europe already has the edge, culturally speaking, over its rivals?

It would be wrong, however, to suppose that either Japanese or American cultures do not show an extremely high level of respect for networks. Japan has developed some of the most sophisticated business networks in the world. The Japanese *keiretsu* system unites companies in mutually beneficial networks, which within an extremely flexible structure achieve some of the scale efficiencies normally associated with vertically integrated single organizations. The system dominates the Japanese economy with the top 6 *keiretsu* linking an average of 30 companies each. Nearly 50% of Japan's top 200 companies are engaged in *keiretsu* relationships. We have also in Chapter 3 charted how America's rise to economic superiority was the extraordinary marriage of individual with collective endeavour, based on the pioneering, immigrant culture that dominated in the period when the economy was built. The immigrant away from old networks of family and locality excelled in the formation of new, alternative networks based on shared values and interests rather than simply blood ties or the accident of geography.

When considering the American or Japanese respect for networks, however, there is one significant caveat that must be sounded. American and Japanese networks tend to be national affairs, rather than international affairs. Respect for networks does not automatically imply respect for difference. Indeed, both the American and Japanese cultures could be seen to be somewhat disdainful of difference. The *keiretsu*, for instance, have been the focus of considerable American criticism on the grounds that they are anticompetitive.

Certainly, the members of a particular *keiretsu* will trade with one another in preference to trading with an outsider even if there is not an immediate commercial logic governing that decision. America, as we have seen, has in the past three decades become an increasingly litigious, rights-based society with a firm and laudable belief in equality. The problem with that belief in equality, as we have identified earlier, is that it denies difference. If we consider the manner in which both Japanese and American corporations have developed internationally then we can see it has been by the assumption that difference is irrelevant. The US practice of simply exiting a country that did not prove amenable to the American approach is evidence of the thoroughgoing belief in the American way of doing business. The Japanese respect for the individual skills of the assembly line worker, which gave rise to manufacturing techniques that substantially undermined the Ford and Taylor techniques that had prevailed in America and American-styled manufacturing businesses, is not matched with a respect for the skills and requirements of indigenous managers. The primary positions in Japanese organizations overseas and, most definitely, at home go to Japanese. Cultural cohesion was a primary enabling factor in the success of the Americans and the Japanese (and, for that matter, the Germans and the British). It will continue to facilitate growth and development, for the culturally cohesive entity (a company or an economic unit) can move relatively faster than one where there is a need to build some form of consensus. However, cultural cohesion in the conditions that we have described is, increasingly, as much a disadvantage as once it was an advantage. I reiterate above the important point that internationalism is giving rise to increased concern to preserve national difference. In an international economy such as we have and will continue to have in the coming decades where there is a high demand for visible respect for difference, America and Japan fall far short of Europe.

A strong and cohesive culture may be able to change direction more rapidly than one where there is a need to build consensus, but can we be sure that the direction in which it turns will be the right one, a new one or merely a turn made in reaction to a situation observed elsewhere? Does a strong and cohesive culture necessarily ensure innovation? As we have seen elsewhere in the text, there are concerns in both the US and Japan that innovation is being eroded. The children of both cultures are rebelling against the standards of their parents and the educational system in America is seen to operate on the basis of the lowest common denominator while that in Japan, which operates on the directly contrary principle and is fiercely competitive and exacting, is seen to be too restrictive, too dependent upon rote. As we have seen European education systems provide European companies (especially ones that assemble international management teams) with highly complementary approaches to problem solving which can only lead to increasingly sophisticated and innovative thought.

I claim above that it is the management of networks that represents the most challenging aspect of the present and future business environment. It is in this area that we can try and assess relative degrees of innovation. In Europe governance has become something of a continental obsession. From a business perspective we have seen the enormous influence of the work of Sir Adrian Cadbury and his committee looking at standards of corporate governance. This work has been important in the UK but has also given rise to a Europe-wide debate and companies around the continent are moving to bring their governance practices into closer alignment with the recommendations made in the Cadbury report. Innovation is leading to a degree of standardization which will improve the decision-making capability and the efficiency of corporate entities without diluting existing strengths. Boards in one country will more nearly resemble boards in another but the skill-sets of the different director groups will remain distinct, although subject to similar regulation. The corporate model has its companion in the political sphere. The emergence of the EU, as we have seen in Chapter 10, is probably the single biggest totem of European innovation. Nowhere else in the world is such consideration being given to the management of a network and for all its faults the EU, in the context of European cultural artefacts, must be seen as paradigmatic of excellence.

From whichever angle we approach Europe we find the linking of the local and the global, whether we look at the Roman Empire or the management style of a corporation such as Unilever or Asea Brown Boveri. We can note different centres of excellence, disseminating that excellence at different periods: the impact of the Italian Renaissance, the French Revolution, of German Romanticism, of the Industrial Revolution in Britain all testify to the ability of Europeans to spread, to network and to share that excellence. In business this is matched by the engineering excellence in Germany, the sophisticated design skills in Italy, the strength of British service businesses. Throughout the history of Europe's shifting boundaries and changing allegiances it is possible to plot distinct nationalities and the enduring importance of language differences with strong local attachment and fierce defence of dialect and minority languages. At the same time Europe has given itself up to the generalized use of an Anglo-American language as a universal. The local and the universal once more in close union. The terms by which we characterize the business environment for the coming decades are the very ones by which we can characterize Europe – the juxtaposition of the local and the global, respect for difference, networks. America and Japan, ironically given the success with which they have built overseas business empires, nevertheless favour the local over the global and lack the European readiness to recognize and defend difference. Measured against cultural criteria Europe would appear to be in the ascendant at the turning point of the millennium. If we accept that culture will indeed confer competitive edge then Europe will move ahead of its prime competitors in the coming decades.

Europe is a collective, a group of equal but different entities which has come together motivated by a form of enlightened self-interest determined to pool expertise, spread risk and innovate. It has the shortcomings of any collective, not least the grave risk of internecine dispute and the unwieldy nature of decision making given the demand for consensus, but the advantages outweigh the disadvantages.

Europe has abundant historical precedent for maintaining a strong position of global power. Moreover, in the substantial efforts made by Europeans to transform themselves from a group of warring nations to a union of trading equals there is evidence of a clear motivation to secure peace, prosperity and stability for the citizenry. It has been an urge for economic union which has driven wider European union and at the operating level of the economy, within businesses themselves, there is considerable evidence of profitable cross-fertilization, increasing integration and close attention being given to the development of a business culture that is distinct from those which have led to economic hegemony in the past. European businesses are, at their best, finding new ways of operating in an international context and in the vanguard of this innovation is a particular breed of international leader who embodies, through an appreciation of difference, often as the product of difference (dual nationalities, early international experience) something of the spirit of Europe. The case can be made with relative ease for an ascendant Europe, capitalizing on the strength of a diverse culture, competing from a strong base against economies where an anachronistic, monolithic culture dominates. The auguries are good, but the outcome will depend upon the willingness of Europeans to recognize them as such. As the 1990s come to a close European union is still in the balance and the chances of European economic success depend very largely on the ability of her politicians and her people to balance the competing interests of nationalism and internationalism, to come into their inheritance and unite once and for all the local and global.

Bibliography

In the writing of this book I have referred to a vast array of printed material, much of it in my daily business life in the form of press releases and newspaper articles. Most of the books that have been important are mentioned in the text. The principal texts to which I have referred are:

Ardagh, John (1995) *France Today*, 5th edn. Penguin, London.
Ardagh, John (1995) *Germany and the Germans*, 3rd edn. Penguin, London.
Derrida, Jacques (1992) *The Other Heading*. Indiana University Press, Bloomington and Indianapolis.
Fukuyama, Francis (1992) *The End of History and the Last Man*. Penguin, London.
Fukuyama, Francis (1996) *Trust: The Social Virtues and the Creation of Prosperity*. Penguin, London.
Hill, Richard (1994) *Euro Managers and Martians*, 2nd edn. Europublications Ltd, Brussels.
Hirst, Paul and Thompson, Grahame (1996) *Globalization in Question*. Polity Press, Cambridge.
Hofstede, Geert (1991) *Cultures and Organisations*. McGraw-Hill, Maidenhead.
Isachsen, Olaf and Berenes, Linda V. (1995) *Working Together – A Personality-Centred Approach to Management*, 3rd edn. Institute for Management Development.
Keirsey, David and Bates, Marilyn (1980) *Please Understand Me – Character and Temperament Types*, 5th edn. Prometheus Nemesis Book Company.
Kennedy, Paul (1994) *Preparing for the Twenty-First Century*. Fontana Press, London.
Pease, Alan (1993) *Body Language*. Sheldon Press, London.
Sampson, Anthony (1996) *Company Man: The Rise and Fall of Corporate Life*. HarperCollins, London.

Index

Adenauer, Konrad 77, 79–80
advertising 65
Albert, M. 94
America
   automobile industry 56–8
   business culture 45, 47, 60–69, 228–9
   business networks 62, 266–7
   business techniques 65–6
   Chief Executives 63–5
   civil war 52–3
   colonization 45–6, 47–9
   corporate growth 51–2
   cultural cohesion 267
   cultural intolerance 13–14
   cultural origins 46–7
   economic future 3–4, 223, 264–5
   education system 221–2
   Europe relationship 45–6, 48–50, 128–9, 130–33
   immigrants 46, 47–9, 52
   independence 49–50
   individualism 19
   industrialization 52–4
   innovation 50–51, 58–60
   neo-American economic model 94–6
   small traders 54–5
   technology development 55–6
APEC *see* Asia Pacific Economic Co-operation
Apple computers 58–9
ASEAN *see* Association of South East Asian Nations
Asia
   common factors 120–25
   Confucian traditions 122
   dominance fears 101–3, 125
   economic decline 124–5
   economic development 101–25
      case studies 106–19
   emerging economies 103–6
   growth circles 118–19
   Japanese influence 121
   religion 122–3
Asia Pacific Economic Co-operation (APEC) 98, 107, 120
Association of South East Asian Nations (ASEAN) 98, 107, 120
attitudes, business 224–9
automobile industry 56–8, 80

Belgium, cultural traits 198
Berlin Wall, fall 127
Bischoff, Win 166, 167–8, 174, 175
Blime, Pierre 218–19
body language, cultural differences 182–3
Braudel, Ferdinand 155
Britain
   civil service 217
   colonialism decline 129–30
   companies, mergers 138–45
   cultural traits 190–92
   economic development 96–7
   education system 214–15
   European Union membership 246–7
   financial institutions 38
   Industrial Revolution 39
   nation state origins 37–8
   national identity 155–7
businessmen
   America 63–5, 67–9

Europe 164–5
  status 227–9

Cadbury, Adrian 238–9, 268
Cadot, Olivier 218–19
CAP *see* Common Agricultural Policy
capitalism
  attitudes 224–5
  international 12
  rise 35–6
cartels 76
Channel Tunnel 145, 234
charisma 59–60, 61, 163–4, 175–6
Charlemagne 30
chemical industry, Germany 80–81
China
  economic development 115–17
  family networks 17
  international growth circles 118–19
Christianity
  European spread 27–9, 33
  Protestantism 35–7
civil service, recruitment 217
Common Agricultural Policy (CAP)
    254
communication, nonverbal 180–83
Communism 127, 211
community, nature 20
companies
  see also corporations
  board structure 236–9
  chairman/chief executive role 237–8
  corporate differences 236–9
  decentralized 148
  European 127–8, 133–51
  headquarters location 137–8
  international 136–7
  leadership 163–76
  market value 103–5
  mergers 138–46
  networks 262–3, 266–7
  ownership 134–6
  small 9
  trading blocs 98–9
Confucius 122
Coolidge, President C. 45, 47
Cornelis, François 167, 170, 171–2,
    174

corporate culture
  America 60–69
  national perspective 159–60
  parameters 160–62
corporations
  see also companies
  America 51–2
  global 7–9, 102
  human element 14–15
cultural isobars 209–11
culture
  communitarian 18
  concept 153–4
  European 207–30
    analysis 202–3
    differences 177–206
    examples 183–201
    models 209–11
  familial 16–17
  individuals 204–6
  influence 13–14
  lifestyle differences 234–5

Danone 134
Davies, Crispin 168, 170, 173, 174, 175
Davis, Peter 143–4, 174, 175
De Gaulle, Charles 130, 246
Delors, Jacques 128
Denmark, cultural traits 200
Derrida, Jacques 23–4, 34
dress code, cultural differences 180–81

east European states, European Union
    membership 253–5
economic and monetary union (EMU)
    248–9
education
  America/Europe comparison 221–2
  Britain 214–15
  business relationship 218–21
  business skills 66, 91, 133
  elites 215–18
  France 188, 213–14
  Germany 90–91, 212
  Sweden 215–16
elites, education 215–18
Elsevier, Reed International merger
    143–4

EMU *see* economic and monetary union
Erhard, Ludwig 78–9
ethnocentrism 155–7
Europe
   America relationship 45–6
   American influences 128–9, 130–33
   business attitudes 224–9
   business leaders 164–5
   colonialism decline 129–30
   companies 127–8, 133–51
      board structures 236–9
   cultural differences 177–206, 207–30
   cultural influence 13–14
   definitions 265–6
   economic future 2–3, 223
   high-tech industries 218–21
   history 23–42
   immigration 251–2
   international co-operation 2, 233–4
   modern identity 42–3
   nationalism 154–7
   networks 266
   reformation 34–7
   single market 233–4
   trade routes 32–4
   unemployment 249–51
European Union (EU) 239–48
   Britain's membership 246–7
   Council of Ministers 242
   Court of Justice 243–4
   enlargement 252–6
   European Commission 241–2
   European Parliament 242–3
   history 240–41
   international co-operation 12–13
   international differences 2–3
   monetary union 248–9
   significance 244–8
   sovereignty implications 11
Eurosclerosis 128
expansionism 34, 37

family businesses, Japan 74
family networks 16–17
financial systems, origins 33, 38
Finland, cultural traits 200–201
First World War 40–41

Ford, Henry 56–7, 67
France
   companies, British mergers 144–5
   cultural traits 187–9
   education system 188, 213–14
   German management comparison 186
   nation state origins 37–8
   national identity 155–7
French Revolution 39
Fukuyama, Francis 16–17, 19–20, 62, 124–5, 255

Gates, Bill 61
General Motors 57–8, 131
Germany
   cultural traits 183–7
   currency reform 78–9
   economic decline 90–93
   economic development 71–2, 74–81
   education system 90–91, 212
   French management comparison 186
   immigrants 251–2
   industrialization 74–6, 80–81
   Japan comparison 72–3, 76–7
   national identity 155–7
   ordnung 184–5
   reunification 256
   Rhine economic model 94–6
Gibson, William 7, 102
Giddens, Anthony 6, 8
global/local paradox 263–4
globalization 6–10
Greece, European Union membership 253

Habermas, Jurgen 6
Hall, Edward 161
Heinz, H.J. 138
high-tech industries, failure 218–21
Hofstede, Geert 159–60, 162–3, 177–8, 202–3
Holland
   companies, British mergers 138–44
   cultural traits 196–7
   financial centre 38
Hollywood 68, 69

Holy Roman Empire 37
Hong Kong, economic development 115
human behaviour 15–16
Hume, David 155
Huntington, Samuel 257

IBM 59–60, 131
imperialism, decline 129–30
individuals, personality types 204–6
Indo-China, economic growth 119
Indonesia, economic development 112–13, 119
Industrial Revolution 39
industrialization, Germany 74–6, 80–81
industry, education relationship 218–21
inequalities, levelling 225–6
innovation
    America 50–51, 58–60
    European lack 149
international co-operation, Europe 2
internationalization 263
Ireland, European Union membership 252–3
Italy, cultural traits 192–4

Japan
    American occupation 82–3
    Asia influence 121
    business networks 266–7
    cultural cohesion 267
    cultural intolerance 13–14
    economic decline 93–4
    economic development 71–2, 73–4, 81–90
    economic future 3–4, 264–5
    family businesses 74
    Germany comparison 72–3, 76–7
    international trade 85–6, 98
    keiretsu 266–7
    labour problems 83
    Ministry of International Trade and Industry (MITI) 84–5, 89
    paternalism 88–9
    Rhine economic model 94–6
    success 86–90
    Westernization 73–4
    Zaibatsu closures 82–3

Jobs, Steven 9, 58–9, 67

Kelleher, Herb 228
Kellogg 137
Keynes, John Maynard 3
knowledge-based societies 223
Kroc, Roy 59

language
    cultural importance 157–8
    German 184
Latour, Bruno 263–4
leadership 163–76
    American 63–5
    charisma 59–60, 61, 163–4, 175–6
    cultural neutrality 165–8
    European 164–5
    examples 166–76
Lessem, Ronnie 209–10
Levy, Alain 147, 166, 170, 172, 174, 175
lifestyles, differences 234–5
listening skills 170–71
Lomax, Eric 260
Louis-Dreyfus, Robert 166, 167, 168, 173, 174, 175
Lugard, Frederick 225

Maastricht Treaty 248–9
MacArthur, General 82
MacDonald's 59
Malaysia, economic development 110, 119
Mann, Michael 28, 42–3
marketing techniques 65–6
Maslow, Abraham 15
mass production 56–7
Melin, Daniel 150
mergers 138–45
migrants
    America 46, 47–9
    Europe 251–2
Miller, Arthur 45, 49
Mitsubishi 74, 82
Mitsui 74, 82
Mitterand, François 25
models, cultural types 209–11
monetary union

Maastricht Treaty 248–9
Roman Empire 27
money markets, international 6–7, 8
Monnet, Jean 130
multinational corporations 8–9, 261–2
Myers Briggs 204

Napier, Robert 168–70, 173, 174, 175
Napoleon Bonaparte 39
nation states
 development 10–11, 37–8
 national/international balance 12–13
National Cash Register Company (NCR) 59–60
nationalism, Europe 40–41, 154
needs, hierarchy 15–16
neo-American model 94–7
Nestlé 135–6
Neubauer, Fred 209–20
Newly Industrializing Economies (NIEs) 107
Nicoli, Eric 166, 174, 175
NIEs see Newly Industrializing Economies
Nietzsche, Friedrich 155
Nilsson, Kjell 167, 174, 175

Pacific Rim, economic future 3–4, 98–9, 103
paternalism, Japan 88–9
Patterson, John Henry 59–60
Peltola, Timo 172–3, 174, 175
Perkin, Harold 219
personality types 204–5
Petrofina 146–7
Philip Morris 137
Philippines, economic development 111
Polygram 147, 166
Portugal, European Union membership 253
Proctor & Gamble 131, 138, 141
professions, prestige 226–7
Protestantism 35–7
Puritanism 49

Rathenau, Walther 76
Redland plc 147

Reed International, Elsevier merger 143–4
reformation 34–7
religion
 see also Christianity
 America 49
 Asia 122–3
relocation, resistance 234–5
Rhine model 94–6
Rockefeller, John D. 55, 67
Roman Empire 25–31
Royal Dutch, Shell merger 138–40
Russia
 America comparison 54
 nation state origins 37–8

Sampson, Anthony 68–9, 89, 132, 137
Schroders plc 146
Second World War 41
Servan-Schrieber, Jean-Jacques 132
Shell, Royal Dutch merger 138–40
Singapore, economic development 114, 119
Sloan, Alfred P. 57–8
South Korea, economic development 110–11
sovereignty, European Union implications 11
Spain
 cultural traits 194–6
 European Union membership 253
Standard Oil 54–5
Sweden
 cultural traits 198–9
 education system 215–16

Taiwan, economic development 108–9
Taylor, Frederick W. 56–7
Thailand, economic development 109–10, 119
'think global, act local' 13, 149
Toyota 89
trade
 historical networks 32–4
 single market 233–4
transnationalism 12
triad of economic powers 264–5
trust, cultures 16–20

unemployment, Europe 249–51
Unilever 140–42
United Biscuits 147
United Distillers 134–5
United Kingdom *see* Britain
United States of America *see* America

Valery, Paul 24, 43
voice, cultural differences 181–2

Wanamaker, John 55
Watson, Thomas J. 59–60
Weber, Max 35–6, 164
welfare systems 250–51
Whyte, William H. 61, 68
Wilson, Woodrow 45
Wozniak, Stephen 9, 58–9, 67

Zevin, R. 8–9